☀ A Celtic Childhood ☀

A
Celtic
Childhood

➤ ⬅

Bill Watkins

Ruminator Books
ST. PAUL • MINNESOTA

Published by Ruminator Books
1648 Grand Avenue
Saint Paul, MN 55105
www.ruminator.com

ISBN: 1-886913-43-9
Library of Congress Control Number: 00-090853

10 9 8 7 6 5 4 3 2 1
First paperback edition, 2000

Cover design by Randall Heath
Book design by Wendy Holdman
Typesetting by Stanton Publication Services

Printed in the United States of America

Dedicated to my father, who never lived to see the Celtic Revival,
and to my mother, who did

Special dedication to my Native American friend,
Ingrid Washinawatok,
who gave her life in the pursuit of peace and justice,
Colombia, March 4, 1999

Preface

In a Scottish library, on a wet afternoon in 1972, I finally finished reading Frank O'Connor's autobiography, *An Only Child*. The postscript puzzled me: "Written in New York 1958–60." Why would an Irish writer go to America to write a book? My answer came in a crowded Wisconsin kitchen on Thanksgiving Day in 1995.

"Bill, why don't you go upstairs and write something? What is it your mother says? 'You're neither use nor ornament here!'"

In the stillness of the airy bedroom, an exercise book lay virgin and mocking under my quivering pencil. Without warning, a torrent of images cascaded through my mind, finding release in a swift scrawl of spiderous graphite. Seven chapters later, the Thanksgiving holiday was over, and the first book in my trilogy, "The Once and Future Celt," was under way. Like O'Connor before me, I had forged the understanding that being too close to your subject can be distorting and that distance, indeed, brings forth focus.

Acknowledgments

My thanks go to the following: In Minneapolis, Patrick O'Donnell, Kieran Folliard, Tim Fitzgerald, Kevin Finger, and all the crew at Kieran's Irish Pub; the staff, musicians, and regulars at Molly Quinn's; and Liam Óg Watkins, Matthew Lamphear, Kristi Johnson, Ethna McKiernan, and Mary Byers; in St. Paul, Jim Brooks, Mary Sue McFarland, and Seán T. Kelly at the *Irish Gazette;* Dermot and Molly O'Meara at Irish on Grand; Nick Potter, Jerry Brennan, and Jim Rogers; Pearl Kilbride, Amy Bell, and Dallas Crow at Hungry Mind Press; and Chad McNally; Chris Dale in Los Angeles; Johnny Carr and Seán Hannon in Berlin; Andy M. Stewart, Dick Gaughan, and Robbie Coltrane in Scotland; John Dingley in Wales; Danny Watkins, Jer and Eithne O'Leary, and Sean O'Driscoll in Ireland; and Cara and Amber Watkins in England.

Special thanks to my Wisconsin girls: Ma Muehlbauer for giving me the embryo of an idea and Katie Muehlbauer for being the midwife of the ensuing four-year pregnancy.

Glossary
of Words and Phrases and Their Derivation

Acting the gussie: fooling, being silly (probably from *acting the goat*)

Adam and Eve it: believe it (*rhyming slang*)

Amadawn(s): idiot(s) (Gaelic: *amadan*, fool)

An Buachaill Caol Dubh (un buckle kyl doo): the dark slender boy (Gaelic)

Avast!: Stop! (Dutch: *houd vast*, hold fast)

Banjaxed: surprise attack (Gaelic: *banaghaisge*, the surprising feats or exploits of a woman)

Barney: an argument or fight (British slang)

Blackshirts: British Union of Fascists, founded by Sir Oswald Mosley in 1932

Blaggarding: being disruptive or undisciplined (from *blackguard*, the soot-faced pot stirrers and fire tenders of a medieval army)

Blenching: flinching, drawing together, especially of eyebrows (Old English: *blencan*, to deceive)

Bloke: a man (Gaelic: *buachaill óg*, young man)

Bobbyhowler: a moth that batters itself to death on a light fixture

Bollocks, bollix: hot ashes, used as a curse (Gaelic: *beolach*, live ashes)

Boreen: a lane usually overhung with trees (Gaelic: *botharín*, little road)

Bosch: World War I slang for the German army (French)

Box: smack or hit (Old Gaelic: *bosc*, to hurt; origin of the term *boxing*)

Brummy: a native of Birmingham (Brummyjum), England

Buachaill on Eirne: the lad from Loch Erne (Gaelic)

Bum gaff: derelict house unfit for shelter (Gypsy slang)

Bumsteer: a noisy chap (Gaelic: *buamasdairish,* a turbulent fellow)

Butty: sandwich, from bread and butter (British slang)

Cabbage crates: green-brown camouflaged aircraft (World War I RAF slang)

Cantle: the rim or edge of something (Scots)

Ceol an Gael Abú! (key-owl un gale aboo): Forward the music of the Gael!

Chélidh (kay-lee): impromptu musical gathering (Gaelic)

Coddin': chiding or chaffing (Irish slang: Codology, joking, putting someone on)

Comhaltas Ceoltóiri Éireann (kowltass key-owltory airann): the Irish traditional folk music and dance society

Craic (krak): fun, also witty conversation (Gaelic)

Crikey: a contraction of "Christ help me"

Croesus: Celtic king of the Lydians, noted for his wealth (sixth century B.C.)

Croix de Guerre: French military decoration for gallantry

Cuirassiers: French light cavalry (from *Cuirass,* armored breastplate)

Culshie: a country person, a peasant (Gaelic: *culcheumnaich,* backward)

Dagda: father of the Celtic gods

Designtly: by design, on purpose (Irish)

Doolally: to go mad at someone (Hindi: *Deolali,* a military lunatic asylum in Bombay)

Duffer: an unlearned person, a dunce

Earwig: to overhear or eavesdrop (British slang)

Eejit: idiot (Irish)

Empire Loyalists: right-wing 1950s movement against colonial freedom

Flash Harry: a famous wartime spiv, or black marketeer (World War II slang)

Fleádh (flaa): festival (Gaelic)

Fleádh Cheoil (flaa key-owl): music festival (Gaelic)

Fong: a kick (Limerick slang)

Gaatch: someone's way of walking, gait (Irish)

Gallowglasses: warriors in the service of an Irish chieftain (Gaelic: *galloglach,* stranger soldier)

Git: a fool (from *get,* an archaic form of *bastard*)

Glic: wise (Gaelic)

Gombeen: a sort of village idiot (Irish)

Gorsedd: Druid enthronement (Welsh: *gorseddu,* to enthrone)

Gossoon: a young lad (Gaelic, *garsun*)

Hessians: mercenary soldiers recruited by the British from Hesse in Germany, renowned for their brutality

Hold your whist! Shut up! Shush! (Gaelic: *éist,* listen)

Hookers: prostitutes (Dutch: *hoeker,* an old sailing vessel)

Huckstered: cheated by a greedy salesman (Dutch: *hoekster,* retailer)

Iechyd da! (yacky-da): Good health! (Welsh)

Keelhaul: maritime punishment involving dragging a sailor under the ship's hull by a rope passed under the keel. Few survived this ordeal. (Dutch origin)

Keening: the wailing for the dead (Gaelic: *caoin,* lament, cry, weep)

Kibosh: the end, from the judge's black cap signifying the death sentence (Gaelic: *caip bas,* death cap)

Kidney: temperament or humor

Knackered: tired out (British slang)

Langer: penis (Irish)

Langers: very obviously drunk (Irish)

Memsahib: the wife of an English officer (Hindi)

Milesian: Irishman (ancient descendant of Mil, king of Celtic Spain and Scota, daughter of the Egyptian pharaoh Nectanebus)

Moggy: a scruffy-looking stray, usually a tabby or feral cat (perhaps from Welsh: *mwg,* smoky, a common name for a cat)

Muileann d' Or (moolin door): mill of gold (Gaelic)

Natter: idle talk often during knitting (British slang, probably from knit + chatter)

Nawney: Irish slang, the meaning of which my mother *still* won't tell me!

Nicked: stolen (British slang.)

Nuxed: dead (British slang.)

Oggin: the sea (from *floggin the oggin,* sailing the hogwash)

Orangeman: Protestant bigot, follower of King William of Orange

Paggering: a severe beating (Gypsy, probably from Spanish: *pagar*, to pay out)

Palaver: idle or lengthy talk (Portuguese: *palavra*, speech.)

Pen and ink: stink (rhyming slang)

Plantangenet: name of the royal house ruling England from 1154 to 1485 and descended from Geoffrey, Count of Anjou, who liked to wear a sprig of broom in his hat (Latin: *Planta Genista*)

Pong: a terrible stink (perhaps from Chinese *pong chi*, a loom for weaving cloth with fiber from the malodorous silkworm)

Pooky my breeks: shit my pants (Gaelic: *pocaich mo briogais*)

Prat(s): foolish person(s)

Quotha!: Forsooth! (archaic, more contemptuous form of Indeed!)

Rakes: lots of, an abundance (Irish)

Ransacked: to search thoroughly (Gaelic: *rannsaich*, search)

RUC: Royal Ulster Constabulary, British armed police force in Northern Ireland

Scallywags: petty criminals, jokers (Old Norse: *skjalla-weg*, a swaggering loudmouth)

Scarper: run away (Gaelic: *sgapadh*, to scatter)

Scouse: a native of Liverpool (from *lobscouse*, a seafarer's meat stew)

Scran: scavenged food (probably from Old Norse: *skrann*, lean, slim pickings)

Second sight: the Celtic gift of seeing into the future

Shanks's pony: using your legs; walking (British slang)

Sinne Fianna Fáil, Atá fá gheall ag Éirinn: Soldiers are we, Whose lives are pledged to Ireland (Irish national anthem)

Skivvy: a kitchen maid or pot washer (British slang)

Slán leat (slaawn lat): good-bye (Gaelic: *Slán*, go safe. Origin of U.S. term *so long*)

Spivs: ne'er-do-wells, idlers, black marketeers (from *spiffy*, well dressed)

Splice the Mainbrace: to give the crew extra rum ration for good work

Spree: to have fun (Gaelic: *spraoi*, to make sport)

Taking the mickey: to mock, literally, taking the piss (Latin: *micturire*, to urinate)

Tanner: an old silver sixpence (Gypsy: *tanno*, coin)

Tat: scrap metal (Gypsy: *tot*)

Teddy-boys: violent youth gangs, wearers of Edwardian (Teddy) frock coats

Ticketty-boo: That's fine (Hindi: *tikai babu*, it's all right, sir)

Tinker's cuss: an inferior type of malediction

Tipplers: people enjoying small amounts of drink (Old Norse: *tipla*, a wee drop)

Tír na nÓg: land of eternal youth—heaven (Gaelic)

Tosser: a small coin (British slang)

Tosspot: derogatory term for a drunkard (probably from *despot*)

Tubal-cain: the first blacksmith (Genesis 4.22)

Wabe: the grass area around a sundial (perhaps from Scots: *wab*, a web)

Wanker(s): equivalent U.S. term *jerk off*

Wizard prang: spectacular raid (World War I RAF slang)

✦ A Celtic Childhood ✦

⤞ Chapter 1 ⤝

"DOUSE THE LIGHT THERE, LIAM."

"What's that, Nana?"

"The light, yer mother left the light burning. Would youse ever quench it for me? I don't like touching them yokes, the bloody squitch stung me once when the old crock cover fell off it. Put the heart crossways in me, tobeJasus!"

"I'm comin', Nana," says I, scraping the old green spindled-backed chair across the flagstone floor and over to the light switch. With the fearless dexterity of a five-year-old, I climb up. *Click!* The kitchen's solitary, fly-encrusted lightbulb goes off.

"You're a good boy, Willie, so ya are." Nana sits down at the scrubbed pine table and begins humming to herself. Her eyes, just as soft as the golden era of gas mantles, are intently fixed on the job in hand. She lovingly fills the oil lamps with tangy-smelling paraffin and then adds a pinch of table salt, "so's the glass won't blacken."

"Yes, yer a good wee lad for your nana, Liam."

"He's a good boy—where the good boys don't answer," cries my mam, sweeping in from the garden with a wicker basket full of dry washing.

"Come here," she says, plucking me up like a rag doll and standing me back on the chair.

"You look like no one's child."

I squirm. She tucks in my shirt and pulls my shorts straight.

"And look at yer socks—mother of God! Yer like a ragamuffin."

"They won't stay up, Mammy."

"No," she says. "The elastic's perished. Go'way and play outside, 'tis a lovely day—go on! Yer like a hothouse plant stuck inside of the room

⤞ 3 ⤝

on a grand day like this. Gowanoutnow, while the going is good."
She claps her hands as if shooing chickens out of the kitchen.

"And don't be playing by the drain—ye'll get the scarlet fever!"
says Nana.

I drag the green kitchen chair outside and lay it on its back on the grass—there now! Next I take the short window-cleaning ladder and place it on the front legs crosswise. This becomes the wings of my biplane, just like Captain Biggles in the comics. Suitably attired in what I think pilots wear, I sit cross-legged on the chair back and thus am able, by leaning left or right, to bank and turn my plane. This is great craic altogether, and the top legs projecting forward from under the ladder are my machine guns, which despite the occasional jam, strike terror into the cold heart of German air ace Baron von Richthofen and his flying circus.

The back garden disappears in the clouds of my imagination as my trusty Sopwith Camel tears across the turf and, with a gentle pull on the stick, speeds like an arrow into the rare blue skies over Ireland. Soon I am in enemy airspace over Belgium.

> *I know that I shall meet my fate*
> *Somewhere among the clouds above;*
> *Those that I fight I do not hate,*
> *Those that I guard I do not love . . .*

W. B. Yeats is reading his First World War poem to me over the radio as I glide like a war hawk above the green fields of France.

"Did you get that, Willie?"

"I did, Mr. Yeats. What's it called?"

"'An Irish Airman Foresees His Death.'"

"Roger Wilco, Mr. Yeats—a nice poem!"

"Willie! Willie, do you heed me?"

Through the static-filled ether another voice is calling on my frequency, a faint familiar voice from far, far away.

"Willie! Are ye deaf, ya wee bugger?"

"Is that for you or me, Mr. Yeats?"

"I think it's for you, Liam!"

"Roger, over and out!"

A quick glance about the sky, no sign of the Hun, make a turn for home, once more descending into the green patchwork quilt of Mother Ireland to land next to the threaded silver embroidery that marks the course of the ancient river Shannon.

Engine spluttering, I straighten the rudder and ease the nose up. The voice in my earphones is still calling, shrill above the din. A sudden crosswind tears at the airframe and flips my crate over like a flapjack. As the starboard wingtip jars in the soft earth, the aircraft tears itself asunder. Pulling myself from the mangled wreckage I saunter toward Fighter Command HQ. At the kitchen door I glance back at the carnage. What is it they say? "Any landing you can walk away from is a good landing." 'Tis true for you!

"Willie! I've been calling you for ages! Go ye up to Paddy King's for the evening newspaper and fetch back half a stone of spuds from Fred Rice's. You can get yourself a patsy-pop for going."

"I will, Mam, and I'll take the handcart."

Mam wraps a silver shilling in the note, which reads: "7 lbs. potatoes please Fred, Put them in Liam's cart—Thanks."

I meander up the road, hard by the Shannon wall, where rows of hungry seagulls wait for our dinner scraps. Behind me I pull my two-wheeled cart by one handle.

In my other hand is a large copper penny with a Celtic harp on one side and a chicken on the other. This coin is an inch across and four of them weigh an ounce, but more important, this is the price of a patsy-pop, which is a kind of frozen orange juice on a stick—perfect rations for a fighter pilot on such a hot day.

I balance the cart handle on the worn boot scraper outside of the shop and, with trepidation enhanced by squeaking rusty hinges, push open the huge red door with its moldy brass handles.

A shaft of daylight and myself creeps into the earthy gloom of the greengrocer's emporium. It is dank and smells like a cemetery. Standing on tiptoes, I place the note and its shilling on the black oak counter. My penny escapes and for a while rolls in diminishing circles before shuddering to a stop. I snatch it back to the safety of my pocket as, in the eerie darkness above me, an enormous face and two gigantic hands appear floating, seemingly detached in the dingy light. With a puzzled look at me and then the note, the face says, "What are ye dressed like that for, ya eejit? Do you have the earache or something?"

Looking around cagily, I catch sight of myself in a Jacob's Biscuit mirror. Sure I am a quare enough sight for such a fine warm day: silk scarf tied around my neck, a rubber swimming cap on back to front, and Mam's furry earmuffs over the top of it.

"So I'm still wearing my flying gear, mister! What of it? You should be grateful that fighter aces like me are here to stop the Bosch from making off with your spuds!"

"A foighter pilot, are ye? Glory be! We can all sleep safe in our beds tonight, knowing that Holy Ireland is being protected by Fly-by-night Foster, or is it All-Day Murphy?"

The room shakes as great cannon shots of laughter echo around the earthen vault. Even in the cool dark an angry red flush stings my face and neck. Mute rows of cabbages transform into wrinkled green choir-boys silently mocking my embarrassment. Pallid cauliflowers like freshly trepanned skulls jeer and jostle with needled-nosed carrots to get a better view, whilst sly parsnips thrust forward raggedy roots to eavesdrop on the fullness of my discomfort. I am anxious to quit this turnip-filled tomb with its guffawing owner tumbling several pounds of prize King Edwards into my cart.

"There are old pilots and bold pilots, but there are no old, bold pilots." My inner voice comforts me as I make the safety of the sunlit portal and bang the door out on my tormentor.

Across the road Paddy King's is a haven of sanity. The shop is bright and airy and romantically infused with the rich aroma of printer's ink, aniseed balls, and black Balkan pipe tobacco. I take my place in the queue behind the ample backside of old Mrs. Morrisey, who although she smells of fish paste and old cabbage water, gives excellent cover as I surreptitiously pore over a *Captain Biggles* comic. There was the chiseled-jawed fighter ace striding from his battered biplane, chummed as always by the ever-cheerful Ginger and his Scottish sidekick, Jock.

"That was a wizard prang, sir! I saw the Jerry spin out of control just as you let fly with the Hotchkiss guns."

"Yes, Ginger, but that Hun in the sun nearly took your tail off, old boy!"

"Aye, Captain, but you were there to save the day as usual," Jock chimes in.

"What is it you want, Liam?"

"Word has come of Jerry massing for an attack on the line of the Somme River."

"Liam!"

"We must move quickly and get as many cabbage crates ready to fly as possible."

"LIAAM!" The magazine, like its hero, shoots skyward and I discover myself standing alone in the middle of the newspaper shop. Mrs. Morrisey is gone.

"Ooh, sorry! The *Limerick Leader,* please, Paddy, and a patsy-pop for going."

"Here," says Paddy. "You can have this old copy of *Biggles Flies at Dawn.* I can't sell it with a torn cover. Wasn't your uncle Bill MacDonagh in the Royal Air Force?"

"He was, sir, yes, a tail gunner in Lancaster bombers."

"Fair play to him—he did well to survive. He lives in London now, so he does?"

"He does, sir, in Hammersmith, sir."

"Your dad's away in the army, isn't he?"

"He is, to be sure—somewhere in England, so."

"But you want to join the air force and become a pilot when you grow up?"

"No, sir, I want to go to sea and be a sailor, that's all."

"You could be a navy pilot, so you could. No? Don't fancy that? Well, regards to your mam and your nana anyway, off you go home now. Jasus, will ye just look at the cut of you. You look the part—*Biggles Flies Undone.*"

Ah yes! That's more like it, a bit of respect from the civilian populace, a patsy-pop for going, and a free comic to boot.

God is in his heaven and all is right with the world as I lie next to my crashed plane reading my comic book. Biggles is not so lucky. He has been shot down and is recovering in hospital. As he lies there, surrounded by pretty French nurses, he dreams of his boyhood days in England and tries to remember back to his earliest recollections. He can only see back as far as his third birthday party. Jasus! I can do much better than that. I can remember it all, from day one! Let me see, what did happen?

I came into this world on a snowy April morning in 1950, an event I recall very well. I am told that many people can remember their birth but, it being a disagreeably messy experience at best, choose to forget.

Life is a sea of blobs and wiggly dark shapes moving in a blue light. Of sounds, too, and voices. I feel unbearably cold and I hear a voice saying, "Move Mrs.Watkins to isolation." All is blue and cold.

My mam is very ill and I have been a difficult birth. Luckily for my mother, she is able to have her confinement in Britain as my father is in the British army. She also can take full advantage of the free medical treatment that was not available in Ireland in those austere postwar days. I am christened William after my Irish grandfather and James after my Welsh one. These forenames translate into Liam and Seamus in the Irish tongue.

Whilst Mam is recovering in the hospital they give her two bottles of Guinness a day "to thicken the blood." Since I am breast-fed and prone to hiccups, my mother blames the stout. Either way, I thrive and my mam is soon up and about and on the mend.

The day comes when we are to return to Limerick. I am three weeks old and a testimony to the newly formed National Health Service. Mam is fit and feisty, which is unfortunate for the hospital discharge clerk.

"Ma'am, where it says nationality of infant, you've put Irish. If the child is born here it should say British." Mam is well able for him.

"If a cat has kittens in a baker's shop, does it make them currant buns?"

Later that day we take the boat train to Holyhead in Anglesey, Wales. Waiting at the quay is the ferry boat to Ireland.

After we set sail, my mam takes me out on deck, wrapped up in a plaid shawl for my first sense of the sea. From my woolen cocoon, I remember the salty tang of it well. It is the start of a love affair.

We arrive in Limerick in a big cloud of steam and wonderful smells.

It's smell that best weaves the tapestry of time into the endless knot we call memories. The use of this sense is still the best transportation across the decades and grand for pinpointing events, places, or even people—though there's some smells you would probably like to forget!

We take a horse-drawn sidecar taxi here to my grandmother's house in Thomondgate. This is to be our home, on and off, for the next five and a half years.

Any excuse for a party. Our homecoming is a big event! I am passed around a circle of smiling blobby faces that I later know as my aunts, uncles, and grandparents.

Over the next few weeks, although I sleep most of the time, I try to make sense of my surroundings and am conscious of my need to communicate with my family. It seems that with a little effort on both sides, a fine chat might be had.

The river Shannon lies thirty feet from our front door behind a low wall. At this point, just in front of the salmon weir, she must be a quarter mile wide—or so it seems. One stormy night, my mother takes me to an upstairs window and stands with me in her arms. The river is wild in flood; crashing and boiling on the rocks below, and a dull clanging pervades the house. Its cause is the tidal flap on the sewer main, which empties straight into the Shannon. I try to say "vibrations," but my infant tongue can only manage "bulberations."

My startled mother takes me downstairs to the kitchen, where she tells the assembled tribe, "The child just said 'bulberations' as plain as day!"

Soon a sea of blurry faces are asking me:

"What are bulberations, Willie?"

"Say 'bulberations,' Liam!"

I give up trying to converse sensibly with my folks and resort to the *goo-goo, bow-wow, choo-choo* noises they seem more comfortable with.

There is a strange gray box in the corner of the kitchen that has pipes going in and out of it. I am now old enough to crawl, but have trouble holding my head up for long periods. I notice that when my aunt Frances puts the kettle on the stove, the magic box started up clicking and whirring. I make a beeline for it and for the first time get to it before being grabbed from above by an overprotective minder. I rear up my head to take a bloody good look at my prize, and my rubber neck gives out. *Thunk!* I split my head open on the corner of the gas meter.

The shock jolts me back on my haunches. I sway to and fro, blood streaming into my eye, but I feel no pain. What is far more interesting is that half of my visual field has taken on a lush red color. All at once, pandemonium breaks out and I am snatched up by screaming adults with terrifying looks on their faces.

"The child! Oh, Holy Mother—the poor child!"

This puts the fear of Jasus into me and I start to cry. Though many long years have passed and gone, lying here on the battlefields of France, I still bear the battle scar of my encounter with the ferocious killer gas meter! It was great to be able to remember such a lot of the past. Poor old Captain Biggles could only remember his third birthday party; I was ahead of him in that respect and had war wounds to prove it. I lie on my back and stare up the arse of a skylark, frolicking in the azure firmament above. In my head my own comic strip is forming. What happened after the gas meter? Ah, yes! I turned one year old.

There I am sitting in a high chair at my first birthday party. Now the faces of my family have much more form and features, and I am able to tell one from another.

My grandda, Willie MacDonagh, is a lovely, quiet gentleman, who has a fine head of soft white hair and a merry twinkle. He makes me the present of an aerodrome made of brightly painted tinplate, and when the handle is turned, little airplanes with tiny propellers fly around in a circle about a central pivot. All of the adults have great sport with it, but I want to play with the solitary flickering candle on my birthday cake. From my position of honor at the head of the table, enthroned in my food-splattered high chair, the candle entices me. It is so bright, playfully dancing, and by hook or by crook, I am going to eat it. It is in reach and everyone's attention is taken up by the airplanes. I grab it, it is mine. *OWEEE!* The bloody thing bites me!

"Willie! Willie, are you daydreaming again? Get up off that wet grass, ye'll get piles. And don't forget to put away that ladder an' bring in the chair an' wash yer kisser. It's time to go to mass."

"What, again?"

"Yes again, and enough of yer moaning—yer worse than yer father!"

"Why do we have to go to mass all the time?"

"Because we're Catolicks. You should be thankful that we're not like the godless pagan English, hammering on the pearly gates while Saint Peter cocks a deaf ear to them! Come on now and be a good boy, and we'll maybe go on a mystery tour at the weekend!"

I shuffle to and fro with the bits of my plane in some contentment. Things are indeed looking up. Partaking of railway mystery tours beats the socks off of going to mass any day. The mystery tours are a great laugh altogether, and on the following Saturday the whole family troops down to Limerick station and boards the waiting train. Most of the men drink stout and play cards, whilst the older womenfolk chatter, natter, and knit away in shawly groups and the younger ones sit studying the railway maps, speculating on the possible destination of the trip. As we clatter along the iron road the railway carriage is filled with singing and folks clapping their hands in time. Us kids run wild from one end of the train to the other, not knowing or caring where we are bound.

After about an hour, we steam to a screeching halt in the small Tipperary town of Cahir during a thunderstorm of biblical proportions. Two hundred or so passengers scurry into the town to find the funfair and amusement park waterlogged, the shops and cafés shut, and the pubs closed for the holy hour. The only thing open to visitors is a ruined castle, which, being open to the sky, affords no shelter. There is almost a riot. The men, some of whom were now the worse for drink, are wanting to lynch the train driver and his fireman for what they think is a practical joke. It takes three local policemen and the parish priest to calm things down. Eventually we reboard the Mystery Express and the train crew comes out of their hiding place to take us back to Limerick.

On the way back home, Mickey Galvin tells a story about his poor old mother in Galway, who at the age of eighty-two, comes down on the train to visit him one summer in Limerick. Well, Mickey, a bachelor, was a great outdoors man, and he couldn't imagine his elderly mam wanting to go hiking or bicycling. So the second day, at a loss to know what to offer her in the way of entertainment, he takes her on a mystery tour. Only this time, the mystery train was going back to Galway! As she recognizes her home town, she looks at him, with tears welling up in her eyes, and says, "Could you not have let me stay on for just a couple more days, son? I won't be any trouble, son."

Disaster or not, you couldn't beat the old mystery tours!

The weather had broken, as they say in these parts, and it was soft over Clare. Great white cumulous billows of wind-lashed clouds sail up the Shannon like a fleet of Spanish galleons. I stare at the wan puddles they leave in their wake, whilst rivulets of silver-gray rainwater saturate my runway. No chance of flying a sortie in this deluge, so I play cards with my teddy bear. He wins by cheating.

A sudden rake of excitement in the house. My father is coming to see us. He is on leave from the army, and he hopes to slip into Ireland quietly for a few days and see his son for the first time. Mam is excited.

"Now you'll see something!" she says, reading his letter in the far corner of the kitchen. "I hope he gets into the country all right."

"What do you mean, Mam?"

"Well, Willie, Ireland stayed neutral in Hitler's war and soldiers from either side weren't welcome here. So with the whole shebang just after finishing, the government do be frightened by rumors of spies and secret agents and God knows what and especially suspicious of British soldiers. Godhelpus, hasn't Ireland suffered enough from the British soldiers? Your father will have to keep a low profile."

"Jasus! Reg keep a low profile? Go'way! Ye might as well be asking a leopard to change his spots!" As it turns out, Nana's words weren't far off the mark.

It being near Bonfire Night, the November fifth celebration of the failure of Guy Fawkes's attempt to blow up the English Parliament in 1605, as tradition would enlist, Dad brings me over some fireworks. How is he to know that such harmless amusements are highly illegal in Ireland?

In trying to gain entry at the Irish port of Dun Laoghaire, either his military bearing and service haircut, or his hastily assembled civilian attire, catches the attention of the ever-watchful security police.

"Excuse me, sir! What have you there in that army rucksack?"

"Er . . . it's nothing, just some presents for my son."

"It's explosives, Sergeant!" says the other one, peering in.

"Jasus!" says the sergeant as they hustled him away. "Who's your son? Dangerous Dan the dynamite man, is it?"

My poor father is deported back to Britain. So as luck would have it, I never get to meet him until the following year.

"Well, now!" says me mam. "If Mohammed won't go to the mountain, then the mountain must go to Mohammed, and there, Willie boy, we can kill two birds with one stone, can't we?" I sit on the green wooden chair, nodding assent and dangling my legs in puzzlement. Grown-ups were an odd bunch with their moving mountains and dead birds—it was a trial to keep up. My mother was best left to her own devices and in time all would be revealed. As indeed it was, later that night around the kitchen table.

"He needs to get that eye fixed or he'll be looking round corners all his life."

"We can't let him off to school with the other kids shouting, 'Hey, Willie! Is that yer eye—the white thing?'"

So I was born with a lazy eye, or a cod eye as they say in Ireland. It caused me no grief, for you never miss what you've never had, but my family didn't want me growing up and people taking the mickey out of me. It is decided that I be taken back to Britain for free medical treatment on the National Health Service. As I have no say in the matter, I am stoic.

On the downside, it means leaving all I'd ever known for a while. On the other hand, it meant a great trip on the train and a ride on a ship. Also, the chance to live with my other grandparents for a wee bit and maybe see my dad if he can get leave from his unit.

As the day of departure approaches, all pervading waves of doom threaten to scuttle the frail craft of my optimism. My older cousin Joe explains it best: "Don't be worried, they just cut out yer bad eye and put a pickled onion in!"

We take the steam train from Limerick to Dun Laoghaire, where we board the ancient steamship *Princess Maud,* a floating relic of the 1920s. Mam sings an old ditty as we tramp up the gangplank, arms linked:

Bobby Shaftoe's gone to sea
Silver buckles on his knee
He'll come back and marry me
Bonny Bobby Shaftoe.

Having only the cheapest third-class tickets, we are confined to green cast-iron park benches bolted to the stern deck. There is only a tiny indoor lounge, and it is already packed full, twice over.

At last the great steam hooter blows. The blue peter is struck from the foremast head and we are off, straight into the teeth of a howling gale. To the exposed cheeks the raw wind is like emery paper, but I discover that by changing the shape of my mouth, the wind could be made to play little tunes that only I could hear.

"What are ye pulling faces like that for? Stop it now, ye'll have people think yer fooly, making faces like a fish, ya eejit. Oh, my God, *fish!*" Mam lurches to the rail and shares her breakfast with squabbling seagulls, bobbing on the boiling foam, thirty feet below. At that moment as we cross the breakwater, the wind freshens and the stern fantail is lashed by a following sea. Mad green crests spill over the aft deck rail and threaten to soak us all. Great eddies of freezing Irish seawater swirl toward our ankles, forcing us to sit like gargoyles, knees under chin. As the pilot boat leaves for shore, a bevy of kind sailors appears and within minutes jury-rig a big green tarpaulin over us to keep off the worst of the salt spray and rain. My poor mam continues to be terribly seasick, but I love every aspect of this seagoing enterprise; it awakens some long-slumbering leviathan within me! Fascinated, I watch the sailors brace against the wind, coiling hawsers, stowing docking gear, and checking davits. The old tub pitches and rolls, whilst I, with arms outstretched as a crucifix, ricochet around the aft capstans like a well-upholstered orb in a giant pinball machine. I have marvelous fun trying to keep my balance and come to no harm at all.

"Mam!" says I, "this is great!"

My mam peers out from under her blanket.

"You're in league with the devil," comes her baleful reply.

A big bearded sailor snatches me up in his arms.

"Steady as she goes! Here's a wee fellow who has his first sea legs! One of these days you'll might make a grand sailor, my young bucko!"

He doesn't have to tell me. I am already of that conviction!

We dock in Holyhead the following morning. Mam is still green in the face but after a cup of tea at the station café feels more the ticket. I am still exhilarated, but my joy is short lived.

Mam fishes in her handbag, producing a lipstick-stained white linen handkerchief. Then she dribbles a long plume of spittle onto it and scrubs my face with the resultant infusion. It is a horrible indignation for a sailor to suffer!

"There you are, a cat's lick and a promise to see you through the day."

So, if *that's* what makes me a Catolick, then I could well do without it!

On dry land now, but my little legs could still feel the pull of the ship.

I weave from side to side in my effort to maintain equilibrium.

"Look, Mam, I'm drunk!"

"That's all I need, a drunken sailor to look after, what shall we do with you?"

> *What shall we do with a drunken sailor?*
> *What shall we do with a drunken sailor?*
> *What shall we do with a drunken sailor?*
> *Early in the morning.*
> *Ohray up she rises, ohray up she rises,*
> *Ohray up she rises, early in the morning.*

Arms linked again in song, we skip past the huge, hissing monster of a Pacific class passenger locomotive and find good seats in a carriage just a few compartments down from the coal tender stacked high with its polished jet-black nuggets.

With two sharp blasts of the whistle, the great iron beast heaves his steel connecting rods and, squealing into movement, belches a hoarse roar of steam. Having thus asserted itself, the tamed tyrant gets down to the business of the day and clanks off into the hinterland of Wales. Mam starts to sing a nonsense song to entertain me:

Paddy was a Welshman, Paddy was a thief
Paddy came to our house, and stole a leg of beef.
We went to Paddy's house, Paddy wasn't there.
So I catched him by the two legs, and threw him down the stairs.

"Mam, who was Paddy?"

"I dunno."

"Why was he Welsh if he was a Paddy?"

"I dunno!"

"How can you throw him downstairs if he isn't there?"

Mam begins to snore and I am left to figure out the mysterious Paddy for myself.

Wales speeds by.

"Will you look at that now," says my mam, waking up from her snooze. We are pulling into a station, the name of which is displayed on a sign that runs the entire one-hundred-foot length of the platform. It reads:

LLANFAIRPWLLGWYNGYLLGOGERYCHWYRNDROBWLLLLANTYSILIOGOGGOG

"What does it mean, Mammy?"

"Jasus, don't be asking me. It could be the Welsh word for teacup for all I know. Ask your dad when you see him. He speaks Welsh, so he'll know how to say it."

So there it was, my father, of whom I had heard so many heroic tales, could also pronounce the Welsh word for teacup. My, my.

"Tickets, please, ladies and gentlemen. Tickets, please!" The blue uniformed conductor enters the carriage. He has a thing like a pair of pliers in his hand and a black peaked cap with a badge of a silver lion holding a wheel on the front. The man looks at the small oblong green tickets and punches a hole in each.

"Thank you, ma'am!"

"The young fella wants to know what the sign reads, yonder?"

"Oh, yes, indeed. I wish I had a shilling for every time someone has asked me that. It means 'Saint Mary's Church of the pool of the white hazel, near the rushing whirlpool, Saint Tysylio's Church, near the red cave.' Lovely, isn't it?"

"What about the teacups?"

"Teacups, is it? Teacups, there's plenty of teacups under the other sign over there. Café, see?"

They're at it again, grown-ups! Ask a civil question and they give you nonsense about saints and hazel trees and red caves. The man looks puzzled, Mam shrugs her shoulders, and I stare out of the window as the train moves off.

The boat train continues over the Telford bridge across the Menai Strait and on into mainland Wales. As we round the sea cliffs the enormous battlements of Conway heave into view. The almost perfectly preserved city walls built by the English king Edward the First are dominated by one of the largest and most formidable castles in Europe. I notice with glee that the railway tunnel entrances are all turreted and castellated in the same style as the Norman fortress above.

My mam is less impressed by this masterpiece of Plantangenet military technocratics.

"All that to keep the poor Welsh down in their own country. BloodyEnglish!" She dozes off again.

I am nearly twenty years old before I realize that *Bloody English* are two different words!

The fatigue of my seaborn adventure sweeps over me and I join Mam in restful sleep. I wake up in New Street Station in the heart of the second biggest city in Britain.

Here in Birmingham, I get my first ride on the top of a double-decker bus and sit right at the front so that I can pretend to steer. The view is terrific and the bustling streets teem with lorries, cars, and tram-cars whose sleek steel rails channel through the shiny black cobbled streets like veins of silver. I am even too curious to mind the inevitable spit-soaked hankie catlicking away at my cheeks. This is the biggest city I have ever seen, bigger than anything in Ireland. World War Two was only over eight years since and vast tracts of the urban area are still fireweed-covered wastelands—bomb sites, courtesy of Herr Hitler's Luftwaffe.

"Do they not have horses here, Mam?"

"No, not many. They have a few, but not like over home."

"I don't see any donkeys either, nor dogs wandering the streets."

"No, you won't. The English keep their dogs inside of the house."

"Oh, yes, dogs inside of the house, that will be right! Ha-ha, dogs inside of the house, indeed. I suppose they keep chickens in the parlor, too!"

"Of course they do, and cheeky little sods like you are locked up in the coal hole! Now hold your whist a minute or we'll be missing our stop to get off."

Mam knows her way about the town, and she tells me her story. As a young girl, she had been here during the war, working in a munitions plant making machine guns. As the blitz continued, every night the German bombers were overhead showering death and destruction on the city. One night my mam was too ill with the flu to do her shift. Her roommate, another Irish girl, said she would put her name on the sick list at work and tell the foreman. That night the Nazi bombs found their elusive target and the factory was blown to pieces. Most of the workers were in the basement canteen on their tea break when the bombs hit. The four floors above came crashing down upon them, burying them alive under hundreds of tons of heavy machinery and bricks. The ones who were trapped had not the slightest chance of escape, there being no equipment available on the home front to lift such massive debris. As the weeks went by, the cries of the entombed faded and were still. My mother's friend, whom she had traveled with from Ireland, never returned. Mam gave out a long low sigh, and I tried to quickly change the subject.

"Brick, brick, and more brick! Sure everything here is made of bricks."

"That's true, the English like their bricks, so they do."

"I bet you don't know a song about bricks, Mam?"

"Oh, don't I?"

> *The county jail is made of bricks*
> *And the gates are made of I-ron*
> *With a big tall window and a big strong door*
> *To keep out Boody Byron*
> *When Boody Byron made a fart*

I thought the stink would blind me
Then he made another and I thought I'd smother
For the girl I left behind me.

Never can I beat Mam with this challenge—she has a poem or a song or a bit of old nonsense for everything. I resolve to take in the sights as Mam does the commentary.

"Things are on the move here, by God. After the destruction of six years of war, the entire place has to be rebuilt. Ye could make your golden fortunes here, you couldn't lose! Sure with full employment, being out of work is almost impossible. But some lazy buggers still manage it, just to stay on the dole." Mam goes on to tell me that at this time, there are tens of thousands of Irish workers in England, and the chiefs amongst these fellas are the far-famed Irish navvies, who are mostly unskilled, but fiercely hard-working, short-contract laborers. They are so clever that they can build houses, roads, railways, docks—in fact, anything. They take their name from the navigations or canals that were dug throughout Britain in the last century. Many who start with nothing but a pick and shovel go on to make a good living, and some end up owning their own construction firms or fleets of trucks and then go back and buy big houses in Ireland.

Schools, houses, pubs, factories speed past—even some of the streets are made of brick. It's marvelous. Ireland has little in the way of brick buildings, so all the more noticeable here are the curves and bastions of yellow, red, brown, and the beautiful gunmetal-colored Staffordshire blue bricks. However, if it all looks different, when we get off the bus it smells even stranger. Whereas in Limerick the pervading odors are of leather tanning, horseshit, peat smoke, and the ever-present tang of the river Shannon, Birmingham's atmosphere bears the piquancy of coal dust, gasworks, and asphalt. Sure enough, there are tar boilers everywhere, sending their glorious reek skyward, and around these, little knots of men lean furiously on rakes and shovels, waiting "for the tae to boil." Whether or not they mean the tar in the boiler or the tea kettle sitting on its brazier, you can only guess. Occasionally my mam will spot a familiar face amongst the tarmac gangs and stop to exchange the news about what is happening over home. She smiles at everyone.

"Odd folk, the English. Most like to get on well with the Irish immigrants, but as anywhere, some folk can be awful spiteful and then they call you a Mick or a Paddy or a bog trotter or even a duck egg!"

"Why a duck egg?"

"Well, they reckon that like duck's eggs, one out of every three Irish people is a bad egg. It's all water off a duck's arse to me," says Mam. "Sticks and stones may break my bones, but names will never hurt me!"

Our journey ends at a little group of apartments, squat and square oblongs of urban utility, coy and effete, each rectangular window opaque with lace-curtain privacy, standing sternly above a prim pinafore of red sand bricks.

✦ Chapter 2 ✦

UNIFORMED AND MUSTACHIOED, GRANDDAD JIM WATKINS glares down from his First World War portrait above the fireplace. He has those eyes that follow you around the room, and I am very put off by the stern look of him. He looks like a baddie out of the films.

My granny, Mary-Anne, seems very nice. She is a skinny little woman and has long auburn hair tied up in a bun. Her maiden name was Bentley, and she is of Irish and Breton descent. She tells me that "Gentleman Jim Bentley," the bare-fist boxer, was her father and therefore my great-grandfather and I should be proud of him. She says he was very tough and, when training for a prizefight, would sit at the kitchen table with his fists pickling in hot salty water called brine to harden them up.

An actress and dancer in her youth, she had met my grandfather, Sergeant Major James T. Watkins, whilst he was serving with the Allied army in France in 1915. She offers us tea and while she's out of the room Mam whispers a song in my ear that gives me a fit of the giggles:

> *Mary-Anne the dancer,*
> *Wouldn't say her prayers,*
> *Catch her by the two legs,*
> *And throw her down the stairs*
> *The stairs went crack!*
> *Mary broke her back!*
> *And all the little ducks went,*
> *Quack! Quack! Quack!*

Mam points to a photograph on the mantelpiece. It shows a woman in a long skirt and buttoned boots, pushing a huge-wheeled baby carriage from which two moonfaced boys grin toothless smiles. In the background, two older boys in knee breeches hold ancient bicycles almost as tall as themselves.

"That's your granny there, and the baby with the squashed nose is your dad. The younger one is your uncle Ronny and the two other boys are your uncle Harold and your uncle Jimmy. When was this taken, Mary-Anne—about 1920?"

"It would be around 1922. Ronny was just a year old, Monica."

Mary-Anne arranges the tea set, which has hexagonal china cups and saucers, very posh indeed. I'd never seen the like. With a gurgle, the hot brown infusion swirls in the silver tealeaf strainer and a tippet of milk is added from a fine floral jug. Mam picks up a pair of silver tongs and drops a small white cube into her cup.

"It's sugar," she whispers, answering my questioning look. The tea has a taste all its own and is very nice. Perhaps it was Chinese tea—we had nothing like it in Ireland. Granny and Mam both sup at the tea with their little fingers pointing stiffly out from the cups. It looks very odd and is called manners. Gran gives us biscuits along with the tea, the sort the Americans call cookies, but I'm warned against dipping them into my cup, as that's called *bad* manners.

After tea, Gran sits chatting with my mother and I take this as my cue to explore the room, which is warm and cozy with heavy braided velvet curtains and a coal fire. I've never seen upholstered chairs before, or the big fat seat called a settee. In Ireland, chairs are made of wood and don't have matching flowery cushions all over them. Here, each armchair has a white linen handkerchief draped over the top. Mam says these are called antimacassars and are used to keep men's hair oil from staining the fabric. One corner of the room contains a harmonium, which I'm not allowed to play with, and a long bookcase with the titles showing through the leaded-glass doors. Opposite, two electric reading lamps in the shape of bronze soldiers hold green glass lampshades above an old Singer sewing machine, and in the farthest corner, the wireless talks quietly to itself and an attendant audience of beautifully ornate antique glass paperweights. For all the novelties, it is the coal fire that intrigues me the most. Being only used to the slow smoldering glow of a peat fire, this is altogether quite different. Queerly shaped twisted tongues of flame flicker in a dainty dance from the black nuggets. Hissing jets of coal gas squirt out from their cracks, gray and vaporous, then catching light, jig and gyrate in ragged crescents of orange, red, and yellow. Veins of intrusive copper ignite, sending arcs of iridescent blue shooting up the chimney, and the sulfurous tang of soot provides the atmosphere with a new and subtle aroma. I am mesmerized.

There is a noise in the hall.

"Here's Jim now," says my gran, tucking a loose piece of hair behind her ear.

I hide behind the settee to avoid being seen by those cold staring eyes. The door opens, and, instead of the Joseph Stalin character from the photograph, there enters a smiling, round-faced, bald old chap, with wire-rimmed glasses and a walrus mustache.

"Hello, Monica," says he, looking around. "Where's the young fellow? I've got something here for him."

I wiggle out of my hiding place and am presented with a small toy army tank. It is made of tin and is driven by clockwork. When allowed to run, it trundles along and suddenly flips over in a mechanical somersault. It is brilliant, and so is my granddad Jim for finding it for me. He says it was made by German prisoners of war, who were very clever at such things, and to beat it all, they made everything out of old sardine tins turned inside out. The tank is vividly painted with bright colors and held together by a system of slots and lugs. I later learn to undo these tags with a teaspoon, and it is true—they were old sardine tins and you could see the labels with fishermen painted on them!

The ice is broken and Granddad Jim is my best pal. I spend many hours sitting on his knee while he reads to me. He sees little merit in kiddies' books and only reads to me from the likes of George Eliot, Sir Arthur Conan Doyle, and Francis Brett Young.

"You're putting an old head on young shoulders, Jim."

"Nonsense, Mary-Anne, he's better reading this than that drivel in the comics."

Granddad is also very keen on Sir Walter Scott and, particularly, the *Waverley* novels. He has a great love of anything Scottish, and my grandparents spend most of their holidays up there.

When Granddad Jim isn't in the mood for reading, he tells me stories of his childhood and the rich history he grew up with, long ago.

"Did you know I was born in Bleddfa in the heart of Welsh Wales, where our people had held land since before the Roman invasion? Oh, yes, indeed! The battle of Pylleth was fought on our ancestral land centuries ago, and the great Welsh patriot and freedom fighter, Owain Glyn Dŵr, used our hidden valleys as a base to attack and harry the English in 1400. A very great man, was Owain. A Celtic hero to be proud of!

"Well, in the late eighteen hundreds, you see, the Great Western Railway Company began to forge its iron sinews into the heart of wild Wales, and legions of Irish navvies flooded into the construction camps and shantytowns that sprang up along the railhead. They needed the work, see? I was only twelve and had just left school. Ever the enterprising, I made lemonade and sold it by the pint to the thirsty workers. Loved it, they did! So anyway, one hot summer's day when I was plying my trade amongst the rail crew, a near parboiled Irishman stopped his toil and leaning on his pick wiped the sweat from his brow. He began to sing 'There's Trouble in My Native Land,' a song now sadly lost, I believe. Soon there wasn't a man jack working on the entire cutting. He finished his song to tearful applause and cheers. As an encore and to lift the heart, he launched into this old Napoleonic war song.

> *'Bad luck to this marching*
> *Pipe claying and starching*
> *How neat we must be to be killed by the French . . .*
>
> *Now I love "Garryowen"*
> *When I hear it at home*
> *'Tis a marvelous tune, with an elegant lilt,*
> *But the strength of the beat*
> *Doesn't sound half as sweet*
> *When you're facing the French and about to be kilt.'*

"After some remonstration, the foremen and gangers got the men grudgingly to resume work, and the young James Watkins—that was me, you see—was left with an experience that I never forgot and an unquenchable thirst for Celtic music that stayed with me ever since. You know, I love to hear your mother sing those antediluvian Irish songs."

"That's typical of Jim . . . use ten words where one would suffice."

"I'll give you one word in a minute, Mary-Anne, that you won't hear in church!"

This new life in postwar Birmingham is full of oddities and exotica. There is marmalade, which I didn't care for; and bread and goody, which I did. The latter is made of broken-up crusts of bread soused with hot milk and finished with a wee dusting of brown sugar. It is a great favorite of my granddad Jim, who eats it twice a day, and later on I am to find out why.

Soon I am settled in and begin exploring. The back garden teems with blackberries, red currants, black currants, and gooseberries, or goosegogs, as they are commonly called. My gran makes a lot of jams and jellies, and I like to help her in the kitchen, which she always refers to as the scullery. One chilly morning, Mam puts together the sticks and paper makings of a fire and stares into an empty matchbox.

"Were out of lucifers, Mary-Anne."

"You can get a light off of the geyser in the kitchen, Monica." Mam goes out of the room only to return puzzle-faced a minute later.

"There's no one in the kitchen, he must have left!"

"No, she means the water heater, Mam, the thing on the wall by the sink. It's called a geyser."

Luckily, I had previously been introduced to this bizarre apparatus by my granddad Jim. It has a little blue flame that just peeps out of its burner, but when the hot tap is turned on—*whoosh!* The entire thing lights up with hundreds of gas jets. Very spectacular! But how on earth does it know when to flare up? I give it a wide berth anyway, in case it is some way in league with its Irish cousin, the dreaded gas meter, and it takes a notion to attack me.

I settle into life in 1002 Warwick Road, Acock's Green, Birmingham, like a cat with a new cardboard box. There is still no sign of my dad and thankfully no mention of the eye hospital or pickled onions.

The whole town is abuzz with talk of the forthcoming coronation of

Queen Elizabeth II, or the "Old Baked Bean," as my granddad Jim calls her in rhyming slang.

"It's a shame you Irish don't have a royal family," says the woman at the grocery shop.

"We've more sense," says my mam. "And anyway, if we wanted one, there's more royal blood in my little finger than in the whole lot of them jumped-up buggers!"

The shop girl is scandalized, and my mother sweeps out of the grocer's like an empress—royal finger and all.

"They make me sick, with their sucking up to the royalty, bloody bunch of inbreeds who wouldn't piss on you if you were on fire! They should have more sense. BloodyEnglish!" Mam is in an acidulous mood, and she pokes her tongue out at the Union Jack banner proclaiming the message "God Bless the Queen."

"God bless my old aunt Fanny! And that bloody awful dirge they call a national anthem—Jeesus! It gives me a pain in the nawney!"

"What's the nawney?"

"Never you mind."

Through the red, white, and blue bunting–filled streets we march to the sweetie shop. I'm in good spirits because this is to be my once-a-week treat. Mam swings her arms like a trooper and sings the stirring Irish national anthem, "The Soldier's Song":

> *Sinne Fianna Fáil*
> *Atá fá gheall ag Éirinn . . .*

Wartime rationing is still in force, and I have my own identity card and ration book. There are coupons for clothes, meat, fish, and eggs, but at my age, it is just the sweet coupons that interested me. I only get two a week, though, and even then they don't buy very much, Godhelpus!

May is the white-haired old lady in the little Victorian confectionery shop at the end of the street. She always seems to enjoy my weekly visit to her sweet-smelling emporium, which looks like a scene from a Charles Dickens novel, all dark oak, polished brass handles, and bull's-eye glass windows.

"Is it your usual then, Willie?"

She knows it is.

"Yes, please, May, two marshmallows, one in a bag and one in my hand."

I think she gets a kick out of my childish ways and funny Irish accent.

Confectionery remains rationed until I am seven, which does me no harm and indeed did well to keep me out of the dentist's chair. Of all the things I miss about the old country, it was the patsy-pop that I could really go for, but there was none to be had hereabouts, more's the pity. On my return home, I will be straight up the road to Paddy King's, to purchase for a penny what could not be got for love nor money in pagan England.

The road back from May's sweet shop is festooned with large colorful enamel advertisement signs screwed to the dark red brick on every street corner. Mam reads every one of them out loud, so I can learn the big words.

"Tizer the Energiser!" the one showing a big bottle of pop reads. Next to it a cheeky-looking monkey stares at his reflection in a newly scrubbed frying pan: "USE MONKEY BRAND SOAP!"

Across the street, a large orange-and-black sign entreats us to "Drink Brooke Bond Tips . . . the Tea you can really TASTE!"

"Drink VIMTO," demands a purple-tinted bottle of pop.

One large and colorful sign depicts the Holy Father sitting in the Vatican supping beef tea. Mam reads the slogan: "Two things Infallible—The POPE and BOVRIL!"

And like a call from back home in Ireland: "GUINNESS IS GOOD FOR YOU!"

The rag and bone men come around in their horse and carts, blowing old brass bugles and calling out, "Rags, bottles, and bones." If you give them something useful they would often swap you a balloon or a goldfish. In these years after the war, little goes to waste. All metal is recycled, and each family has a pig bin to put waste food—potato peelings, rotten apples, or what have you—for the wee porkers. I like the horse and carts clip-clopping along the cobbled streets and the way my granddad Jim scurries after them with a bucket and shovel to collect shite for his roses.

Entering the hallway of the house I realize something is different.

The air smells of cigarettes and there is a large army kit bag in the hall. I run into the living room to investigate and fall straight over the sausage-shaped draft excluder. As I lie sprawled facedown into the red-and-brown Chinese carpet, a voice in the air above me says, "OOPS-a-daisy!"

I arise tearlessly and towering above me is a huge soldier in full dress uniform. He is like the ones I've seen in the toy shop, but to me, he seems sixty feet high! His trousers have a red stripe running down each leg, and he has a brown mustache.

I do not know what to make of him or the long steel and wood thing he has with him. It looks like a toy gun but is of a weight that surely none could lift. He tells me it's a Lee-Enfield Mk. IV 303 rifle. He picks me up and gives me a kiss—he needs a shave.

This, then, is my dad, Bombardier Reginald Watkins, a noncommissioned officer of the Royal Artillery, home on leave before parading as part of the guard of honor at the queen's coronation in London. It's odd to see him with my mam. I feel a bit jealous.

Some days later Mam and Dad take me shopping. It is our first family outing.

Dad carries me up on his shoulders and I get a first-rate view of the world from above the top of my dad's head, plastered with this shiny Brylcreem stuff. Dad has his attention fixed upward at me and fails to notice the ice cream sign straddling the pavement. He promptly falls over it. This projects me in an arc, cometlike, from his grasp. But being well upholstered against the chilly spring air, I bounce along the sidewalk like a rubber beach ball, all with little ill effect.

The next minute I am snatched up. My father is furious. He dives into the nearest shop door, towing me in the air behind him.

"Are you the manager?" he demands.

"Yes, sir. I am indeed," says the man in the white coat, venturing a discreet smile.

BANG! My father hits him square on the nose. As the ill-starred shopkeeper slips gently to the floor, my father is roaring at him.

"You stupid bastard! The child could have been killed!"

"Reg! Reg!" My mother is pulling at his arm.

"Bloody stupid place to leave a sign!"

"Reg! For Christ's sake!" Father, in his "battle fury," takes no notice.

"REEEGGG!" Mother is desperate. "YOU'RE IN THE WRONG SHOP!"

Dad produces a wiggly face like one of the cartoon characters from the news theater and looms over the counter.

"Sorry, pal, my mistake!" He comforts his cowering victim, then he is gone like a shot from a gun, us following.

A few days later we go downtown on the bus and into an imposing-looking building that smells of iodine and disinfectant. I don't like it one little bit.

The doctor at the eye clinic gives me a ragged, old one-eyed teddy bear to hold, which does nothing at all for my confidence. Then, sitting me in a giant, cold, leather chair, he wheels over a thing that shines a bright light into my eyes. After some poking about in a drawer, he leans into me, peering into his space gun. I can see right up his nose!

"I'm afraid the right eye will always be weak, Mrs. Watkins, but he'll most likely grow out of his squint."

"Very good," says Mam. "Will he have to have glasses?"

"Indeed, yes, and he'll have to wear a patch over his good eye to force the other to improve."

Well, this was great news! No pickled onions, and I always fancied glasses because clever people wear them. Apart from this, I have the bonus of a pirate's eye patch that makes you grow "out of your squint," whatever that was. It all seems very grand and it looks like the visit is worthwhile after all. He even lets me look into his space gun, but all I see is a round blob of light.

On the way home we venture into the fish market. The building is just walls now, open to the heavens, the roof having been destroyed by German bombs in November 1940. I eat three plates of cockles drowned in malt vinegar, which I then drink. It is lovely!

By the time the spectacles arrive, I have quite forgotten about them. Granddad Jim comes in with a big pile of mail.

"Your gig lamps are here, Willie."

Mam slowly opens the parcel, putting aside the brown paper and string, and there they are, little round specs with . . . Agh! Horrors! PINK RIMS!

"I can't wear these, they're for girls!"

"You bloody well shall and you bloody well will, by crikey! No son of mine will ever look a gift horse in the mouth!"

I have no idea what she is talking about, but I know better than to argue. To add insult to injury, a special plaster sticks them to my face, so there is no escape from the poxy things. I look in the mirror, wishing to see a scientist-type chap reflected, but instead, staring back dolefuly at me is the village idiot.

Mam must be feeling sorry for me. She takes me to see *Bambi*.

"We better test your new glasses," she says.

I wanted to test them with a hammer.

At any rate I knew it was Mam's custom, after the movies, to go next door to the Oxford Restaurant. There they serve the finest sausage and stuffing in the world, and it is my favorite. The forest fire rages, Bambi's mother dies, Mam sobs into her handkerchief, and I sit in the darkness, my stomach rumbling like a volcano, dreaming of sausages and stuffing.

"Have you no heart at all, child?" Mam says, appalled at my indifference.

"Sure 'tis only an old filum," I say, the steam from the sausages condensing on my glasses and gravy running down my chin.

"What did you feel when his poor mother died?" she entreats.

"Hungry," says I.

Mam shakes her head in resignation, and the dreaded lipstick-and-mascara stained handkerchief makes its appearance.

"You're a muck savage," is her final word on the matter, as she spits on the hankie.

Dad, resplendent in his best uniform, says he's going off to London, "to look at the Queen," like the old nursery rhyme would have it. Mam and I go with him to the railway station, where he mingles with a great squad of other soldiers all dressed the same. The military police won't allow civilians onto the platform, and Mam and I have to wave from behind the iron railings. There is a huge press of people, cheering and waving flags at the troop train. But I'm crying. With all the soldiers looking so much alike, I can't see which one is my dad anymore. My mother doesn't notice me until I get my head stuck in the bars of the gate and howl even louder. In the ensuing panic I miss the final departure of the London Coronation Special altogether, as I'm busy being scolded for sticking my head through the bars and getting my ears rubbed with stinky soap by the stationmaster.

I'm still crying when we get on the bus to go back to Granny's. Mam says Dad is only going away for a few days and I'll see him soon enough. I'm not convinced.

We go to the Freemans' house to see the coronation on a new televisor. I am very excited, as I have never seen a TV in action. Granddad Jim tells me that television had begun transmitting from Alexandra Palace, London, in the late 1930s, but the broadcasts were suspended at the outbreak of the war. The coronation of 1953 is the BBC's attempt to reestablish the service, and thousands, like the Freemans, have bought new television sets for the special occasion.

The house is as crowded as a wasp's nest, as this is the only TV in the entire street. Everyone has been invited, and the Brits are in a festive mood. There are sandwiches and pop for the kids, and beer and spirits for the older folk.

A great silence falls upon the eager crowd. Mr. Freeman checks his pocket watch and, with somber ceremony, switches on the television. The set begins to warm up and after what seems like an age, the sound comes on first with a loud drum roll and everyone stands up as a fuzzy picture appears. A mournful, lethargic tune fills the room like a funeral march. The TV image sharpens. It shows a man in military uniform, standing on a stone column.

"There's my dad!" I shout, pointing with certainty at the granite statue of Admiral Lord Nelson standing atop his pillar in London's Trafalgar Square.

"Quiet, child! Have you no respect for the national anthem?"

"No, it gives me a pain in the nawney!"

✦ Chapter 3 ✦

THE SEASONS TURN AND DAD GOES BACK TO HIS UNIT. THERE is much weeping, and I want to go with him. He tells me I must stay behind to look after my mam on the trip back to Ireland, as she is such a poor sailor. Once again, Dad disappears from my life, and two days later we take off for my other home over the water. This time sailing from Liverpool on the B+I steamer *M.V. Munster.* The crossing is pleasant, and Mam is able to sit inside, as third-class accommodation is far superior to the old S.S. *Princess Maud.* The voyage is much longer, however, and it is nighttime when we sail up the treacle-black river Liffey and dock amid the golden glow of Dublin's North Wall pier.

The city is afire with neon signs, the first I have ever seen. One in an alley off Dame Street shows a before-and-after baldy man, frowning under his naked neon dome, then seconds later—Exulted!—colorfully crowned with his flashing electric wig!

"I bet you don't have a song about a baldy man, Mam?"

> *Hey there baldy over there*
> *What's it like to have no hair?*
> *Is it hot or is it cold?*
> *What is it like to be bald?*

"Got me again, Mam."

Another spectacular display is at the end of Grafton Street. It takes up the full parapet of an entire block and depicts a cheery neon pig frying two sausages in a pan. The piggy, having decided the bangers are ready, gives them a flick and *Wheeee!* The pair of links loop the loop across the building and land square on the plate of a smiling diner.

"Give me a song about sausages, Mam. I bet you can't."

Oh, the next time you visit your grocer
Tell him no other sausage will do sir.
The next time you visit your grocer
It's Donnelley's Sausage for you.

"Oh, Mam, you're a terror!"

The train ride down from Dublin is a cozy affair. We have the compartment to ourselves and lollop across the brown-braided seats, as snug as seals on a sandbar.

In the dim carriage light, Mam fishes out a copy of the *News of the World*.

"'Twill be nice to be home again, eh, Willie?" She flicks through the newspaper.

"'Twill so, Mam, but why is it home when we have a home in England as well?"

"Ah, well, that's the Irish for you—always on the move, taking their homes with them on their backs like a snail." She nods agreement with herself and ruffling the folds of her gossip sheet, reads aloud the curious headline: "'HOW THE WELFARE WORKER'S MODEL WIFE FELL FOR THE CHINESE HYPNOTIST FROM THE CO-OP BACON FACTORY.' Jasus, who'd of thought it . . . shocking . . . *tut-tut!*"

Mam turns over the pages to be shocked and reshocked again and again. Although I doubted the wisdom of distracting my mother from her weekly dose of scandal, I'm left in some puzzlement by her previous explanation and venture another query.

"Mam?"

"What now?" says the distracted voice coming from behind the newspaper.

"Mam, I don't get it. What's the thing about the snail? What does it have to do with us having two homes—and what on earth is that story you're reading?" Mam's paper crumples into her lap. She stares at me like a cat about to pounce on a field mouse and chastises my interruption with a bit of poetry:

"You are a funny fellow," says a puppy to a snail.
"As far as anyone can see, you haven't got a tail."

"My tail is not a waggy-one. It's in my house upstairs,
And I don't poke my nose like pups, in other folks' affairs!"

Jeez, that's rich coming from Mam, who not only minds her own business but kindly accepts the burden of everyone else's besides.

"The priest says it's a sin to read that newspaper!"

"Does he so? Maybe he's feared there'd be a story about him in it."

I wake up in a brightly lit Limerick station. A taxi ride through the streets proves the worth of the taxi driver, who is telling us of the great electrification scheme going on all over Ireland since the building of the hydroelectric plant on the Shannon at Ardnacrusha.

"Sure the 'lectric light is a marvel, missus. It don't be flickering like the ould gas lanterns, and you can see for miles with it."

It's true. Lights twinkle out in the darkness, way off on the hills of Clare, and it's hard to tell where the streetlights stop and the stars begin.

The car arrives at Nana's house. Electric light spills from every window.

On entering the old homestead, I notice a change of smell. The aroma of peat smoke is still present, but the sweet tang of warm paraffin oil no longer wafts from the now redundant kerosene lamps.

My relatives greet me with a flurry of head pats and "My, hasn't he grown, Monica." Behind their heads, a big new painting of Jesus gazes down from the top of the stairwell, illuminated by a red neon crucifix glowing beneath. After the teapot has made its second circuit around the kitchen table, I excuse myself and sneak upstairs for a surreptitious peek at the mysterious holy picture.

Jesus' long brown hair curls down to his shoulders and his bearded mouth is fixed in a benign hint of a sad smile. His blue eyes are whirlpools of sorrow as he points to the raw red thing sticking out of his bared chest. Stuck through with jaggy, spiked thorns and sur-mounted by hot flicks of flame, the heart-shaped object on Our Savior's breast is a fearsome sight. What could it all mean? I wasn't going to ask my folks and get called an ignorant pagan again. I'll have to work this one out for myself. What did it mean? Then it dawns on me. Of course! This must be what the grown-ups call heartburn! Flushed with the pride of discovery, I look for confirmation on the little brass name plaque fixed to the gilt frame beneath. In the dim bleed of light from the neon cross, I trace out the letters with my finger, making the sounds like Granddad Jim had taught me: T . . . H . . . E . . . S . . . A . . . C . . . R . . . E . . . D . . . H . . . E . . . A . . . R . . . T.

"The Scared Heart!" I find myself whispering in the blood-colored gloom.

Poor Jesus, with heartburn to contend with, it's little wonder he looks so melancholy. 'Tis true what Mam says: "He suffered for the sins of the world."

Later, as I climb the stairs to my bed, I glance once more at the sore-looking sacred heart and pray that Jesus might be allowed a glass of Andrew's Liver Salts to ease his pain.

The next morning, in the full brightsome of day, Christ appears much more at ease with his complaint and seems to have a merry twinkle in his eye. Ah, there's great power in prayer, I'm thinking, as I dive downstairs to a fried Irish breakfast that would give a goat indigestion.

The kitchen door opens and in comes a bicycle. Behind the bicycle is a smile and behind that, in his postman's uniform, is my uncle Seán. He is always laughing and joking and acting the gussie with us kids. He's like a big kid himself, and he speaks lovely Irish.

Breakfast done with, I am sitting in the peat house, just off the kitchen, trying to build an igloo with rectangular blocks of turf. It is grand to be home and busy constructing something. It's no easy matter getting the cuts of dried peat to stack in concentric circles and my previous attempts lie like the ruins of the ancient monks' cells on Skellig Island.

"You'll get fleas, playing in that turf," says Seán.

I grin like a gombeen.

"Here's a tosser for you," he says, flicking me a silver sixpenny piece.

I miss the catch—and it is consumed by the piles of peat.

"You'll have your work cut out for ye, finding that!"

And I do, but it was worth six patsy-pops!

"The boys will be over later and we'll all go to the pictures," says my uncle.

"Terrific!" says I, and spend the rest of the morning scratching around in the peat for the elusive sixpence. At last I see the glint of it just as the back door almost leaves its hinges, and the querulous circus of humanity known as my cousins fall, flop, and flounder on the kitchen floor.

These are Joe, Mikesy, and Willum, my aunt Frances's boys, all screeching and squabbling, like cats in a passion.

"What's all this, lads? I never heard such a din!" Seán picks up his dinner plate left warming above a hissing pot on top of the ancient gas stove.

"Mammy said I was to hold the sweetie money," says one.

"No, she didn't! She said I could!" says another.

"Well, I'm the eldest, so it should be me!" joins the third.

"Enough! Enough!" says Seán, still smiling. "It goes to the quietest!"

This psychological ruse has instant efficacy and the Buckleys sit at the table like the three wise monkeys, Hear No Evil, See No Evil, and Speak No Evil.

I emerge from the store triumphant, holding my tanner coin aloft.

"There now," says Seán, "who says there's no money in farming?" He removes the saucepan lid covering his meal and stares at the food with a convulsive shudder.

"Did yer mam cook this for me, Willie?"

"She did, Seán. It's Tuesday, so it's chops, peas, and potatoes. Is it all right, so?" He shudders again.

"Would you ever get a fork and mash up them peas for me? I can't be atein' them like that, they give me the heebie-jeebies, they do."

So it was true after all, what Mam had told me, a long time ago, that Uncle Seán wouldn't eat anything round! I suppose that on this occasion Mam had forgotten about the peas, but sure enough, word had it that he couldn't face a baby spud, or a wee tomato, nor button mushrooms, nor any of their ilk. Cherries, peas, pickled onions, and gobstoppers all fell foul of his spheraphobia and were immediately mashed into a mushy pap or dismissed to the bin of seagulls' scraps. He would have hated brussels sprouts, but there were none of them to be had in Ireland. Still, it takes all sorts to make a world, and Seán finishes his pulverized repast with relish and we strike out bold for the Treaty Stone.

Outside St. Munchin's Church we meet up with Nana, my mam, Seánin and Martin Franklin, my aunt Maura's lads. We are soon joined by cousin Breda, who, like me, lived at Nana's house. We all troop up to the Thomond cinema or the "Flea Pit," as it was known. It was the sort of place you might want to sit on a newspaper and wipe your feet when you come back out. On Saturdays you could get in to the pictures for a jam jar, and it was fun to see the lines of rowdy kids trying to smash each other's jelly jars for devilment. Anyway, we see Errol Flynn in *Robin of Sherwood,* and it is mighty!

For the next few weeks wee wild lads in Lincoln Green terrorize the locality with homemade bows and arrows and try to rob the rich and the poor, too, for that matter! Cinema is all the rage and acting out the stories is the most thrilling thing in the world to small lads with more imagination than common sense.

Evenings around the kitchen table are great craic all together. We play cards and have beetle drives and there are stories, always stories. My favorite are the Fleádh nights. These get-togethers, impromptu as they are, happen as often as not at the end of the month, when money is running short. A crate or two of stout arriving at the house will sooner or later give rise to a mighty night of story and song. My folks all do their party pieces, as like as not in the old Irish language. Mam sings "Ar M'Eiri Dhom Ar Mhadin," which means "I Arise at Morning," then maybe recites "The Siege of Athlone," both from the Williamite wars. Maura offers "Bridgín Bhán Mo Stór" (Bright Bridget My Treasure) or "Maidrín Rua" (The Little Red Dog—The Fox, in other words).

Grandda plays jigs and reels on the wooden flute and beautiful slow haunting airs such as "Rosín Dubh" (My Small Dark Rose—a secret freedom song, in which Ireland is portrayed as a tiny rose), or the "Coolin," a lament for the ponytail that the ancient Celts wore until its banning by the BloodyEnglish!

I like to sit quietly under the table and bother no one, as my more vociferous cousins get sent home for blaggarding or off to bed for falling asleep. Sitting in my tent of legs and ankles like a hermit in his cloister, I hear Grandda recite *The Sixpence,* an uproarious tale of a day in the life of a coin and all the people whose hands it passed through. My lovely grandda, Willie MacDonagh, has a great voice for lilting and a generous supply of Celtic songs and tall stories for all social occasions.

One I particularly liked and made well to memorize was "Dinny Burns the Piper." So here follows a wee snatch of it:

In the year '98 when our trouble was great,
It was treason to be a Milesian
And the blackwhiskers said that we'd never forget,
And our history tells us there were Hessians,
In these troublesome times; everything was a crime
And murder it never was riper
In the town of Glensheed, not an acre from Meath
Lived one Dinny Burns the piper.

Neither wedding nor wake would be worth a shake
If Dinny was first not invited
For at squeezing the bags, or emptying the kegs,
He astonished as well as delighted.
In these times poor Dinny, he could not earn a penny
Martial law had him stung like a viper,
And it kept him within, till the bones of his skin,
Were grinning through the rags of the piper.

Nana's favorite song is "Long Shadows on the Grass" and it is woefully sad. She also sings "Ching Chang Chinaman, Chop—Chop—Chop," which is a funny Victorian music hall song. Sometimes, when in a more mellow mood, Nana croons a slow haunting air called "The Spinning Wheel," which tells the tale of a secret courtship in sumptuous imagery. It so easy to picture it all in the mind's eye and it moves me to have memories way beyond my own childish experiences.

After hearing these songs so many times over in childhood, I find that they have slowly sunk into my head through some wonderful Celtic osmosis.

I especially like the strong, stirring lyrics of Canon Sheehan's fine old song "Seán Ui Dhuir a Ghleanna," or John O'Dwyer of the glen, as it is in English. This song has a special meaning for us, for our little house stands on the very spot where, legend has it, he forded the Shannon in 1690, and, in consequence, our old Shannonside house was called O'Dwyer's Villa:

> *After Aughrim's great disaster*
> *When our foe in sooth was master*
> *It was you who first plunged in and swam*
> *The Shannon's boiling flood.*
> *And through Slieve Bloom's dark passes*
> *You led your gallowglasses*
> *Although the hungry Saxon wolves*
> *Were howling for your blood.*

This is all wonderful stuff. I love history, and my little world was saturated with it.

King John's castle, dating from the 1200s, glowers at us from across the river. This was the same Bad King John that the English barons forced into signing the Magna Carta in 1215. Grandda Willie has a book about it and one evening proceeds to give us a lecture and all.

"Hm . . . hm . . . the Magna Carta. This charter of English liberties has over the years been much vaunted, by some politicians, as a bill of rights. Even a cursory reading of the text shows that it is no such thing; sure it guarantees rights mostly for the nobility and the bigwigs, not the ordinary folk who were mostly slaves, serfs, and villeins!"

He reads: " 'For the holding of general council of the kingdom . . . we shall cause to be summoned the archbishops, bishops, earls and the great barons of the realm. Furthermore we shall summon our sheriffs, bailiffs and all others who hold us in chief.' In other words, let's keep it in the family!

"They're still the same and the legacy lives on in the nonelected, hereditary House of Lords. The Americans had the good sense to rebel against this lot and elect their upper house. Anyway, after King John had grudgingly signed the Magna Carta, the barons of Merrie England decided they now had the power to get rid of the bugger once and for all. So with their wonderful sense of English fair play, they dumped the mad monarch on the necks of the poor Irish in that castle yonder. And do you know what happened then?"

"No, Grandda."

"He died of a surfeit of lampreys."

"What's lampreys?"

"They are boiled eels! And he ate so many of them that he burst! Too good for him! The greedy old sod! As if the English royals weren't revolting enough, the antics of some of the commoners were just as bad!" He went on to tell me of the time in Irish history called the Curse of Cromwell, no book this time, he spoke only from memory.

"Opposite the castle stands the house where Oliver Cromwell's equally nasty successor and son-in-law, General Henry Ireton, set up his headquarters in 1651. He and his army besieged the walled township of Limerick in an attempt to starve out the native Irish defenders. The English Roundheads and self-styled Sons of God were spoiling for more blood after taking part in the infamous massacres of men, women, and children in Drogheda and Wexford in 1650. With God Is Love painted around the mouths of their cannon, they began their bombardment.

"After six months, the remnants of the plague-ridden garrison surrendered. Five thousand had died of the epidemic and thousands more in the defense of the walls. After reassurances to the contrary, Ireton had most of them put to death. And, as if the murderous excesses of these Puritan English bigots was not enough, the few survivors were shipped as slaves to the Americas—the first of those unfortunates to be sent there!

"However, fate had a trick up her sleeve and within the year the foul Ireton died of the same plague, screaming for a priest, as the story goes and too good for the rat. Even the English eventually had their revenge upon him; Ireton's body was exhumed from its place of honor in Westminster Abbey and, to add insult to injury, burned at the gibbet on Tyburn Hill, shortly after the fall of Cromwell and the restoration of King Charles the Second."

Grandda takes a long pull on his pint of stout and starts afresh.

"Up at the end of the street there stands the Treaty Stone of 1691, commemorating yet another bloody siege and the subsequent treaty with the English under William of Orange, in which terms the Irish people would enjoy civil and religious freedom if the city's garrison of some fifteen thousand agreed to surrender and take ship for exile in

France. With their commander, Patrick Sarsfield, the survivors of the siege boarded a fleet of French ships and sadly departed for the Continent. As soon as the sails were out of sight, the English broke every article and covenant of the agreement, and so Limerick became known as *the city of the violated treaty*."

He thumps the table and sits down. We all clap and cheer, and he takes a bow.

Mam, as ever, knows a song about those events so long ago and strikes up:

When William stormed with shot and shell
At the walls of Garryowen,
In the breach of death my Donal fell
And he sleeps near the Treaty Stone.
That breach the foeman never crossed
While he swung his broadsword keen.
But I do not weep for my darling lost,
For he fell 'neath the flag of green.

Mam says, "You can't spit without hitting a piece of history around here."

"And neither is it the dry old stuff of books either!" says Seán. "The castle is always there as a reminder of a ruthless enemy, and d'ya see the bullet-riddled houses along the Shannon wall? It was the Black and Tans did that, in 1920."

Nana sups her tea and tells of the day when a woman walking with her was shot dead by the Black and Tans at the end of our street.

"Those whore's melts were recruited from every jail an' mental asylum in England, supposedly to fight the IRA. Bunch of bloody cowards they were. They kept well away from our boys, an' spent most of their time getting langers in the pubs an' refusing to pay for it, too! This day they get ordered out of a bar by their senior officer an' they're like a pack of wild animals, cursing an' firing at anything that moves an' threatening to shoot their own commander. They grabbed poor Joseph O'Donoghue an' dragged him off. Next day he was found with eighteen bullet holes in him. The Tans see me an' another woman running up Farron Seon. The bastards start shooting at us an' me with baby

Frances in me arms. I hear the woman next to me cry out. I look around an' she's lying there dead in the gutter with the drunken bastards laughing at her—may they roast in hell!" She stares out of the window, teacup in hand.

"Jasus sure they shot the mayor of Limerick, poor Michael O'Callaghan, in front of his whole family! Nothing but a bunch of blaggards and murderers, Godhelpus! What sort of mothers brought them into the world at all?" Nana sighs, the memory of those awful days of British occupation still vivid in her mind; she smiles over at Frances.

It was Sunday, and Sundays had a rare, brisk quality about them. Necks were scrubbed and inspected for tide marks, then without further ado, off to morning mass at St. Munchin's.

"Mam, why is the church called Saint Munchings? Was he a priest that was always eating?"

"No, his name was Munc-een, which is Irish for a little monk."

"It's a quare name anyway. Why was he so famous?"

"Sure, didn't he build the church yonder and put a curse on the Limerick people that wouldn't help him erect the steeple? It was left to some strangers who were passing by to help the poor old monk, and he said that from that day forward, strangers would always prosper in Limerick at the expense of the local population, who were a lazy bunch of goodfornothings. There they are—look, idle buggers, still as he left them!"

She points to the huddle of men sitting around the steps of the Treaty Stone and on the parapet of the Thomond bridge, waiting for the Treaty bar to open. The granite blocks of these archaic landmarks are polished to a fine luster over the years by the languid attentions of a million recumbent backsides squirming the minutes away till opening time. She sings:

> Saint Munchin was pleased with the job
> And laughed with devout satisfaction
> He gave every stranger a bob
> Along with his best benediction
> "May the strangers henceforward!" he cried

"In Limerick fast prosper and flourish
While like a bad foam on the tide
The natives will dwindle and perish
With plenty of nothing to do!"

"Does that mean we're cursed, too, Mammy?"

"No, no atall! Sure the curse was on Limerick and we live in Thomondgate, which is in County Clare. UP CLARE! AND DOWN THE RABBLE!" Mam punches the air with her fist, then crosses herself demurely when she sees the parish priest staring at her.

We go back home to a great feast of a meal, which was either breakfast or dinner, I don't know. Afterward, I take the scraps out to the squabbling seabirds that line the Shannon wall. You're not allowed to eat or drink before taking Holy Communion. I'm too young for the sacraments, but I starve along with the others. "'Tis good for your immortal soul," says Mam. I am usually as hungry as the seagulls.

The night service, or benediction, is a much more enjoyable undertaking. You are fed for a start, and kneeling before the looming alabaster statues is less unpleasant on a full stomach. The challenge is to stay awake! I like going to church better when I don't have to leave a nice warm bed. I love the singing in Latin and having the smell of incense around, but the second part of the service is a bit mystical and scares me.

God lives in a big, gold, spiky thing inside a round-topped house called a tabernacle. The priest goes up to the altar, opens the door of the tabernacle, draws back the curtain, and takes out the spiky thing. Then, holding it above his head, he recites some old incantation or other and turns to face the pews. He thrusts the spiky thing straight toward us. Mam and Nana make the sign of the cross, and I, peeping through my fingers, see the "eye of God" staring right into my sin-ridden soul.

I knew I had sins, but I didn't know how or why I got them. My nana, who I considered to be a living saint, was forever going to confession, but why was that? What could a God-fearing, righteous woman possibly do each week that required such frequent penitence? I decided to ask her straight out.

"Nana, what have you been doing so bad, that you must be telling the holy father?" Nana is momentarily stunned by my directness and looks uneasy.

Mam and Aunt Frances take up the job.

"Yer, come on now, Mam, what have you been up to?"

"Well . . . ," says Nana, with a sheepish grin. "I called Paddy the butcher, a . . . a . . . robbing bugger, Godforgivemeforswearing! An' he is so, so he is! Trying to sell me scrag end of mutton an' charge me for lamb!" She is fuming with indignation at the thought of being huckstered by a mere meat merchant.

"Anyway, the sin's on his own head," she said, tying on her plastic rain hat.

"The good Lord will forgive me—an' kick his arse into the bargain! So he will, Godforgivemeforswearing. Robbin' bugger, that he is, so he is!"

Behind my agitated grandmother, I can see Mam and my aunt making for the front door with their shoulders heaving with silent mirth.

Nana, Nelly Kelly, as she was born, is a great feast of a woman and a joy to be with. Although she never drinks liquor, she enjoys the company of those that do and loves a party. She can dance a jig and play the mouth organ at the same time. I never recall her having anything but white hair and a merry twinkle in her eye. Her laugh is ludicrously infectious, and almost anything will set her off into fits of giggles.

Mass being over, Mam and Nana sit in the kitchen, eating periwinkles, both of them helpless with laughter, recounting tales of Limerick's many odd characters and likewise their antics.

The cast of quare ones, as these worthies were known, was as never ending as the stories. Nana kicks off.

"Do you remember 'Old Wirey,' the quare fella who rode the bicycle all festooned with wires and sundry contrivances?"

"Oh, Jasus, how could ye forget him? He had dynamos, lights, horns, and all connected by curly wires, sticking into his pockets and coming out of his sleeves and up his arse and God knows where else. Sure he looked like Frankenstein's monster!"

"What do think he gained from that paraphernalia?"

"I dunno, but he was always as nice as ninepence to talk to."

"He was. He's dead now, TheLightOfHeavenToHim, so he is, and he had no one belonging to him. Do you remember the other old man? The fella who the same time every day walked up Lovers Lane outside of the house. I would see him from the kitchen window. He had a curly walking stick, the poor old chap, padding along in slow motion like a snail going to Jerusalem. 'Here's Mickey-walk-aisy,' you kids would all shout—Godhelpus, the poor crater!"

"Oh, God, yes! And do you mind the other unfortunate soul who had the spinal condition that had him bent nearly S-shaped?"

"Here's-me-head-me-arse-is-coming."

"That's him, and when the pair of them met in the lane from the opposite ends—oh, Jasus! It was like the clash of the Titans."

"Ah, now, the gaatch of the pair of them. They would meet in the middle of the lane and say hello. Then they'd be into odd maneuverings, trying to get a-past one another. 'Twas like a couple of old swans doing a courtship dance. They'd be shuffling this way and that to get the advantage, then all of a sudden break off the engagement and slip past each other like as if nothing had happened."

"Oh, good gentle shepherd, we won't see their like again."

"Unya-Conya was another quare hawk. Mind him sitting in his pew at the mass, rocking himself backwards and forwards, eyes shut tight, crooning away—*Unya-conya . . . unya-conya . . . unya-conya* . . . no matter what the hymn, his response was always the same—*Unya-conya!*"

"Maybe it was Latin, Mam?" I offer hopefully.

"Aye," says Nana. "Bloody bog Latin."

"It was always a blessing when he rocked himself to sleep."

"And the other bloke, what was his name? Steve-Mack. Remember how he was forever late and he always managed to come in the church just as the choir were singing the hymn to the Virgin Mary. 'Immaculate . . . Immaculate,' they'd be singing. 'Steve-Mack, you're late,' we'd be giving him, but he never took no notice."

"Danny-the-bags, coming home from his job at Rank's flour mills. He would be covered in fine white dust, and when you asked what he had been doing, he'd say, 'Bagging fog!' or 'Bagging daylight into a dark cellar!' He was a good sport, and he would beat his coat with his flat cap, sending up clouds of flour. Right enough, he was a good old stick."

At Hassett's Cross lived the legendary Jim Hassett. I never met him, but he was constantly referred to in our house. Whether some article of clothing was too big or too little, it would fit Jim Hassett. Whoever he was, he must have had the Druids' power of metamorphistic shape-changing to fill such a position in local folklore.

The majority of these souls were harmless, but as in all societies there were some bad-uns and some were positively malefic.

One such was Clack-a-Bone. He was a cantankerous old body who hated children and, even in passing, often dealt the unsuspecting a violent blow with his stick. He had an orchard dripping with apples, which was a terrible temptation to the young kids every autumn. A scrumping raid on his domain was always a risky business. If you were spotted, he would erupt with surprising agility from his back door, screeching: "I'll clack yer bones! I'll clack yer bones!" and demonically waving his cudgel. If caught, you could expect an unmerciful thrashing. All this, however, added to the dare factor and thus the thrill of it.

Another great dare is to climb over the Shannon wall and shin down the telegraph pole stay-wire. At low tide the river bank gives up its treasures. I find six of the Dutch General Ginkle's cannon balls that had bombarded the walls of Garryowen in the 1690–91 siege of Limerick that my grandda had told me about. I give them into the museum in town. Also one day, I see something round sticking in the crack of a rock. It is a bronze badge depicting a phoenix rising above a fire, surrounded with Celtic knotwork. A scroll underneath bore the Gaelic motto, "Forfaire agus Cairiseact," which I take to mean, "Watchful and Loyal."

From the same wall I fish, using just a reel of line and a big wormy hook with a lead weight. I catch an eel, which wraps around my wrist as I try to unhook it. I think it's cute and take it home as a pet.

"Get that slimy thing out of my house an' don't you bring serpents in here again!" Nana chases me out with the yard broom. I can outrun her, but others I can't.

Sabu Binn is a nasty piece of work, and teasing him is very dangerous and thus highly daring. I am far too small for this enterprise, but go along and watch from a safe distance as the older boys get near enough to the house to shout obscenities.

The upstairs window flies up and a head appears, cursing and blinding like a soul in the throws of demonic possession. What makes this apparition more bizarre is that the head wears a First World War German spiked helmet. He looks like a demented Kaiser Wilhelm! If he was good and drunk, it was certain he would remain in the house, but if not, he will give chase and an awful hiding to anyone he catches. This at least gives some respite to his own wife and kids, whom he abuses violently, in public as well as in private.

Like many of his ilk, he does no work himself, but his frail wife works as a skivvy to keep him in beer money. For her pains, she is forever sporting black eyes and bruises.

One day she brings home some Jeyes fluid, a powerful drain cleaner, in an old Guinness bottle and leaves it on the table. Sabu staggers in and downs it in a one 'er. He dies an agonizing tortuous death as befits such a tyrant and is no bloody loss to anyone, according to my nana.

"TheLightOfHeavenToHim," she adds in divine supplication.

Directly over the river stands the Island Field, or St. Mary's Park, as the city fathers had renamed it. We, on the Clare side of the Shannon, call it Hollywood due to the pageant of odd and exotic people who make up its populace, the likes of which you might only see on the silver screen. Ironically they have the last laugh—sure didn't they give us the great Irish actor Richard Harris.

It is pleasant to lie at night with the windows open, looking at the dancing lights of the Island Field across the roaring Shannon and smelling the tang of the distant sea.

Mam tells me stories like "The Colleen Bán," about an unfortunate girl seduced into robbing her father of his life's savings in 1820, then horribly murdered—drowned by her callous suitor. "Murder will out," as the old ones say, and sure enough her body was discovered floating in the Shannon. The rope knot tying the poor girl's neck to a large stone came undone—as indeed did the wicked plans of the young squireen, who danced the Devil's Jig on the gallows. This time there was no mistake about the knot, a looped noose of thirteen turns. The hangman knew his trade well.

In the warm darkness, my mother tells me tales of Drunken Thady and the Bishop's Lady and of the pig who went out to dig one fine day in Roscommon and the Kilkenny cats, who were so ferocious that they would fight each other until only their tails were left. Before I go to sleep each night, she teaches me how to count in Irish and say my prayers, like a good little boy. This simple life seems as endless as the hot summer, but with the first cries of autumn a cold wind blows in from the east and with it comes unexpected news.

"There's a letter here for you, Monica. It's from over in England." Uncle Seán shows me the new threepence stamps with the queen's face on them. Mam reads the letter and sits down with it open in her hand; she is trembling.

"Is it from me dad, Mam — is it?"

"Go outside and play, Willie."

"But Mam, I want to see the letter."

"Go on now and don't be annoying me, you bold boy, or I'll break you in half and fight the pair of you! Go out now, before I scatter your ashes to the four winds!"

I go out into the yard and sit under the kitchen window. I can hear the news.

"It's Reg. He's out of the army and has borrowed enough money to set up house in a . . . in a caravan!"

"JESUSMARYANDHOLYSAINTJOSEPH!" interjects Nana. "You'll be living in a trailer, like a tribe of gypsies, Jasus! A gypsy caravan, is it? Whatever next?!"

My heart sinks. I sit on the kitchen wastepipe with the familiar smell of the stinky drain wafting around me. Like any Catholic in trouble, I take to praying.

"Please, God, don't let them take me away from here! I'll be good and I won't moan when I go to mass, I promise!" With my eyes tight shut and my fist white-knuckled with clenching, I am oblivious to all but my little world of misery.

"Jasus, child, what ails ye?" says a voice. It's my uncle Paddy, looking in from his job on the Salmon Weir. "What are ya doing down there? Ye look like yer taking a shite!"

In a desperate attempt at staying behind with my family in Ireland, I take to my bed and feign illness. My folks are not to be kidded so easily and give me a dose of cod liver oil that gets me well acquainted with the bathroom. Even the prospect of the long sea voyage fails to rouse my spirits, proving that blood is thicker than water. When the morning of departure finally comes, I howl unmercifully, like a banshee with a bellyache. Through the blurry torrents of tears I see someone take a photograph of me and that sets me off.

"Don't ye be taking pictures of me when I'm crying—I'll kick the shins off ya!" All the effect this threat has is to raise a roar of laughter at my expense. Raging at this further indignity and very distraught, I rail on at them. Why could they not understand? I didn't want to be amongst strangers in a strange land, where I only knew my grandparents and Miss May at the sweetie shop. It was all so unfair!

Mam tries to drag me out of the door, but I hold on to the kitchen chair. How can I leave my old green plane? That faithful friend that has flown countless dangerous missions and carried me through the maelstrom of dogfights with the fearful Red Baron.

"The taxi's here, Monica."

"Come on now, Willie. You can see your dad tomorrow."

"NO! I don't care, I'm not going!"

"The taxi's waiting—come on!"

"No, I'm not going!"

"We can stop at Paddy King's for a patsy-pop!"

"OK, then!"

What can't be cured must be endured, especially when Mam puts things into proper context with the bribery of a patsy-pop.

The train heaves forward with a gaseous grunt, as over the orange glow of my ice lollipop, I watch distant Limerick City dissolve into a languid lake of gray mist, dreamily supporting the pugnacious turrets of King John's dark castle.

Mam looks very glamorous and has no shortage of admirers on the passage over the water. Some of the more optimistic men buy me sweets and sodas, in order to get acquainted with Mam, and I'm not about to complain to anyone.

Mam is less impressed by the amorous attentions of these hopefuls.

"They can try as they may and a fat lot of good it will do them. Men—bunch of goodfornothings, they're only after one thing! *Tut, tut, tut,*" she says, raising her eyes briefly to heaven. Mam wraps her coat around her knees and reads her *Ireland's Own* magazine. She seems sad.

I'd quite forgotten my woeful departure and thrill as the great steamship plunges into a rhythmic roll.

"Oh, my Gawd!" says Mam, looking green around the gills and clutching her stomach. I take great solace in sailing again on the high seas. For some unknown reason it gives me a tremendous feeling of adventure tinged with a distant memory of sadness.

It is a night crossing, and my poor mother, prostrate with mal de mer, lets me go out on deck in the company of one of her once hopeful Don Juans.

"Yer mother's not much of a sailor, Liam. Sure the sea's calm enough this night!"

"'Tis true for you. Me grandda says she get can seasick standing on a wet carpet."

For what seems like an age, I stand in silence with the kindly stranger at the stern rail, somehow knowing that my great adventure was about to begin.

A gigantic seagull flutters almost motionless against an ink-black sky. I could taste the salt spray, see the green and red navigation lights of the passing ships, hear the *whoosh!* of the bow wave, and gazing back to Ireland, see the solitary finger of Howth Head lighthouse, sweep the sea and flicker out, like a lone birthday candle.

❧ Chapter 4 ❧

EIGHT MILES FROM STRATFORD-ON-AVON AND THREE FROM Henley-in-Arden, at a bend in the A34 trunk road in the green rural heart of England, nestles the ancient and picturesque village of Wootton Wawen. A Celtic cross stands before the square tower of the eleventh-century Saxon church, recording the fallen of two world wars. Opposite, a row of black-and-white Tudor period houses winds down the hill and halts at the Bull's Head tavern built in 1320. The church and its environs straddle the top of a low hill, where once the Druids practiced their rites. Behind the hill and almost hidden from view by a blaze of exotic imported trees, somber and time-worn, towers the gray solid mass known as Wootton Hall.

This Georgian pile was indeed built by one of the King Georges to keep his mistress Lady Fitzherbert well away from the wagging tongues of the London court. Now in more austere times, it had been converted into apartments and is surrounded on three sides by a caravan site. In the old kitchen garden, which once supplied fare for milady's table, amid a crisscross of cinder track roads, stands a sixteen-foot green caravan.

"This is it, our first family home!" Dad is fired full of boyish enthusiasm. He opens the door and we go in. It smells of wood and varnish and seems larger inside than out. It has two folding beds, a stove, a bottled gas cooker, and a tiny sink. Mam turns on the water tap and nothing happens.

"Where's the water?"

"I'll get it connected tomorrow," says me dad. He never does.

"There's no toilet either!"

"Jasus, woman, would you ever be aisy. I'll dig a bloody soak-away as soon as I buy meself a spade." And dig one he does—five years later.

Despite her reservations, Mam soon gets used to our new home. "There's not room to swing a cat! At least there's no place to lose anything, and I suppose we won't be throwing any parties."

"Why would anyone want to swing a cat?" Mam was fussing about storing my meager belongings, so I thought it best not to ask.

"Your job will be to get buckets of water for washing and cooking, Willie. We'll need one in the morning and one at night. The tap is just over the road. OK?"

I wander over to the freestanding water tap and try to turn the big brass handle.

It won't budge. I climb up the wooden support and try again, to no avail. Then I slip, and a jagged razor-sharp piece of metal gashes my left leg, almost slicing off my calf muscle. Dad sews the flapping skin back into position, and I nearly bite the arm off my teddy bear with the pain. He does a grand job, albeit without the proper tools, disinfectant, or anesthetics. So once again, without provocation, an inanimate object has made a direct attack on my person for no apparent reason. Gas meters and water taps and anything with pipes are in conspiracy against my well-being and should be judged accordingly. I have a new battle scar but have become very wary of such apparatus.

I am laid up for a while until my leg mends and I can resume my aquarian duties. As the hot summer days suppurate, the drain below the water tap effuses a deathly stench as people empty their shite buckets and piss pots down the grating. In winter the plastic bucket chafes the calves of my legs raw and tips icy splashes of freezing water into my Wellington boots. Often the tap freezes up, and I have to melt snow and ice to fill the tea kettle. The joys of living in rural England!

As I grow older and stronger my water-gathering task is made easier by my ever resourceful father: he kindly buys me another plastic bucket to hump about.

Most of the young people I have met so far have been very nice, but some tend to take the rise out of my singsong Irish accent. I try to talk like an Englishman, but that makes matters even worse and Mam steps in.

"Ner'mind dem bunch of eejits," Mam says. "They don't know 'A' from a bull's arse about nuthin', all talking like they've a mouthful of plums—bollocks to 'em!"

It's only when my ear gets attuned to the angular speech of the British that I realize Mam uses words and idioms that no longer exist in modern English. Mam's everyday speech is full of quaint colloquialisms.

"I was after seeing Mrs. Arrowsmith down the market. She was coming-a-past me. When I saluted her, she didn't recognize me atall. I don't think she did it designtly, so she didn't. Mind you, that daughter of hers, the tatty-headed one with the pencily eyebrows, she wouldn't give you the steam of her piss since she got herself a bloke. You should see the gaatch of her, all airs and graces, fur coat and no knickers, the durty hewer!"

Mam's language is rich and sometimes puzzling; the more I get used to hearing the local people talk, the more I notice her peculiar way of putting things.

"The weather is a wee bit adjacent today, Willie, mind and take yer raincoat. I'd run you to school on the back of me bike, but I'm after feeling a little previous myself."

I become a bit self-conscious about my own accent, especially after being sent down to the pub to call my dad home for his dinner. I am about five years old.

I open the barroom door and there, surrounded in a haze of blue cigarette smoke, are Dad and his "boozing pals," as my mother calls them.

"Come away out of dat, and don't be drinking all dat porter!" I shout with all the authority I could muster.

"Out of the mouths of babes and sucklings!" quotes one of Dad's mates above the din, and my enjoinder is greeted with hoots of laughter and derision. At a total loss, red-faced and shamed, I run away home crying.

Mam uses a lot of words and phrases that I mistakenly take to be commonplace.

"Don't ye be deifying me with that brazen face, you bold boy, or I'll give you a lifter under the chin and a fong up the arse!"

It is oftentimes a struggle to crack the nut of my mother's meaning, and many is the kernel of connotation that escapes me entirely. Maybe she did it to tease me.

"Mam, what have we got for dinner today?"

"Currant cake and great sport!"

"Mam, what can I get to eat?"

"Shit tied up in a whisp to frighten you naked!"

"Mam, what's for dinner?"

"The full of yer hole of roasted snow!"

Sure Maxim's of Paris could not boast a more exotic menu!

"Mam, I don't like carrots."

"If you hadn't it, you'd ate it."

Well, as the old saying goes: "If the English love to hoard words like misers, the Irish love to spend them like sailors!" And likewise in Mam's peculiar patois: "If we all had the makings of ourselves, we'd be beautiful!"

"You'll be starting school next week, so we better get you some decent clothes," says Mam.

We have taken the bus into Stratford and it is market day. I dread the thought of school. There would be dozens of kids taking the mick out of my accent. We turn into a shop that proclaims "Back to School Sale." A very tall man who looks like an undertaker comes forward, rubbing hands that are long-fingered, parchment white, and bony. He has a cadaverous visage that gives him the appearance of a skeleton with skin stretched tightly over it, and a plummy English accent that you could butter a muffin with.

"Kin eye help you, Modom?"

"Yes, please, the child needs a school uniform."

"Which educational establishment will he be attending, Modom?"

"Wootton Wawen Roman Catholic," says Mam.

I am kitted out with short gray trousers, a white shirt, navy blue sweater, socks, and a black blazer jacket. These are the first new clothes I've ever had, and they even smell new. I look in the mirror, very smart, like a sailor.

"We have a large selection of school caps, ties, and pocket crests. Would Modom care to see?"

"Modom would!"

The man rummages in the big wooden drawers; for some reason he has a cloth inch tape around his neck, no doubt for measuring corpses. He hums away to himself and after some ferreting, produces a blue-and-yellow striped tie and a blue badge with a gold Celtic cross, embroidered with the letters A.M.D.G.

"Ave Maria Deo Gratias! That's Latin," the gaunt gargoyle of a shopman informs us.

"Oh," says I, my nightmare closing in. It was bad enough being stuck with a load of English kids, but now there was Catholics and Romans as well—all speaking Latin!

"What are you looking so worried about? Ye'll all be dressed the same at school, so no one will take the mickey out of your clothes. Isn't that right, sir?"

"Indeed, it is, Modom. Clothes maketh the man, Modom!"

We walk through the town. I'm glad to be out of the shop with its spindly proprietor. The air is warm and moist on the banks of the Avon. American tourists watch the rowing club scull their way through sedately swimming swans. Mam sings us through the Tudor shops of Market Street, past the Shakespeare Memorial Theatre, and up to the bus station:

> Bobby Shaftoe's gone to sea
> Silver buckles on his knee
> He'll come home and marry me
> Bonny Bobby Shaftoe.

The feared day arrives, and Mam dresses me for school. I feel awkward in my new getup, and my stomach is churning. Mam takes me down on the back of her bicycle, and I am presented to the head mistress; the dark, tall, obsidian-eyed Mrs. MacArthur.

"Nora, come ye hereabouts and look after this wee laddie," she burrs, in what I later find out is a Scottish accent. I try hard to choke back the tears as I see my mother wave good-bye and disappear up the road on her great clanking bicycle.

"Don't you be giving me any trouble now. I'm two years older than you and I'm a school monitor," says Nora. She is very bossy and bears an uncanny resemblance to Lassie the Wonder Dog. She gives me a board with little wooden pegs in it and a small wooden mallet.

"You tap the pegs through the board."

"Then what do I do?"

"You turn the board over and tap them back of course, ya idiot!"

"I'm not doing a stupid thing like that! Do ya take me for an eejit or something? I can read, you know, real words and everything!"

"If you don't do it, I'm telling miss and you'll get the cane across yer arse."

She grabs me by the collar of my new shirt and I give her a slap of the wooden hammer. She is shrieking and caterwauling and everyone is looking over. Then the head teacher pulls me out to the front of the class by my earhole. She shouts and bawls at me, but I could make out little of what she is saying on account of her accent. I do catch the word *hooligan,* however, as I know people of that name back over home. For punishment I have to stand in the corner until break time. This is very tedious, and my legs hurt. I try to stand on one leg like a stork, but I fall on my arse and get another row in Scottish for gooning around. When playtime comes I discover my new status as a holy terror has done me no harm at all. The other boys gather around eager to meet the new-comer. I am relieved and even a bit grateful to Nora.

"Where are ya from?" they ask.

"Ireland."

"Sure most of us at this school are from Ireland, ya eejit! What part?"

"Limerick City."

"Me too!" says a lanky lad with black hair. "County Limerick, that is."

"Me and my sister are from Kerry." I grin and nod.

"We're from Dublin," says one of a bunch of obviously related freckle-faces.

So fate has cast the dice and here I am, in the land of the stranger, surrounded by my own people, the far-flung children of the Gael. Despite my foreboding, my first day at school ends happily with me sitting four to a table with my newfound friends, Jeremiah Daly, Liam Cosgrave, and Steven O'Donnell.

"All the kids at school are Irish, Dad! Except a little French kid called Jean-Paul something or other. How is that?"

Dad looks up from his newspaper and regards me with curiosity.

"Their parents come over to lift the corn harvest and the potatoes and such like. Then when the season's over, they just stay on. They're what's called migrant laborers except most of them have stopped migrating. Of course they'll all be Catholics, being Irish, and the French are left-footers, too!"

"Why do people call Catholics left-footers?"

"Because they dig their spades with their left foot, of course!"

The school is unique and picturesque. Started by the monks in the Middle Ages, it is housed in an old flour mill and sits in the fork of two rivers. Behind the main buildings is a mill pool where great thrashing fish consume our leftover dinner scraps. The playground is full of mature trees—oak, ash, and beech—and is great fun to cavort around in, when the leaves lie thick in the autumn. There are two green corrugated iron bicycle sheds and two rows of outside toilets marked *Boys* and *Girls*. The main schoolroom is a single long hall with windows to the south that had been a flour store in its time. It is divided into three areas by two thick black velvet curtains.

At the end of this is the infants' room, where I found myself. My teacher is a tall, gaunt, kindly lady called Miss Hathaway. She is a descendant of Anne Hathaway, the wife of William Shakespeare, and had lived in the same house that they had once occupied. Enthusiastic and rightly proud of her heritage, she tells us much of the history and folklore of the local area and it is fascinating.

"Wootton Wawen is an old Saxon name meaning the 'Woodland of Woden.' He, you will remember, was a pagan god," she goes on. "The Saxons settled here and eventually became Christians. Some of your Irish monks were responsible for that!"

"Did they build the flour mill, miss?"

"I don't think so—or maybe they did. Anyway, they built the church that still stands on the hill yonder."

"Were they Protestants, miss?"

"No, no, they were Catholics."

"But the church is a Prody church!"

"It wasn't then. That was hundreds of years ago, before the Reformation."

"What's a reformation, miss?"

"Miss . . . ?" "Why . . . ?" "What . . . ?" "When . . . ?" A dozen hands shoot up with a dozen questions. *Clang-ker-clang!* goes the school bell, and as lively as eels, we spill out past our weary teacher into the sunlight.

The other components of the teaching staff are the accident-prone Mr. Bury and the dinner lady, Mrs. Dunscombe, whose son, Tommy, becomes one of my best friends and as a result I get bigger helpings at lunch. The operation is masterminded and directed under the eagle eye of the formidable Mrs. MacArthur, who in her own words, "Will brook no nonsense from you unruly lot!"

The parish priest comes around twice or more a week and the nit nurse once a month. She checks our hair for *visitors* and he checks our *souls* for sins. The *souls* in question were pieces of white paper pinned to the wall with our names printed underneath. If you misbehave or are found guilty of some heinous crime, such as talking in class, a small black blob is added to your record. If your sin is more serious, like cursing or giving cheek to the staff, the blot is larger. I was always a bit of a tearaway, and as a result my *soul* usually looks like the backside of a Holstein cow.

The priest teaches us two subjects: religious instruction, where we have little idea of what he is talking about, and moral instruction, where *he* has little idea of what he is talking about.

Dad objects to me being schooled by the priest and tries to argue with Mam.

"Bloody rubbish! What do they know? A Catholic priest advising you about sex is like a vegetarian telling you how you want your steak cooked."

Not that sex is ever mentioned by our priest, but he is very heavy on "the sins of the flesh" in his Sunday sermons. He seems to take a great delight in recounting the interminable horrors that await the sinful in the next life. We are told, for instance, that as Catholics, we would of course make it through to salvation, but our sins require a time in purgatory. In this place of lost souls, flames come out of the taps when you try to wash your hands.

There were venial sins—swearing, white lies, and the like—which could be forgiven with ease, and mortal sins, which killed your soul stone-dead. The latter included murder, rapine, blasphemy, and worst of all, becoming a Protestant, whatever the hell that was.

Every Wednesday we go through our own purgatory. This takes the form of morning mass at the little chapel in the graveyard behind the school. The building is unheated, and in winter we suffer greatly, kneeling without hassocks on the cold terra-cotta tiles.

Each week we pray for the conversion of Russia, not that one of us knew where Russia was or why it required converting. This is the secret of the smug priest. Eventually curiosity gets the better of me and I resolved to ask Mam.

"Mam, who are the Russians?"

"The Russians is it? Sure they're worst than the Germans! They murder priests and everything!"

Suddenly I look upon these Russians in a new, benign light.

"Ah yes!" I think, remembering a recent beating I'd received from the cleric.

"They sound like the boys for me, all right!"

Only Miss Hathaway refrains from dealing out corporal punishment. Even the dinner lady is capable of giving you a crack with a soup ladle if you are naughty.

The final authority is the florid-faced priest, who when telephoned in the most serious cases, screams down the hill to the school on his bike and like an avenging angel, delights in dealing out wicked bone-splitting raps from his long bamboo cane.

This day the cantankerous cleric is doing his rounds of the school, when he begins to inquire what various children want to be when they grow up.

"I want to be a holy father like you," offers Joseph "the saint" Ryan, sitting coyly under his spotless *soul*.

The priest's blue-jowled grin beams down apostolically upon him.

"Little creep!" I whisper to Jerry Daly, who lets out a stifled giggle.

Father spins around. "Well, Daly, what do you want to be?"

"A fireman, Father."

"H'em. And you, Watkins?"

"A sailor, Father," I say, with what I thought was a nautical grin.

He shakes his head and mutters, "Godless lot." For balance, he turns to one of the girls. "Elspeth O'Neill, what about you?"

I suppose he is hoping for the answer, "A nun, Father." If so, he doesn't know wee Elspeth O'Neill.

"I want to be a striptease dancer!" she blurts, her eyes like big blue saucers.

The priest looks like he'd been stung by a wasp.

"Now, child, I'm sure you don't even know what that is."

"Oh, I do, Father! It's a woman who takes her clothes off in front of men!"

The priest's visit was cut mercifully short by a hastily remembered appointment—elsewhere!

Mr. Bury takes us for science, in which I have a great interest. He is tall and gangly with a pointy nose and a mop of sandy brown hair, both of which accentuate a pair of peering brown eyes that give him the aspect of a perplexed rat looking out of a hayloft.

He does have an odd way with the world, and it sometimes seems that inanimate objects conspire to frustrate his efforts and thwart his every turn.

In common with the other teachers, Mr. Bury seldom partakes of the free school meals delivered each day, but prefers to make his own food in a small kitchen attached to our cloakroom. I witness him put a tin of baked beans on the hot plate of the cooker and then go searching for the can opener. Perhaps he had forgotten about Boyle's law and the expansion of hot gases. There is an enormous bang and the air is full of flying beans. The hapless young teacher spends the rest of dinner hour scraping them off the ceiling.

A week later, he plugs in the electric tea kettle and leaves it to boil on the wooden cloakroom floor. The first frost of winter has frozen some of the water pipes, and myself, coming in from the outside toilets, goes to the sink to wash my hands. I turn on the tap and expectantly hold the soap under it. Instead of water, a nasty hissing sound issues forth. *"Aargghh!"* What the priest said was true: the flames of purgatory are coming out of the pipe! I instinctively leap back, and my heel catches the spout of the boiling-kettle, which obligingly empties its bubbling contents into my shoe. Severely scalded, I am off school for a good few weeks. Maybe it was a punishment from God, but it sure was nice to be lying snuggly-buggly-boo in my bunk, far from the chilly chapel with its bare stone floor, icy arctic drafts, and frozen specters of unconverted Russians.

Whilst I am settling down to my new school, my father tries his hand at being a traveling salesman for a leading fire extinguisher company. He is sent to Morcombe Bay in Lancashire for training in shock sales technique, a startling new 1950s concept that works something like this.

After gaining entrance to someone's abode, the trick is to immediately grab a coat or scarf, spray lighter fuel on it, and set it aflame. As the horrified owner stands agape, the salesman, with a flourish, whips out the extinguisher and—*fooosh!*—the fire is out! The carbon tetrachloride base of the appliance leaves not the slightest trace of damage on the material.

All is going well and the tactic is proving effective. Dad has won some small orders from housewives and shopkeepers, but he decides that a big order might ensue from one of the many-roomed, stately Victorian mansions that dot the local vicinity.

Briefcase in hand, he walks the long, tree-lined drive to Manstell Manor. The only resident is His Lordship, an old retired Indian army officer. Dad is met courteously enough by the lord, who takes him into the gun room.

"What have you to show me, young man?" he says, in an affable enough fashion.

With a lightning sweep of the wrist, Dad snatches off the old chap's hat, douses it in petrol, and sets it alight.

"What the—?!" The general is caught completely off guard by this assault.

"Now the GREAT MOMENT!" shouts Dad, grabbing the fire extinguisher from his bag. He points it at the blazing hat and depresses the handle. *Phut! Phsssh!* A tiny whiff of gas escapes from the empty cylinder. "Bugger!" says Dad, all fingers and thumbs, trying desperately to screw on a fresh refill. The bug-eyed general stares at the funeral pyre fast diminishing on the marble floor.

"My hat! My favorite hat!!"

Dad looks up to apologize, but too late.

His Lordship, beetroot purple in the face and eyes like hot rivets, is reaching for a fine double-barreled shotgun. "GET OUT OF MY HOUSE! GET OUT!!!"

Dad needs no further encouragement—the sound of the gun being loaded is enough. He grabs his stuff and flees for his life through the front door. As my father sprints in Olympic fashion down the tree-lined drive, buckshot whizzes about his ears and clips leaves from the poplar branches. Behind him, like a charging rhino, the old boy is still running down the path, roaring. "GET BACK TO RUSSIA, YOU BLOODY BOLSHEVIK!"

✦ Chapter 5 ✦

SLOW — SCHOOLS, DEMANDS THE BLACK-AND-WHITE ROAD sign, depicting the torch of learning surmounted by a large red warning triangle. I stop dead in my tracks and stare at it as if I had never seen it before. Suddenly the revelation comes to me that I pass this sign at more or less the same times every day. I had not thought about it before, but the days were cyclic and so too were the weeks. From the peculiar feeling this dawn of realization gives me, I make a small mental jump into intellectual no-man's-land.

I perceive that somehow it's all connected. The days, weeks, months, and years, too — all planned out by some unseen hand, some mastermind. It must be God! Every morning I pass the school sign and each afternoon I go past the other way. In between times, I labor under the jurisdiction of Mrs. MacArthur and the school rules, but when I pass the sign on my way home, I am *free!* This sense of freedom is uplifting but hard to understand. Time becomes a fuzzy observance that I try to come to grips with. It is best measured by food. I know what day of the week it is by what is on the dinner table. It is said that a man's stomach is the best clock you can have, but we had a calendar too, which, when times were good, seldom varied:

> SUNDAY: Roast beef, pork, lamb, or chicken, served with boiled and roasted potatoes, greens and gravy. Dad traditionally cooks this repast.
>
> MONDAY: Cold meat from the Sunday joint, homemade pickled onions, steamed spuds, and English mustard.
>
> TUESDAY: Chops, peas, and potatoes, with Sunday's gravy.

✦ 63 ✦

WEDNESDAY: Gammon, broad beans, potatoes, and lashings of bacon fat poured over it all as a gravy. (My favorite!)

THURSDAY: Belly pork grilled, baked beans, and mashed spuds.

FRIDAY: Fried fish and chips, served in newspaper with pickled onions, malt vinegar, and salt.

SATURDAY: (Winter) Irish stew, hotpot, or beef stew. (Summer) Fresh salads from our own garden.

We have the typical Irish appetite for potatoes and eat pounds of them every week. I would sometimes even eat them raw like apples. There were, of course, changes to the routine, as in the traditional boiled bacon and cabbage for Saint Patrick's Day and other Irish occasions. None of us has ever even seen a turkey, so it is roasted chicken for Christmas with sage-and-onion stuffing. Our meager rations are sometimes supplemented by nocturnal hunters called poachers. These gentlemen provide us with various game dishes like pheasant, venison, and salmon. These are bartered for with Dad's home-brewed beer.

The biggest changes in the family diet are brought about by our occasional dips below the poverty line. Dad is fired from his job due to setting alight the old general's hat and because his temper gets the better of him and he tells his boss that he doesn't suffer fools gladly and to stick the nozzle of his fire extinguisher up his arse.

He has always tried to grow enough potatoes, cauliflowers, cabbages, and kale on his allotment to see us through to better times, but supplies are low and he's drunk all the home brew. He sits moodily, the stub of a cigarette fuming in his nicotine-stained fingers.

Mam, with a wizardry to shame Merlin, conjures up a Sunday dinner for three out of two ounces of corned beef and some spuds.

This severe trough in our fortunes is marked by the daily ingestion of bread and dripping. Great pallid gobs of white pork fat spread cold on crusts and sprinkled with salt are better to eat than look at. For a change I try a "dip in the fat," which is the same idea, only hot. Condensed milk, dribbling like candle wax from the tin, alternates with brown sauce to make a sandwich filling.

Lean times have come upon us. Dad goes off cursing to the labor exchange to look for a job. Ominous black clouds leaden the sky, and I watch the blue flame on our tiny gas cooker fade into a wee peep as Mam tries to boil the kettle for the tea. A heavy rain is thundering on our thin aluminum roof, making lighting a campfire out of the question. Mam dons her raincoat and ventures outside. She stands at the back of the caravan, furiously shaking the gas bottle; the flame rallies for a moment, then splutters into oblivion.

"What's happening, Willie?"

"It got bigger, then it went out, Mam."

"The curse of Saint Malachy and the seven fiery devils to it. I don't think I've enough money for a refill!" She sits back at the fold-down kitchen table and pours the contents of her little leather purse onto the linen tablecloth. There are no banknotes and more miraculous medals of the Virgin Mary than coins. A gray slanting light from the side window picks out the normally invisible logos on the white linen cloth. "Ranks Flour Mills—LIMERICK" spells the ghost of the bleached-out imprint.

"We're one and ninepence short. Come on, Willie, and we'll see if Aladdin will give us a recharge on tick." I find the bottle-changing wrench, and Mam screws the brass regulator away from the cylinder. The rain subsides as we load the gas bottle onto my soapbox cart and trundle our way through the dripping trees, down to the storeroom where a little wizened woman who reeks of heating oil sells bottled gas and kerosene to the site dwellers. In the stinky darkness the wee witchlike wife sits wrapped up like a tattered mummy, wearing an odd assortment of men's clothes. She is completely permeated with paraffin. She huddles dangerously near a single hurricane lamp to read a faded newspaper. She is a walking Molotov cocktail, but this was her normal way. "Like Aladdin in the magic cave," Mam once said, and so the nickname stuck.

"Hello, Aladdin, would ye ever give us a refill for the gas? I'm needing to cook my husband's tea and I'm just one and nine short, but I can pay you on Thursday."

"Then you can get your bloody gas on Thursday."

"I thought we were friends?"

"We are, but there's no sentiment in business, Mrs. Watkins." The old vendor pushes the door closed against the wind. Mam stands dejected, on the verge of tears; the thin drizzle has started up again. I am embarrassed for my mother and annoyed that she has been rebuffed in such an offhand manner by a human lampwick. Betwixt anger and frustration I kick into the gravel surface of the old stable yard with the toe of my boot. Something odd is glinting pallidly up at me from the stones. It looks like a small set of chain links about three inches long. I bend down and pick it up. The crusty verdigris that holds the coins together crumbles and seven threepenny pieces separate in my hand. I stare in disbelief at the brass bits, exactly one shilling and nine pence.

"Mam! Look what I've found—one and ninepence. It's just exactly what we need!"

Mam takes the money from my trembling hand. Her eyes are large and round.

"Oh, thank you, thank you, Saint Jude, thank you!" she cries skyward.

"Saint Jude, me arse! It was me that found them, right over there, in the ground!"

I knew little of the patron saint of lost causes, but over the years I have heard my mother invoke his help on my behalf so many times, that along with Saint Anthony, the saint who helped you find lost items, they become invisible members of the family.

Back at school I tell my story to the priest during my communion class. I get the feeling that he doesn't believe me.

"What is Saint Jude the patron saint of?" he asks.

"Is it the obscure?" I offer, remembering something my granddad Jim had read me.

I pass the sign on my way home from school. I'm free again, free to explore my environs. I stroll toward the ivy-grown limestone mansion.

An ancient bronze sundial stands on a hexagonal stone pillar in a grassy wabe at the front of the great hall. I climb up to watch the shadow creep imperceptibly across the roman numerals incised on the plate. It has almost reached IV when the great bell of the old Saxon church chimes four o'clock. Looking up, I lose my footing, and the world spins through sky and garden as I spiral down like an autumn leaf to destruction on the ground. The interruption of the force of gravity knocks the wind from my lungs, and I lie stunned and sickened by the sudden stop. Unable to cry for the numb pain that has become my universe, I lie on my back, staring up through the branches of a giant redwood tree that towers one hundred and fifty feet above the park. No one has seen me fall except a long, lean marmalade tomcat, who now scampers toward me and begins licking away the salty tears running down my cheeks.

"*Purrow*," says the cat, as it rubs along my grazed legs. I stretch out a hand to stroke it and it bites me, dancing off sideways.

"*Perrow, perrow.*" He comes back, nuzzling my face and causing me to pull myself up to get a better look at it. What a quare orange moggy this was. One eye missing, the opposite ear missing, one incisor broken off, and only half a tail. He tumbles about in my lap, teasing and playing like a kitten. If I move my hand too quickly, he bites me, then licks the same spot whilst purring like a well-oiled sewing machine. Having distracted me from my painful plummet, I recover enough to stand up. This he doesn't like and repairs posthaste to the thick rhododendron bushes from whence he had come.

From his green hidey-hole he meows at me balefully until I sit down again, and, purring away, he rejoins me. We become firm friends and after some cajoling he follows me all the way home, where I secrete him in the cupboard underneath my bed.

"There's an awful pen and ink in here! It smells like cat's piss!" My dad's face is all screwed up like a sucked orange. Oh, my God! I'd forgotten about the cat.

"I'm off to get the water, it's bath night," says I, anxious to get out of the van.

"Yea, if that's you that's making that pong, you need a bloody bath! Leave me some water for a good wash tonight. I'm going to put in a few hours on the allotment, bastard-trenching my potato patch, then I'll be fit for a couple of pints at the Bull's Head. I think I'll grow some sprouts this year. D'you know your mother's never eaten one?"

"Neither have I. In fact, I've never so much as seen a sprout. Cheerio now, so!" I take off toward the tap with my two plastic buckets. As I splash my way back, I see Dad, two empty beer bottles in hand, swinging his way up the cinder track road, with a garden spade on his shoulder.

"It's OK, puss, he's gone!" I open the cupboard and with a flash of furry orange, the imprisoned cat shoots out of the caravan door, leaving an airborne slipstream of watery yellow shite in its wake. The small red fireside carpet, the front step, and myself are liberally coated in a malodorous defecation that only a frightened feline or a dyspeptic demon could be called on to produce. *Now* what can I do? Mam is due home soon, and it is Thursday—belly pork, beans, and spuds—but apart from that, it's bath night, which means boiling rakes of water, standing naked on a towel, and washing yourself down from head to toe. All this and the house swimming in shite! I throw the red mat into the garden and wriggle out of my black jeans and tartan shirt carefully, so as not to spread the poom all over me. There is shite on the wee pearly buttons, so I can't undo them. In pulling the shirt over my head, the stench just an inch from my nose makes me gag. No time to get dressed! I put a kettle full of water on to boil and hide my clothes in the old traveling trunk, rusting in the garden outside. In a fluttering panic, I begin to scrub away at the pungent excrement on the step. Luckily, a dousing from a full water bucket does the trick and flushes the offending feces from the linoleum. The red mat is a bigger problem. I try to wash a bit of it, but it makes the cat shit spread. Standing in my ragged underwear in the junk-filled garden I must have looked a pretty sight.

A girlish giggle erupts behind me. I spin around to see the nice little Burmese lady from the corner caravan.

"What are you doing all naughty like this? Hee-hee-hee!"

"I'm trying to get the stain out of this rug and it won't shift."

"Let me see. Oh, stinky stink! It is shit! It is shit!" She lets the mat drop and leaps backward. "SHIT! IT IS SHIT!"

"I know what it is! How do you get rid of it?"

"Oh, so sorry! Dry by the fire and brush it off with firm brush. But brush hard, very hard. It is SHIT!"

When Mam comes in the mat is clean and dry, the deposit having left the carpet in little clouds of khaki dust with each fervent stroke of a wire suede brush. The little square enameled stove is lit, and I am drying myself in front of it after my strip-wash. Mam is somewhat taken aback.

"It's not like you to have a bath without being yelled at. You must be courting. That's it—you've got a wee girlfriend somewhere!" I go red and Mam sniffs the air.

"There's a queer stink in here. I know we're hard up, but has your father been smoking those horseshit cigarettes again?" I stay red, as red as the mat I'm standing on.

I didn't see the motley old mouse hound for a while. No doubt it was off on its rounds of erstwhile benefactors, burgling, begging, and biting the hand that feeds it.

My rotund friend, Fatty Roger, and myself stroll in chitchat cheeriness up to our caravan to find the war-torn ginger tomcat sitting on the front doorstep, back leg erect, studiously licking its hole. Roger recognizes him.

"That's Candy, that is. He's a wild cat, fights with foxes and badgers and everything! You can't stroke him, you know. He'd have yer hand off!"

"Get on out of it! *I* can pet him. He's my pal, so he is!" I put my hand out and the moggy turns into a hissing ball of ear-back malevolence, rolling onto his side and lashing the air with sickle-sharp claws. I leap back in dismay.

"Some pal you've got there." Fatty Roger chucks his school cap at the cat, who shoots into the dark shadows beneath the van from whence his one eye gleams like a coal and a low growl curses our impudence. We go into the caravan and raid the food cupboard. Under a plate I find two cold pork chops, which we wolf down with dry bread and mustard, totally oblivious to the fact that they are all my mother can afford for the dinner. Mam is furious when she comes home. Roger runs, leaving me to my fate.

"For Jasus' sake, Willie, you can't keep bringing home other people's kids and feeding them! We've hardly enough food for ourselves, and Roger's people are well off compared to us. And anyway, it's not as if he's wasting away, is it?" She is right enough. Like most kids I never think of where food comes from or how much it costs.

"I'm sorry, Mam. I didn't know it was Dad's dinner. It's just that Roger said he was awful hungry."

"He's always hungry. He's like a bloody termite! Jasus, he eats his poor mother out of house and home. BeGod she can't keep up with him for sure. He's a big lad so, and it's plain that he makes great use of his food, but he gets plenty to eat at home."

"Well, I'll not do it again, Mam, so I won't."

"Good lad, you're too bloody generous to others altogether. One of these days you'll give yer arse away and ye'll have to shit through yer ribs!"

Mam is always very forthright in her use of language. When first I heard my teacher talk about something called cursive, I thought of my mother.

I go into the sitting room, where curled up on my dad's black coat is the purring form of a sleeping marmalade tomcat.

"Arggh! Get that mangy bugger out of here!" Mam begins doing the Highland fling and throwing everything at hand at the swiftly departing pussycat. Like an amber arrow, he shoots out of the open window and away toward the shrubs lining the main road.

"Durty bugger, he is! Look where he was lying on your father's coat. Look—bloody HOPPERS!" There in the warm dent left behind by the rudely awakened Candy, a small colony of cat fleas, having lost their host, is wandering about aimlessly.

"Did you bring that scruffy specimen into the house?"

"No, Mam. He must have jumped in through the window."

"Well, I believe you, thousands wouldn't! But if I see that flea-ridden bleeder again he's going to get a fong up the arse that will knock him into the middle of next week! Right, watch this carefully. Ye might have call to do this yourself one day, the way you carry on!" She goes over to the sink and picks up the soap. Slowly she walks to the spot where the old moggy had been lying, and, *dab-dab-dab* with the bar of soap, the fleas were gone! Mam turns the underside of the bar toward me and there are the tiny parasites imbedded in the bottom, firm prisoners of the carbolic soap.

"That's them wee buggers nuxed!" She smiles with all the primeval satisfaction of the ancient huntress and, stepping outside, scrapes them off onto a fence post, singing:

There was an old man at the fair
He didn't know what he was at
He was taking them out of his hair
And cracking them on his old hat!

She takes up a washboard and places it in a zinc bucket full of suds on the kitchen table. Mechanically she rubs away at the grime in my school shirt collar.

"You know there's people in America have machines that can do this."

"Goway! Machines that can do the washing, whatever next?"

"'Tis true, and they have refrigerators and vacuum cleaners, too. Even the poor people have them, so they do!"

"Why would you want to clean a vacuum? Sure Mr. Bury says, there's nothing at all in a vacuum."

Mam picks up the basket of wet clothes and pulls a puzzled face. She shrugs her shoulders and steps down into the garden.

"Oh, Jasus! It's me that's over!"

Mam slips on her duff whilst hanging out the washing and, in trying to stay herself, plucks the washline like an archer with a giant bow. This has the effect of launching all of the unused clothes-pegs skyward from the rope like a salvo of Minuteman missiles. She is not best pleased! Two straight lines like a number eleven appear on her forehead as she struggles up. The warning sign of the number eleven bus!

"What are you laughing at?"

"Nothing, Mother."

"Well, if you laugh for nothing, you'll laugh a bloody lot for a halfpenny, you cheeky young pup, you! And don't be giving me any of your old guff or I'll box yer ears for you. Now get this garden tidied up and dump some of this bloody junk. It's like Duffy's Circus here with all this crap lying about. Get rid of it!"

Loaded down with a heavy heart, old wind-up gramophone parts, and empty paint tins, my wooden box cart squeaks a weary mile to the trailer park rubbish dump nestled in the heart of the wilderness. I chuck the garbage onto the pile and go for a look-see about.

The dump lies in a wide clearing surrounded with trees and shouldered by nearby Top River, a straight stretch of water that had been, long ago, channeled in artificial banks as a tributary of the river Alne. This supplied the giant heron lake at the head of the wilderness, which feeds in turn, by means of a waterfall, Bottom River. Brown and turgid, this watercourse sluggishly bisects the wild woods, making the dump an island accessible only by one of three ancient stone bridges. The whole area is about a mile square.

I root around in the detritus of the dump for treasures. Nothing big, mind—I don't want Mam putting on her number eleven scowl and giving out to me again about the amount of old tat in the garden, half of which was my dad's junk anyway.

Overhead the round leaves of the poplar trees whisper and rustle in the light breeze, and from afar a strange whooping, yelping noise carries on the west wind mixed with a sound like a castrated car horn. Intrigued, I scamper up to the riverbank, where my view westward is not encumbered by the trees. There is a queer-looking beast swimming at full tilt down the dappled waters of Top River straight toward me. Ten yards away the beaverlike creature abruptly turns to its right and hops onto the grassy bank, shaking fine mists of water droplets from its pelt. It pees briefly in my direction and, seeing no threat, dives into a culvert and swims through the watercress patch to where the stream enters a nearby tarpaper hut. "Water Works—Keep Out!" reads the sign above the half door.

I glance back upriver, where a blur of red dots is moving about and the unmistakable baying of hounds mingles with the cries of huntsmen and the sharp bugling of the hunting horn.

What could all this carry-on be in aid of? Then it dawns on me. Oh, my God! This must be an otter hunt and they're chasing that wee beastie. It also occurs to me that the dogs are way ahead of the huntsmen and would get here first, probably tearing me to shreds in the process! You couldn't fool me! I'd seen the like in the film *The Hound of the Baskervilles. Arggh!*

Adopting the instinct of the beast pursued, I crash through the undergrowth to the refuge of the mysterious hut. The otter has wisely wriggled under the half door and is hiding behind a thing that looks like a big porcelain lavatory bowl, except this gives out a regular banging noise as it gushes water from out of its top. I bolt the top half of the door shut and climb on top of the shack. In no time at all my sanctuary is surrounded by a garish tangle of snarling dogs, and I am in fear of my mortal life.

"Come on now, Saint Jude, get me out of this one. I'm sorry I claimed the finding of the one and nine, so I am!" I lie face down on the asphalt roof. The tarry smell reminds me of those first visits to Birmingham, oh so long ago, and now I am to be ripped asunder by these devil's hounds. "Oh, Saint John Bosco, pray for us!"

"BECK! Beck, I say! Orf hownds, beck off!" In the pandemonium of trumpeting horns and hysterical dogs, two black-gloved hands appear over the cantle of the roof, soon to be followed by a red-jacketed man with a face like boiled shite.

"OH, DEM IT ALL! It's not the scent—it's jest some bloody kid!" bellows Shiteface. "CALL ORF THE HOWNDS!" he shrieks to the harbinger, who dutifully lays about the squabbling pack with a nasty-looking long whip.

The querulous gaggle of inbreeding moves off, man and dog alike. Only when they are far removed from the cover of the wilderness, way out in the lush open meadows beyond, do I wiggle myself down and open the door of the shed. To my great relief, the little brown otter is still there, his wee eyes glinting like chocolate buttons. We regard each other with benign interest. I feel we are brother survivors with something deeply elemental in common. As to who has saved whom? It doesn't matter a tinker's cuss. The point was, we are both free.

Later I ask my dad about the queer tarpaper hut and its weird machine.

"Oh, that's a Montgolfier water ram, the nearest thing ever invented to a perpetual motion machine."

"But what does it do?"

"The water runs down a slope, where it picks up energy from gravity. This hits the low-pressure diaphragm of the hydraulic ram, which pushes up, forcing some of the water at high pressure through a valve and into the pipeline. It's where our tap water comes from and all the taps on the site. Ingenious, eh? It was invented by the fellows who made the first manned balloon flight at Paris in 1783. The other nice thing is you can grow watercress in the gravity run because cress only likes to grow in shallow, fast-running water."

"OK, know-it-all, stop filling the child's mind with pumps and balloons and watercress and lay the bloody table. The dinner's ready." Mam's chide is leavened by the fact that Dad has found a job and the number eleven has disappeared from her forehead. Practical as ever, she is cooking: chops, peas, and potatoes. Hurrah! It must be Tuesday!

"Dad, why do them people hunt the otters?"

"Those upper-class twits will hunt anything! If you ask me, they're still lusting after the days when their aristocratic Norman forefathers hunted down people like us and hung them. They'd rather shoot peasants than pheasants. Bunch of bloody oxygen thieves!"

"They didn't have any horses with them though."

"No, they only use the horses for the fox hunt. Oscar Wilde rightly called them, 'The unspeakable in full pursuit of the inedible!' He wasn't too far off the mark, as usual. D'ya know, Willie, the misfortunate wee fox was introduced to Ireland by the English just so they could hunt the poor bugger. That's how it became a symbol of resistance to the downtrodden native Irish!"

After the unexpected events of the day, I knew fine how it felt to be hunted and I didn't care for it.

The evening meal arrives at the table in its welcome cloud of savory steam. Gratefully we tuck in to the best feast we have had in a while, accompanied by the sound of my mother singing an old Irish song: "An Maidrín Rua"—The Little Red Fox.

There he was in my mind's eye, having outwitted hounds and hunter alike, boldly lying in the bulrushes with his two little ears sticking up:

> Maidrín rua, rua, rua, rua,
> An Maidrín rua atá dána,
> An Maidrín rua 'na luí sa luachair
> Agus bárra a dhá chluais in áirde.

→ Chapter 6 ←

THE AUTUMN IS GIVING WAY TO WINTER. MR. BURY LIGHTS the potbellied stove that heats the whole school, and soon the entire place is engulfed in acrid smoke. As luck would have it, crows have made their nest in the chimney during the summer, and the smoke is going everywhere rather than up the stack. It is imperative to put out the fire. The unfortunate teacher lifts the fire extinguisher and stares at it: *non comprende*.

This was my moment to leap up from my seat and take charge of the situation.

"This is how you do it, sir!" I strike the knob as I had seen my father do.

I manage to put out the fire and soak the teacher in one fell swoop. I sit down a hero!

My heroics do not last for long—pride comes before a fall.

Mam wants me to wear a particularly ghastly cream-colored Aran sweater that has been sent to me from Ireland. I hate it and when she won't take no for an answer, I tell her that it will get me picked on in school. This is an out-and-out lie, but she demands the name of the bully. In my panic, I name the last person I'd talked to in class, thinking it would go no further. My mam, outraged, marches me to school and demands satisfaction. The child quite rightly denies it, but I am too craven to recant. As the poor innocent lad is flogged across the backside, he stares at me with such a lost, pleading look in his eyes. I look away in shame and guilt; his hurt will heal, mine won't. I do my all to make amends after this awful experience, and myself and the victim of my dishonor become firm friends. He is a gypsy lad named Paul, and his people have left the highways and byways to settle down for a while in the heart of England. Their eldest girl is at university, a thing totally unknown to us. They live in two caravans connected together in an H shape by a central veranda. There are lots of kids in the family, and it becomes my second home. For the first time I hear a recording of Tchaikovsky's *1812 Overture*. I am spellbound. "Good Golly Miss Molly," by Little Richard, has me jitterbugging around the room. Dinnertime is a feast of the bizarre. I eat hitherto unheard of things like spaghetti bolognese, sago pudding, and hedgehogs roasted in balls of clay, which helps pull off the prickly spines when you break them open. Under the supervision of the eldest lad, Nicky, I learn how to take car engines to bits and motorcycles to pieces and reassemble them with not too many pieces left over. Happily I dwell with these gypsies in their wonderful, surreal pied-à-terre and as a result spend less time at home.

Mam has an important announcement for me.

"I'm going to have a wee baby!" She grins.

This is great news. I have always wanted a brother or sister. Mam gets bigger day by day and knits lots of little woolen things from the old socks and jumpers that I unravel for her. She packs a suitcase and tells me it's time to go and get the baby. I want to go with her, but I have to stay and run the household. Dad is away at work. A car comes, and my mother waves at me as it drives her to the hospital. In an old drawer I make up a crib and put my teddy bear in it to keep warm for the baby.

Dad comes in late and won't eat his dinner. He is very drunk and holds me so tight that I can't breath. He rocks me back and forth, all the time crying and muttering in Welsh. The smell of stale beer and cigarettes is horrible, and the rocking motion makes me gag. I am terrified, and glad when he finally goes to sleep. Women call at the caravan and ask me what I need. Days pass and Dad still comes home stinking of drink; he lies awake half the night. I hate the acrid sting of sulfur from struck matches as he lights the roof of the caravan with the orange glow of another cigarette. Please, Mam, come back soon!

Mother comes home alone, there is no baby with her. My little brother, Keith, had lived only four days. He only comes home to be buried, and even then I never see his face. Mam says he looked like an angel. His coffin lies in the corner of the caravan until Davy Windle has finished digging the tiny grave at the back of our school chapel. After he was gone into the earth, Mam sits for hours cradling my teddy in her arms and singing, "Shule, shule, shule, aroon." A lament for a lost loved one, as heavy as the cloud of misery that hangs above the corner where we live. The keening notes drift upward to heaven and into a lifeless sky, as gray as my mother's face.

Something has to be done to turn the luck: Dad sobers up.

"I've got a better site," he says, turning up one day on a old Ferguson tractor. After much palaver and arsing about, he pulls the caravan some fifty feet to the shelter of a tall ivy-grown red brick wall. Mam, still mourning her loss, is singularly unimpressed. I also notice with gloom that this move puts me even farther away from the water tap.

"This thing here," says me old fella, pointing to an old army ammunition box bolted to the wall, "is an electricity hook-up and we shall have electric light!" Mam is almost impressed and raises an inquiring eyebrow.

"What about the toilet then?" She likes asking awkward questions and is enjoying twisting my dad's tail. It is good to see her smile again.

"All in good time, woman! Didn't it take God seven days to make the world?" This divine allusion from my atheistic father is calculated to rile my devout mother, and it works.

"Seven days, me arse! What would a pagan like you know about it? He worked six days and on the seventh he rested, ya bloody heathen! You do it all arse backwards, one day's work and six days' bloody rest— mostly in the public house!"

Dad puts his thumb up to his nose, waggles his fingers and speeds off on the little gray tractor. I try the same gesture at Mam and get a slap round the earhole for my pains.

Months later, Dad, true to his word, installs a single forty-watt bulb in the caravan. Mam says, "Whoopee!! We're back in the twentieth century!" But I miss the yellow gas light burning hoarsely in its fragile lime mantle. On the other hand, we now have a socket to run the ancient Sobell valve wireless that has sat in its box for over a year. With this aid, we can tune in Radio Eireann from its transmitter in Athlone and get the Irish news from home. The BBC has a lot of plays and on Sunday mornings runs *As I Roved Out,* a program of traditional folk songs from all parts of the British Isles and Ireland. This is presented by A. L. Lloyd, the famous folk music collector, and features many old songs that we know. Sadly, the tuning cord eventually breaks and the radio remains stuck on the frequency of some European station that plays the "Harry Lime Theme" from the film *The Third Man,* over and over again. We soon have enough of that. The wireless goes into Dad's "must fix it pile," where it stays until I fix it myself, many years later.

Winter is now upon us, but we are cozy in our little environment. Mam asks me to help tidy up the rest of the garden before the snow comes.

"Now let's get you wrapped up," she says, tying a scarf around my neck. "We don't want the damp to get you!" I glance nervously over my shoulder as the wind shakes the bushes behind me.

My large tin trunk has been left outside in the elements and is disintegrating with rust. Mam forces it open and inspects the contents. Shaking her head in disbelief, she picks up my cowboy suit, a present from my great-uncle who's a cop in New York. It is green with mold and in tatters.

"Oh, dear, look at all this stuff. It's ruined." She holds up one of my picture books. The cover slides off and the pages are all in decay.

"What causes all this, Mammy?"

"It was the damp, son."

A cold shiver runs through me. So the damp has been in our garden, causing havoc while we lay asleep in our beds!

"It's a good thing we lock our door at night, Mammy. Only the other day I heard the neighbors talking of a murder! Did you hear old Mrs. Mackay was found dead in her caravan? Oh, yes, they say it was the damp that killed her. Yes, it was the damp all right. Why don't they get a posse together and hunt it down, Mammy, before it gets us all?" Mam shoots me a queer look.

"You'd better go inside, I think you're coming down with something," she says.

"Hellooow!" The queer figure I had been idly watching as it trudged through the snow turns out to be my dad. The tracks behind him have a definite wavy quality, and his nose is red. He has a bow saw in one hand and a hip flask of brandy in the other.

"Come on, get your coat! We're going to cut timber for a rustic garden fence."

Off we march into the wilderness, that magical enclave of wild nature, now a stretch of ice-covered scrub bushes, frosty silver tree trunks, and frozen lakes. We cut several lengths of sapling about ten feet long, then with much grunting and swearing on my dad's part, we drag them home. On the way back, we see two big brown hares sitting in the rays of the setting winter sun.

"We'll come back for those buggers tomorrow—with a gun!" whispers my dad with an expeditious wink. Blue shadows fill our footprints as we march home through the snow in the indigo twilight.

"Here's the shotgun, Reg, and six cartridges. They're all I have just now."

"Ticketty-boo, sahib," Dad answers. I notice he often speaks to his old army chums in strange words and phrases; sometimes Arabic or in this case, Hindi, meaning: "That's fine, sir."

We crunch our way back to the wilderness, while Dad gives me a lesson on the etiquette of firearms.

"You *never* point a gun at anyone, always assume a gun is loaded, never carry a loaded gun with the safety off, and when hunting, always break a shotgun at the breach."

"There's one!" says Dad. The .410 discharges its shot, and the big brown hare falls still in the snow. I get such a fright from the bang, and because my ears are still ringing, I don't hear my dad say, "Hold this!" He thrusts the single-barreled shotgun into my hands, and I, totally unprepared for its weight, watch helplessly as the barrel spins round and sticks in the snow.

Dad is running over to his kill as I retrieve the gun and brush the snow off of the long blue barrel. He has not seen me drop it, and I say nothing.

"Now," says Dad, "this is what you do." He takes the one back leg of the hare and pushes it through the sinew of the other, forming a carrying handle.

"You hold it," he says, and reluctantly I do—at arm's length.

A little farther off, Dad motions me to be still—he has spied another. As he raises the newly loaded gun and takes aim, a miracle happens! The hare I'm holding suddenly jerks and kicks so violently that I let go of it and it takes off, zigzagging across the snow. The damn thing had only been stunned! I am even more stunned and take off running in the opposite direction. At the same instant, Dad fires and the end of the gun, packed with snow, mushrooms out in splinters.

It was a long walk home, with Dad muttering darkly to himself. As we reach our caravan he suddenly brightens up.

"Get my tools, Will, I have a plan."

For the next few hours my father saws, files, and smooths until the gun looks as good as new. Then with a blowtorch, he tempers the barrel until the metal is the same beautiful, uniform, blue color all around.

"There, he'll never know the difference," he says with some pride, scrutinizing the gun, now three inches shorter.

The next day we take it back to his mate. There is a unsuspected fly in the ointment, however. The owner takes the gun and is set to notice nothing until, to my Dad's wiggly-mouthed chagrin, he produces a case for it. Dad shuffles nervously as the man puts the gun in its walnut box. The man blinks, stares again, and utters, "The f—ing thing's shrunk!"

"Oh," says Dad, used to thinking on his feet, "it must be this cold weather!"

"What!" says his pal. "I've never heard of such a thing." Dad warms to his ruse.

"Do you know aught about the coefficiency of gun metal alloys?"

"No," says his mystified friend.

"Well, there you are. It's ten below out there!" Dad's superior knowledge wins the day and we leave his pal scratching his head.

The next summer, his mate duly reports that the barrel has never recovered from its mysterious shrinkage.

"Aye," says Dad. "That was a bloody cold winter!"

It is fast approaching Christmas. Dad has found a decent job as a signalman for British Railways. All is very pleasant at school, and we spend a lot of time making Christmas decorations and rehearsing for the school nativity play.

I had long wanted to have a go at acting and hoped for a star part. It was not to be. Like so much in life, I am passed over for someone whose only talent is not getting into trouble. The best parts go to those with the most spotless *souls*.

Amongst these chosen few, Mary O'Malley is given the part of Jesus' mother because she is the only Mary in the school. The fact that she is extremely timid and can't remember her lines is glossed over by the first-time director, Mr. Bury. The saintly Joseph Ryan is a triumph of miscasting for the same reason, and although he is playing Mary's consort he is too shy even to hold her hand.

I wanted to play King Herod, but Mr. Bury cut that role and I am given the only remaining speaking part—the innkeeper! Well, at least I have an apron, so my costume won't be expensive.

We rehearse in the school, but the play is to be held at the Firemen's Memorial Hall in nearby Henley-in-Arden. As the opening night approaches, I notice that the leading players are almost fainting with fear at the prospect. They should be more like the shepherds, who are scallywags and, with no lines to say, are having a ball. Even the angels, whose elaborate wings never seem to want to stay on, are having fun. I am in my element and delight at Mr. Bury as he strides around, wringing his hands and intoning, "This is going to be a disaster!" For once he was right, dead right!

During rehearsals the shepherds watched their flocks by night around a pile of rulers, which was their makeshift campfire. Now on opening night, Mr. Bury, our resident Jonah, builds a pile of twigs center stage to add a little realism. For color, he wraps a hundred-watt lightbulb in red cellophane and plugs it in. He flashes it up and it does look very pleasant, bathing the shepherd's faces with a warm glow. We are all set.

The choir are sweetly singing "O Little Town of Bethlehem," and from the scraping of the chairs and excited chatter, we know we have a full house.

At last the houselights dim, the curtain opens, and Mr. Bury's "fire" looks very realistic.

"Go—lighting cue one," comes a whisper. Nothing happens. Dark shapes move around the stage and collide with each other. The audience, sensing that something is amiss, begins to titter.

"Lighting cue one—GO!" bellows the director and the stage lights shoot up to discover an angel, with wings like Pegasus, wedged firmly in the doorway. The shepherds, far from being sympathetic, begin laughing. The determined seraphim, mustering all the strength of an indignant ten-year-old, bursts free of his encumbrance and marches on stage.

"I have come to tell you the Good News!"

"You've given up flying!" shouts an irreverent voice offstage, and the audience is in transports of delight.

"This is not supposed to be funny!" Mr. Bury is nearing the edge of his patience, and his stage whispers are in danger of drowning out the actors' dialogue.

Funny or not, it was getting realistic—he trapped lightbulb had reached the flash point of the cellophane, which had burst into flames.

"Holy Christ!!" shouts a new figure in the play, leaping into the midst of the confused gaggle of shepherds.

"FIRE! FIRE!" The tall man in the shiny brown suit is doing a jerky jig on top of the campfire in front of puzzled actors and audience alike. Mr. Bury has made his stage debut, as a fire dancer!

With great presence of mind, a young actor whose father once worked for a fire extinguisher firm douses them all down with a fire hose and never even asks for thanks.

The curtain closes prematurely on the first act, and Mr. Bury sits dripping and disconsolate in the wings.

I thought it had gone quite well, and the audience seems to be enjoying it. In fact, news of the fun had reached the fire station next door, and the backstage area is now full of men in firemen's gear. They tell us that we can proceed with the show once they have turned off the fire alarm, which is threatening to deafen us all.

Eventually the time comes to do my bit. There isn't much to it, so I make the most of it. "Saint" Joseph knocks timidly at the inn door, his pregnant wife beside him. This was it! I throw open the door and roar, "NO ROOM! NO ROOM AT THE INN!" But before I can finish, Joseph has fled off stage and Mary gets such a fright, she drops the infant Jesus, which had been secreted in her garments, and stares in horror as the Messiah's head flies off, rolls down the raked stage, and lands in the orchestra pit. The final curtain comes down on our pantomime production and likewise on Mr. Bury's career in show business. The befuddled audience is wild with appreciation, and even the firemen are cheering.

Later, as we make our way back in the winter chill, knowing that on the morrow our luckless teacher must explain the night's bizarre events to the stern Mrs. MacArthur, my gift for parody comes to the fore. Borrowing the melody of "Ding Dong Merrily on High," I offer "Ding Dong Bury's Gonna Die." Our little group takes up the chant as we walk the two and a half miles home through the snow.

Our wee school is blessed with two bequests from long-dead estates: the first amounts to sixpence for each child and the second to half a crown. Both are payable at Christmas. This makes a total of three shillings in sterling money and is a princely sum.

An ice cream costs a penny and there are thirty-six pennies in three shillings. The lowest-value coin is the farthing. Even this will buy you a boiled sweet, and there are four farthings to a penny, so the mathematics are simple: 36 ice creams = 144 boiled sweets.

The farthing is a neat little coin about the size of an American penny. On its face side, it has the monarch of the day, whilst the obverse bears the likeness of a wren.

Whether the Royal Mint in London realized it or not, this tiny creature was the smallest bird known to the ancients and is the Celtic king of the birds.

Mam had told me the story of the wren-king back home in Ireland

when I was wee, and so I present it to the class as my Christmas mono-
logue:

> The birds were deciding who should be their leader. "I
> am known to be the wisest," said the owl. "The swiftest
> should rule," squeaked the swallow. "How about the
> most graceful?" asked the swan. In a terrible uproar, each
> pressed his case, except the humble wren, who consid-
> ered himself unelectable on account of his diminutive
> size. He instead went to sleep in the warm feathers of the
> eagle's back.
>
> Knowing his ground well, it was the eagle now who
> spoke. "The title shall go to he who can fly the highest!"
> None dared argue and the contest began. One by one, as
> they climbed and wheeled, the various species reached
> their limit. Soon only the swifts, martins, and hawks
> were left. Still above them, climbing even higher, was the
> mighty eagle. Finally, in a last show of prowess, he flew
> higher than any eagle had flown before. At the very edge
> of his strength, he hovered and the rest of the birds whis-
> tled and squawked in approval.
>
> This awoke the sleeping wren, who flew straight up to
> see what all the commotion was about. The eagle, crest-
> fallen, admitted defeat, and the wren became the king of
> the birds.

In Ireland, the pagan ceremony of wrening still persists. On the day
after Christmas, boys dress up and go hunting for a wren. The object is
to capture one and parade it around the village in a cage. People give you
money for good luck and then the bird is released. It is considered very
unlucky to kill a wren, and if you do, you will be struck by lightning
within the year. I finish the story with a song I also learned from Mam:

> *The wren, the wren, the king of all birds,*
> *St. Steven's Day, was caught in the furze.*
> *Though he is little, his family is great,*
> *I pray you, good Landlady, give us a treat.*

The school term is over for Christmas and we have ten glorious days off! We are all very excited and even the prospect of midnight mass seems thrilling. Indeed, it was easy for the meanest of spirit to feel a little more *bon vivant!* at this time of year.

The big church at the top of the hill, next to the railway station, is very different from the freezing old barn of a school chapel. The statues are all nicely painted and look like real people. The altar boys have incense, and best of all—it is heated!

Christmas Eve comes with a light fall of fine snow that crisps under foot. The bells of the old Saxon church cascade in syncopated peals. This is great! It is nearly midnight, and I am so wrapped up against the cold, I am impervious to the many slips and falls we all have on the way up the hill. Many of the once a year devout traveling with us have just come out of the Bull's Head tavern, and giggling is the common currency of their conversation.

The priest is less pleased at seeing these annual revelers and warns them about swigging from secreted bottles during the mass. The great organ swells into a mighty crescendo, and we launch into "Adeste Fidelis."

The service seems very holy until about the halfway point, when the great nail-studded doors at the back of the church are flung wide open, letting in an icy shaft of air. Everyone turns to see the cause of the draft. I shiver and so does Mam. She recognizes the stumbling figure weaving his way toward the altar.

"Mother of Good Counsel—it's your father!"

Dad has inbibed a little too much of the Christmas spirit and is as drunk as a bobbyhowler. He is wearing both his work overcoat and his khaki army greatcoat, the pockets of which clink with beer bottles. He kneels down in the nave and begins to wail: "Oh, Jesus, forgive a poor sinner . . . oh, Jesus!"

He falls forward, giving his head a mighty clout on the altar steps. Two bottles of stout escape from the prison of his pockets and shoot across the marble floor. Dad goes after them sideways like a crab, all the time grabbing at the air, as they roll out of reach beneath a pew.

"Cummeeer, ye wee bashtards!" Dad slurs. "Whoops! Shorry, missus, was that yer leg?"

The priest, having recovered a little from this unwarranted intrusion, explodes!

"HOW DARE YOU BRING ALCOHOL INTO THE HOUSE OF GOD!!!" he thunders.

Dad wheels around on one foot, blinking in disbelief at the raging cleric.

"Shorry, mister, shorry, God!" Dad shuffles out toward the porch, tucking his prodigal Guinnesses back in his greatcoat pockets. Mam has her head buried in between the leaves of her gilt-edged prayer book.

"Has he gone?" she whispers. He has, for the time it takes him to line up his six bottles of stout in the vestry and return, waving his arms about and smiling like a prat.

"Happy Chrishmash!" he wishes one and all. "Peassh to all men."

"I'll give him peace when I get him home!!" Mam hisses, gritting her teeth into her missal. "I'll give him such peace it'll kill 'im."

The verger, a nervous man, decides to position himself near the telephone in case the assistance of the village policeman is required. In his haste, he neglects to see Dad's choir of beer bottles standing to attention across the vestry floor. He scatters them like ninepins. The unmistakable sounds of disaster send my father scurrying and cursing back up the aisle, where he confronts the terrified verger.

"YOU STUPID FU—!"

To the relief of all, especially the priest and my mother, Dad's voice is drowned out as the organ strikes up with, of all things, "Silent Night."

A Christmas Day truce is observed by Mam and Dad, "for the sake of the poor child." I appreciate it no end and stare at the solitary Christmas present under the tree. After breakfast I'm allowed to open it; it's a small red Dinkytoy fire engine.

Soon my mother, enlivened by a glass of sherry, is in better kidney and laughing about the previous night's doings.

"My God, Reg, you put the fear of the devil into that verger. When me and Willie last saw him, on our way home, he was hiding in the graveyard as white as a ghost!"

"If I'd have caught the bugger, he would *be* a bloody ghost by now! By the way, how do you like your Christmas present, Will?"

I was sitting on the floor, playing with my fire truck.

"It's terrific, Dad. Thanks!"

"We could have used that the night of the play," Mam says and proceeds to fill Dad in on all the disastrous details.

"There's a party at the big hall on New Year's Eve," informs my mother, who has started working as a part-time barmaid there. "It's a western-style barn dance cum fancy dress party. The theme is cowboys and Indians!"

"There's no shortage of either around here," says Dad.

"This will be old Mr. Mayer's last New Year's bash, as he's selling the estate in the spring," she says, pouring another sherry for herself and one for Dad.

The news of the sale saddens me, as I liked the old chap. Even though Mr. Mayer was seldom seen around and was a bit of a recluse, when he did venture out, he was pleasant to chat with and sometimes handed out silver sixpences. Each year, in the country gentleman's tradition of noblesse oblige, he threw a party in the grand ballroom for the estate workers and caravan site dwellers. He did not attend the revelry himself, but would stand at the door shaking hands with everyone before retreating to his lonely rooms above. Mr. Mayer's apartments in the Georgian mansion were spacious and crammed full of bric-a-brac from all over the globe. Mam said he had been well traveled as a youth and had made a lot of money in the United States before coming back to buy the hall. He also told my mother that what he missed the most about America was the pancakes.

In the British Isles, we only eat pancakes once a year, on Pancake Day, or Shrove Tuesday, as it's properly called. Being the start of Lent, this is the time to be shriven of sins and to use up all your flour and eggs before the fasting of the Lenten weeks begins. Last Pancake Day, we remembered old Mr. Mayer and brought some hot pancakes up to him. He was delighted, and although he was Jewish and didn't celebrate the feast day, he said he was very touched by Mam's simple act of kindness. He gave me a wooden camel from Egypt, which I treasure, as a memento of a kindly old man, who, though as rich as Croesus, lived a solitary life and hardly seemed to have a friend in the world.

Mam pours a small glass of sherry for me and gives us the toast: "We have come through some hard times—a happy Christmas and peace on earth!"

"And sod the begrudgers!"

"REG! That's enough of that sort of language in front of the child!"

Christmas dinner over, we all fall asleep where we sit, like giants surrounded by the bones of their slain.

The New Year's Eve party is a great success. A western barn dance scene is created, using bales of hay and old wagon wheels for effect.

Mam and Dad look very fine dressed as cowboys and have their photograph taken by the local paper. Dad has drawn a funny mustache and beard on his face with an indelible marker and finds that it won't wash off. People put a lot of care into their get-ups and everyone sports cowboy hats; Mam wears my hat and belt when she gets up to sing with the band:

> *I'm a rambler, I'm a gambler*
> *I'm a long way from home*
> *So if you don't like me*
> *Then leave me alone!*
> *I eat when I'm hungry*
> *I drink when I'm dry*
> *And if the moonshine don't kill me*
> *I'll live till I die!*

So the year was almost over. I get to go to the kids' party that precedes the grown-ups' fancy dress on Old Year's Night. To my amazement, there in the ballroom of the great hall, I meet with a quare-looking character, the likes of which I've never seen before. My friends say he is called Old Father Time. He has a well-worn, tattered robe of sable, a long white beard, a scythe over his shoulder, and a thing called an hourglass in his hand. I asked him what he is and why he was dressed like that?

"I am death!" comes the voice from within.

✦ Chapter 7 ✦

IN PREPARATION FOR THE SALE OF WOOTTON HALL AND ITS lands, hordes of workmen are recruited to do a spruce-up job on the three-hundred-year-old building.

The hall had been commandeered by the army during the war, and somehow, in the defense of king and country, the soldiers had managed to set fire to the roof. As a result, it was far from weathertight and needed major repairs.

In due course, huge flatbed trucks arrive carrying trusses, A-frames, stringers, and beams. All this makes a grand playground for us kids, both while stored under tarpaulins on the ground or rigged in place on the roof. The laborers, all of whom we know, are for the most part oblivious to our presence and pay us no heed.

One evening, I overhear some of the workmen chatting at the end of their shift.

"So they've finally managed to eradicate the damp, I hear," says a big, red-faced geezer.

"Yes, Mr. Bullivant, and none too soon either. It had eaten halfway through some of the timbers supporting the west wing. We caught it just in the nick of time!"

I am glad of our deliverance, but still curious. I'd never been face-to-face with a real monster.

"Can I see it?" I says to the construction fella.

"See what?"

"The damp, of course!"

"Well no, it's gone, dead! Not a trace left. Kaput!"

"Damn!" says I. "What did it look like?"

"Er . . . it was green and yellow spots mostly, and it really did stink!"

So there I had it, firsthand, from a man who had seen the ghastly murderous beast with his own eyes. The dreaded damp that had terrorized our neighborhood for ages was *dead*. We had been saved from the big stinky thing!

I lie in my bunk at night and watch the myriads of stars in their punctual progression around Polaris. I feel very small, very safe, and very happy.

The day dawns to a new brighter age and with it I arise confident to explore my terra incognita. The first thing is to acquire a trusty steed. This comes in the form of a tall, black, 1910 BSA bicycle. It is given to me by an old lady who'd had it from new. She called it a sit-up-and-beg, but my mam tells me it is a Thin Lizzy. It's a single-geared machine and has mechanical brakes. Although it is old fashioned, I love it.

Dad checks it over and after some tightening and adjusting, he pronounces it safe and roadworthy.

"See this thing, here?" he says, tapping the chain guard with a wrench. "This gadget was invented by your great-granddad to keep ladies' crinolines out of the works." I nod approval. "Now, let's oil her up and when the weather's better, I'll teach you to ride the beast."

Learn to ride, I did, sitting way up in the air on that ancient and venerable old bike. I got a great view of the entire world from up there!

Bright Phoebus vied for control of the northern skies and General Winter, sensing defeat, retreated his storm troopers, southward to the Antipodes. Spring was born.

"Rabbits!" shouts my Dad from his bed.

"What was that?"

"Rabbits! It's traditional to shout 'Rabbits!' on the first of March, for good luck."

"Ah, now, Reg, don't be filling the child's head with superstitious old nonsense. You're as mad as a March hare and you'll have the child as daft as yourself," Mam contends.

After my hunting experience, I'd had quite enough of hares, March or otherwise, but when I look outside, the snow, like the accursed damp, is gone.

"In like a lion and out like a lamb," Mrs. MacArthur says, turning over the calendar page and placing the red marker on March 1st. 1957.

"You're supposed to say 'Rabbits!' miss," I blurt out, as blithe as a butterfly. She turns and fixes me with a viperous eye. My heart stops.

"Beware the hides of March!" she warns me, or it could have been the eyes of March—I couldn't tell with that quare Scottish "Och eye the noo" accent of hers.

"What was that again, miss?" I entreat, trying to get into her good books.

She turns a serpentine stare back toward me.

"I don't boil my cabbages twice," she hisses mysteriously and fills my conviction that grown-ups like to answer proper questions with odd allusions to vegetables! Luckily for me, the old school wireless set crackles to life with an important announcement.

"This is the BBC Schools Service. We begin today's Broadcast of Scottish Country Dancing in five minutes. *PEEP! PEEP! PEEP!*"

"CLEAR THE DECKS FOR ACTION!" Mrs. MacArthur has become transformed. "You there, Patrick Whateveryournameis, stack those chairs!" She has become Captain Bligh! "Clear the tables away! Move it! MOVE IT! Mister Bury! Where are you? MISTER BURY, GET IN HERE!!!"

Mr. Bury, still on his morning break, appears in the doorway. Teacup in one hand and half-dipped digestive biscuit held high in the other.

"Er, what is it, Head? Er . . . um," he bumbles, staring around in disbelief as the normally well-ordered schoolroom is stripped as clean as the gun deck on a frigate.

"I'm still on my . . . er . . . tea break!"

"GET STUCK IN!!" she barks. "The DANCING will start in two minutes!!"

"I . . . um . . . yes . . . em!" All this is as new to Mr. Bury as it is to me and whilst his mind vacillates between incomprehension and hope, the soggy end of his biscuit breaks off and disappears down his shirt sleeve.

"MISTER BURY—DO SOMETHING!!!" she orders, clearing away the blackboard. He does and in his eagerness to please, he tries to do two different tasks simultaneously. Unfortunately, they are at opposite sides of the classroom and his confused corporance, in defiance of the laws of anatomy, attempts to move his bottom half to the right and his top half to the left. Still with teacup and half biscuit in hand, it gives him the appearance of a bemused hula-girl on coffee break.

"Mr. Bury, stop those gyrations and come here!" she says, pointing to a spot on the floor. "That's it—guid!" Clapping her hands three times, she calls, "RIGHT NOW! Let's get fell in. Guid! Guid! Two lines, girls to the left, boys to the right, facing each othe—? Michael Dwyer!!! Do you not know what gender you are???"

"No, miss," he says in all honesty, as we hadn't done gender yet.

"Well, that butters no parsnips with me! Get in line!"

"Mrs. Mack's gone veggie again!" I confide to Steve O'Donnell, who gets the giggles. The teacher spins around, but we are saved as the wireless strikes up with a skirling Scottish march and Mrs. MacArthur, her eyes blazing like Queen Boadicea mowing down the Roman legions, stomps up and down the assembled rows of children, swinging her arms and blowing odd bagpipe-type noises out of the corner of her mouth.

"The Campbells are coming . . . *Puh—Paw—Puh—Paw!* The Campbells are coming . . . *Puh—Paw—Puh—Paw!!*" It is all very unnerving.

The brisk signature tune fades and the lesson proper begins.

"Now each of you take a partner." She grabs Mr. Bury, who pales visibly. To my horror, though I try to maneuver myself down the line, I get stuck with Nora.

The music begins with an eightsome reel, and whether Nora had forgotten the incident with the hammer two years ago, I don't know, but being taller and older than me, she throws me around the room like a terrier does a rat. I am glad when the final *Deh!—Dah!* comes and we all can rest.

Mr. Bury looks like he's been filleted. His body has gone to jelly and he is having trouble keeping it on his chair. One of his legs has taken to doing a solo twitching dance, and with his face the color of an overripe tomato, he is sweating profusely.

The headmistress, however, is bristling like a sergeant major's waxed mustache. Her eyes gleaming like the hot coals of hell, and with a determined stride, she swans up and down the ranks, rubbing her hands with glee.

"Well done! Well done, children, a very guid show!"

This unexpected praise spurs us on to new efforts, and we all get thoroughly into the swing of things; all except the recumbent Mr. Bury, who sits like a broken toy in the corner, nursing a supposed dislocated shoulder and complaining of nausea.

"You should eat more *porridge*, sonny!" Mrs. Mack teases as she circles past the fallen teacher clutching her new dancing partner, the terrified Michael Waterson. In her exuberance she fails to realize that Mike, being half her size, has become airborne; his little legs describe spindly arcs in her turbulent wake.

After half an hour of Scottish country chaos, we file past a proudly smiling Mrs. MacArthur and into the sunlit playground where we sit in little groups, supporting each other like earthquake victims. The aftershocks of the jigs and reels still shudder in our small bodies like tremors, and despite the warm day, Mike's teeth are chattering.

Break over, we troop back into the classroom to find the genie out of the bottle. The florid-faced parish priest is there with an unwelcome announcement.

"Tomorrow there will be a special mass to celebrate Pope Pius the Twelfth's eightieth birthday. Also, his seventeenth year as the Holy Father. You will all attend. There will be NO EXCEPTIONS!" He says the last bit loud enough to drown out our groans.

As if this isn't bad enough, the next subject is the dreaded arithmetic or sums, as we called it, and that is the one subject I have the most trouble with.

Now, it isn't that the idea of adding and subtracting, multiplying and dividing is all that strange. The problem lies in the teaching methods and the British school's standard math textbook. The course work relies heavily on allegory, which is fine for teaching fables or parables, but to me mathematics is abstract and is best dealt with in abstraction.

I could readily understand that $1 + 5 = 6$, but to the Celtic mind, one carrot + five carrots = a bunch of carrots and nothing else. Similarly, $3 - 1 = 2$, fair enough, but the book would ask: "You have three apples in one hand and you take away one, what have you got?" To the Anglo-Saxon, the simple answer is two. To the visually minded Celt, however, you have two apples in one hand and one in the other. Apples and carrots, me arse; I'd rather be fishing.

The lesson begins with a cane being rapped on the face of the blackboard to draw our attention, and Mr. Bury, now on firmer ground, feels like he's back in control.

"John Costello, if it takes one man one hour to dig a hole, how long does it take two men?"

"Two hours, sir!"

"No, no, no! How could it be two hours? Come on, John, think about it!"

"Well," says John, "the second fella would be getting in the first fella's way for a start and then they'd be talking and wisecracking an' carrying on. Then they might stop for a smoke and then—"

"Stop, stop, stop! The answer is simple: half an hour! OK?"

"Noshataall!" continues John. "There'd be no hole dug in half an hour that could accommodate two men with picks and shovels and them both working!"

We all support his irrefutable logic and we know full well that John's dad is a ganger for Ryan Construction and so he knows what he is talking about.

Mr. Bury is stunned to silence, probably lamenting the fact that he had spent all those years at college just to be worsted by a young gosoon from the wilds of Connemara. Mind you, no teacher back home in Ireland would ever be so errant as to argue digging holes with a Culshie.

"They just don't seem to grasp it, Miss Hathaway," our young teacher confided over a cup of tea.

"You should try taking the little tykes for history! I only had to mention Oliver Cromwell and they nearly took the hide off me! They take it all so personally!"

This is true. History to us is a living, breathing beast. A composite of people and events that directly effects and involves our lives. Wasn't Thomas MacDonagh, the poet and patriot, who signed the Declaration of Irish Independence in 1916, a living kinsman, before he was executed by a British firing squad!? He was! Didn't General Sir John Cope, another distant relative, have the good sense to take one look at the Highland Scots' army and run away from the battle of Prestonpans in 1745? He did! Who was it that got hung for organizing the Spithead naval mutiny in the 1700s? Thomas Watkins, that's who! Mind you, Uncle Walter reckons our family are direct descendants of Old King Cole, but that's Uncle Walter for you! Anyway, the English history that we are now obliged to learn is merely a long list of kings, queens, and battles that would put a glass eye to sleep! To us, history is still in the making. On New Year's day this very year, a small force of volunteers of the Irish Republican Army has attacked Brookeborough RUC barracks in Northern Ireland. The gunfight that ensued left two IRA men dead and three wounded. The fallen were Fergal O'Hanlon, aged nineteen, from Monaghan, and the raid's legendary twenty-seven-year-old leader, Seán South, the family of whom we knew well.

> *At early dawn, the Colleen bawn,*
> *Put on her long black veil.*
> *She told me then, of two young men*
> *Who fell on freedom's trail.*
> *The seagulls cried, for those who died*
> *All along the Shannon's shore.*
> *God rest you brave, Seán Sabhat.*
> *We will ne're see you more.*

The funerals for the two young men were the largest in living memory. In Limerick, 36,000 people followed the coffin, including the U.S. ambassador. Seán was buried with full military honors in the same graveyard as countless past generations of my own family. That's the sort of history we are used to—not the despotic antics of some obese, syphilitic, ax-wielding old tosspot like Henry VIII.

The long plod home from school is rewarded by a grand yeasty aroma emanating from the vicinity of our caravan.

Mam is in good fettle, making bread and singing a wee song away to herself:

> *Ireland was Ireland,*
> *When England was a pup.*

And Ireland will be Ireland,
When England's "buggered up"!

"Mam, do you hate the English?"

"Good God, no, Willie. There's enough hate it this world without me stirring up some more. You shouldn't hate anything in this life, except hatred itself. The poor old English, they're more to be pitied than scorned, with their cricket and tiddlywinks and their passion for keeping up with the Joneses. As Brendan Behan says, 'Take them away from their kings and queens and rifles, and they're decent enough people!'"

There is a blue van sounding its horn at the end of the road. The back doors are opened, and old Mr. Westmacote, the greengrocer, stands waiting by his weighing machine, wearing a grubby white apron.

"Willie, go up to the van and buy me five pounds of spuds and a cabbage. I've a lovely piece of boiling bacon and tomorrow is Saint Patrick's Day."

"On my way, Mam. Where's the money?"

"Take a pound out of my purse and make sure you get a nice firm little cabbage."

Shopping bag in hand I saunter up to the mobile shop.

"Five pounds of potatoes, please, and I'll take one of these." I set the small green orb on the weighing scale. The needle hardly moves.

"Do you only want one of them?"

"Yeah, there's only the three of us."

"OK, you're the boss!"

I stroll back to the caravan. Mam stares at my purchase in disbelief.

"Is that the cabbage he gave you?"

"It is."

"Jasus! What sort of daylight bloody robbery is going on here atall? That skinny little thing wouldn't feed a flea, ifeverawomansuffered!" She grabs the goods and storms off to the vendor.

"What sort of a cabbage do you call that?"

"I call it a brussels sprout, madame!"

"WILLIE! Willie! You bleeder, I'll kill you for making me look an eejit!" She chases me back to the caravan to the great delight of the departing grocer.

What is with vegetables? Why are they always trying to get me into trouble?

It's a great day for the Irish! March seventeenth. Saint Patrick's Day is here again and all of the kids in the school have green, white, and orange tricolor ribbons with wee gold harps on them. Everywhere little tufts of wild green shamrock sprout from coat collars. The atmosphere is unusually festive, and even Mrs. Mack, Miss Hathaway, Mr. Bury, and wee Jean-Paul are all decked out with the three-leafed wonder. We sing:

> Hail glorious Saint Patrick, dear Saint of our Isle
> On us, thy dear children, bestow your sweet smile
> And as you look down from your mansion above
> On Erin's green valleys, look down in thy love.

The priest arrives and beams at us during our hymn singing. Father rambles on about St. Patrick being a slave and how he lit a fire to annoy the Druids, then showed the king of Ireland that a shamrock had three leaves, and that's what saved us all. He sets us an essay to write on the subject of "The Real Catholic Meaning of St. Patrick's Day."

I had heard my father say, "It's a good thing to have *real Catholic tastes.*" Hence, ignoring the patron saint of Ireland and his driving out the snakes an' all, I begin:

> Bacon and cabbage is made like this. First you must boil
> a lump of shoulder bacon or corned beef, in a big pan of
> water for two hours, add no salt as it comes out from the
> meat. Then add a chopped up cabbage straight into the
> same pot and leave it alone. Then boil up loads of spuds
> and eat it all together with Colman's mustard on it. Then
> you will have a happy Saint Patrick's Day.

March goes out like a lamb and then 'tis April, just before my seventh birthday.

A bright yellow General Post Office Telephones van pulls into the main drive of the hall and its crew begins rigging poles and wires to a new phone box at the end of the road. It is always a curiosity when a government agency makes a rare visit to our secluded environment.

Mostly we only see the village postman on his red bicycle or the occasional policeman on motorcycle patrol, so the arrival of a GPO van is noteworthy. The post office has a unique place in public life. Not only does it run the postal service, but also the national savings bank and the telephone and telegraph networks.

The linesmen are busy in the field with their cables and poles, and I wander over to take a closer look at the operation. Behind the open back of the telephone truck, much to my surprise, I stumble headlong into my father doing something furtive.

"What are you doing, Dad?"

"Shooosh! Shsh!" He winks and flashes a roll of copper wire that he has concealed under his coat. With a sideways glance at the oblivious workmen, he sidles away whistling the old military march "Colonel Bogey."

The next day the wire is hanging high above our caravan, suspended on a pair of porcelain insulators, between two poles. What could it be? I soon find out.

"Happy Birthday!!!" Mam and Dad usher me into the caravan and there on my bed is a small white box with dials and switches and a pair of earphones. It's a crystal set.

I put on the headphones and tune the dial around. There it is: the BBC "Light Programme" on 1,500 meters long wave! A flick of the switch to medium wave and there is the BBC "Home Service" and, further down the frequency, the "Third Programme." This is truly a mystical experience, the sorcery of which intrigues me.

"Does it have batteries, Dad?"

"No, no, it works only on the signal voltage coming down the aerial wire."

"Is that the stuff you nicked from the GPO van?" Mam's smile fades.

"You said you found that wire! You thievin' bugger!" She gives him a dig.

"I did find it—just before it was lost!"

At night in the darkness, I tune in the world. I can hear stations from all over Europe and beyond. It is totally different from the big wireless set that hums. This is quiet, and the reception is crystal clear. My excitement gets the better of me.

"Dad! Dad! Radio Moscow has just announced that they've launched a spaceship called a sputnik!"

"Go to bloody sleep, Marconi. I've got to get up for work in four hours."

As a result of my ear on the world, I become a walking encyclopedia of news, comment, terrestrial trivia, and litanies of unrelated facts.

"Oliver Hardy died last night," I tell the postman.

"Oh," he says. "What a shame, I liked him."

The school crossing lady is edified by the splendid news that there is now a brand-new tunnel under the Hudson River in New York.

"That's nice, dear. Watch out for the traffic now!"

"Mam, thousands of Hungarians are arriving in Britain. They're called refugees, and they had to get out of Hungary because of the fighting!"

"Yes, the poor hungry Hungarians," she says, looking troubled. She tucks me in and takes off my earphones. I sense something is badly wrong.

"Mam, tell me a poem about Hungary?"

"OK," she says, still distractedly poking the old stove:

Long legged Italy,
Kicked little Sicily
Into the Mediterranean sea.
Germany got angry,
Austria got Hungary
And ate a bit of Turkey,
Fried in Greece."

"Now give me a real poem—the 'Siege of Athlone' or suchlike."

"No, not tonight. I've too much on my mind, son," she says, turning off the electric light to sit quietly in the amber glow from the little stove.

Dad comes home and I wake up a little. They sit sharing a bottle of Ansell's Nut Brown Ale. As I drift in and out of sleep, I try to follow their conversation.

"The priest has given him the last rites," Mam says.

"God, it couldn't have come at a worse time, Monica. With this nonsense going on in Cyprus, I might have to go. The army may call up all the reservists."

"There's never a good time to get cancer, Reg."

"I know," says Dad, putting his arm around her. "I think the world of your da. We've had many's the spree together. You had better get the boat train tomorrow."

The next morning Mam is up early, packing her old brown suitcase. In my sleepy state I don't notice at first, but as she fusses and folds, she is crying.

"So it wasn't all a bad dream then?"

"No, Willie."

"Then Grandda is going to . . . ?" I can't say the word.

"Yes," she says. "Now be a good boy and pack your things."

"Am I going back over home with you, Mammy?"

"No, you're going to your granddad Jim's house in Birmingham for a few weeks." I am strangely relieved. I don't want to see my lovely Irish grandda on his deathbed.

Mam and me take the Midland Red bus to New Street railway station in Birmingham. My granny Mary-Anne is waiting on the platform to see Mam off and take me back to granddad's house. Granny looks as care-worn as Mam.

"Be a good little soldier now for your mammy and don't be bold to your grandma!" I nod up and down, biting my lower lip hard so I won't cry.

From along the platform, the guard waves a green flag and blows a shrill shriek on his whistle. Like the keening of a banshee, the engine's siren wails a mournful farewell and the train slowly squeals away, leaving grandma and me wrapped in shrouds of white steam. When it clears, all I can see is the red oil lamp of the departing carriages glowing like a cinder in the funereal darkness of the long black tunnel.

"Bye, Mam," I whisper to the retreating taillight.

Granddad Jim's house seems huge and scary after the confines of a sixteen-foot trailer home, and to make it worse, I am given a double bed in the spare room. I've never slept in a room on my own before and

I'm very nervous. The lofty oak furniture, dark and terrifying, towers around me, creaking for no apparent reason. I feel alone and frightened. From one wall of the bedroom stares the ghostly face of an old oil painting. It's the portrait of a man in early Victorian garb. He has a lace ruff around his neck and his eyes are dark like damsons. His forehead is adorned with a row of little kiss-curls, his lips are cherry red and in the shape of a cupid's bow; like Mary Pickford or the famous "It Girl," Clara Bow. This, my granny tells me, was my great-uncle Leman, who had been a dandy and who eventually died in a duel, his gambling debts paid on the point of his creditor's rapier. This is not the bedtime story I was hoping for, and I long to be back in my tiny caravan, where, sitting on my pillow with the black Bakelite headphones on, my teddy bear was keeping abreast of the world's events on the crystal wireless set.

Life at the grandparents' place is a lot different than I remember from the last time I stayed there. Grandma seems more remote and can't be bothered with me. She says odd things and wanders about a lot. Granddad Jim is tired most of the time and sometimes very grumpy. I like to look inside the fragrant-smelling walnut writing bureau, where is kept ink, drawing pens, and colored pencils.

"Stop that meddling!" comes the call from Granddad Jim.

"But, what is this thing?" I'm holding a glass paperweight with beautiful nodules of colored coral entrapped in the lead glass.

"It's a lay hole for a meddler. Now put it down before you drop it and it's smashed!" He holds his stomach and moans.

"Willie, make me up some bread and goody, there's a good boy."

"He who asks, don't get. He who don't ask, don't want!" I says in jest, repeating one of his own maxims.

He manages a smile and indicates the scullery. "Go on now, Willie, and be a good lad. I must go and lie down."

When Granny comes home I ask her what is wrong with him.

"His stomach . . . in tatters. What do you expect? Years at the whiskey bottle. Should have spent more time at home with me. Always off swilling down Scotch with your uncles and their cronies at the Masonic Lodge. One foot in the grave . . . bread and milk and Andrew's Liver Salts." She walks nimbly over to the curtains and yanks them open as if expecting to find someone hiding behind them. The doorbell rings and I get a fright!

It's Dad with the grim news that Grandda in Ireland has died and Mam is coming home in a few weeks' time. Then he leaves and I'm sitting at the fireside with Mary-Anne.

"He was here again, you know? That little boy. I saw him looking through the window, upstairs."

"Gran, what little boy? Gran, we don't have a window upstairs. This is a ground floor flat."

"There he is again, looking at me!" She stabs the air with a crooked forefinger and the heart is put crossways in me. I spin on my chair; there is nothing at the window except a pale twilight moon peeping above the lime trees. I am scared. She puts on an old fur coat and goes out.

"Where are you going, Gran?" The bang of the front door is my only answer.

What my granny does in the daytime I don't know. She seems to like going shopping, but all she keeps bringing back is dried yeast and marmalade. We have cupboards bursting with it. I spend many hours each day with Granddad Jim, who now seldom gets out of bed. He says he is very poorly. I make bread and goody for us both; luckily bread and milk are delivered to the house. I sit day by day, reading to him. It makes him laugh when I mispronounce words or read things without knowing their meaning.

Granny is gone more often; time passes; Granddad grows worse. He calls for an enamel bowl and then sends me out of the room. Standing in the hallway, I can hear him being sick. The bowl is full of brown liquid that stinks like cat shit. I pour it down the toilet and pull the chain.

I doze off by the fire. Again Granddad Jim is shouting. He calls for the bowl, but he's too weak to hold it. I put pillows behind his back and hold it as he vomits a bowl full of thick black blood. I flush it down the toilet and ask if he wants some liver salts made up. He nods no. He closes his eyes, but in a weak voice asks for the shoe box from on top of the wardrobe. I get it down for him. It contains a silver-mounted Colt .45 pearl-handled revolver and a small brass padlock key.

"This is for you!" he whispers, giving me the pistol. He asks for a drink of water and I fetch it for him. Taking the small key he puts it into his mouth and swallows it. Then finally, lying back with the palms of his hands flat on the green eiderdown, he says, "You're a good boy, Willie," and then he dies.

Previously in the long talks we had as he lay in his sickbed, he told me not to mourn death, but celebrate life. Alone in the apartment with his body, I didn't know what to do. I wander from room to room like my granny does, just wishing my dad would come. I want to cry, but I can't. As if in answer to my plight, the door bell rings. I nearly jump out of my skin with fright. "Please, God, let it be Dad!"

It isn't Dad. It's two strange men in suits and bowler hats. They push past me. One goes straight into granddad's room and nods to the other one when he comes back out.

"We've come for your granddad's things," says the taller of the two.

The other geezer, a squinty little bloke with glasses like the bottom of milk bottles, tries to engage me in childish conversation. I'm not having any of this old soft soap. I might be just a kid, but I know he is trying to distract me while the lanky one is snooping around the house. I ask the tall bloke what in the name of Jasus he thinks he's doing. He puts a hand on my shoulder and leers at me with a smile like a boiled herring.

"Oh, a little Irish boy!" he smoothes, with what I take to be total contempt. I make a mental note where the revolver is.

"Maybe a clever little boy like you knows where your granddad's secret key is?" he probes in the clipped tones of the BloodyEnglish upper class. I make my way nearer the shoe box.

"Well, tell us, Sonny Jim," says the kipper-lipped one.

"He swallowed it, with a glass of water, just before he died."

"Ah good." They nod knowingly at each other.

"Well, we won't detain you any longer." They pick up granddad's large trunk that contains his sword and weird clothes and walk outside with it.

"His things are in here, we'll look after them," says Squinty, patting the lid.

"Bye-bye, Sonny Jim," adds the fish-faced one, as he pulls the door shut on a seven-year-old boy and a sixty-seven-year-old corpse.

There is a policeman at the door with my granny. She is babbling about the little boy who sets fire to things, looking in the window. He says that my gran is not well and is having delusions. He wants to see Granddad Jim. I show him in. He talks to Granddad Jim for a bit and then just stands there in silence. Then he grabs Granddad's wrist.

"He dead!" he says to me, going all white and big eyed.

"I know!"

"Suffering Jasus!" My father is incandescent with rage. "Those fucking cockroaches come in here without so much as a by-your-leave, take away Dad's Masonic regalia, and leave a little boy alone with his dead grandfather and a grandmother with senile dementia! It's outrageous, totally beyond belief. What the hell do they think they're playing at!"

My two uncles nod and shuffle their feet. Granny doesn't seem to know what's going on and keeps saying that it's getting late and she must make Granddad's dinner.

"It's all a terrible mistake, Reg. I'll see that questions are asked at the next lodge meeting."

"Fuck the lodge—and fuck you both as well!" roars my father, bundling me into the front seat of a waiting car.

On the long journey back to the caravan site, Dad thumps the dashboard of the borrowed car with his fist. I have never seen him so angry. He seems to have forgotten all about me. He just shouts that fuck thing, that Mam said was a soldier's word, and hits the car. For the first time in all this, I begin to cry. Dad's anger is gone. He realizes he is not alone and puts his arm on my shoulder.

"You poor wee bastard. You've lost both your granddads in seven weeks!" he sighs.

So that was just seven weeks. It had seemed like an eternity. I had never fully understood time before. It just sort of happened, like passing the school signpost every day. Now it is all too real, painfully real. I remember the Old Father Time character I met last New Year's Eve.

"I am Death!" he had said—and now death had a face.

↷ Chapter 8 ↶

MAM HAS BEEN BACK FOR A FEW WEEKS. IN HER FRAILTY, SHE seems wizened with worry and is full of distractions. It's been desperate hard on her, with three deaths in the family and poor old Mary-Anne now locked up in a mental home, but as Mam is wont to say, "There's always someone worse off than yourself." To take her mind off things, my mother busies herself with something called relief work. She sorts out seldom-worn clothes and puts them in a pile.

"This is going to be a cold winter like the year before last. The rowan berries are heavy on the trees and that's always a sure sign of a rough winter." I look up from playing with my little red fire engine by the glowing cast-iron stove.

"Aye, but we'll be warm enough, eh?" I am thinking of the big pile of hard, shiny anthracite coal we have just been delivered by Mr. Snell the coalman.

"Yes, we're all right, but what about the poor refugees up at Snitterfield? They need everything and the poor misfortunes have nothing. Do you have any toys you don't play with anymore, or things you've grown out of? There's little kiddies up there with bugger all and sure Christmas is only a couple of weeks away."

"Yeah, I've a rake of old toys and things. I'll round them up so."

We pack a big bag of stuff and hitch a ride on the Red Cross collection truck that is doing the rounds. In twenty minutes we are at the old RAF base that serves as temporary shelter and housing for the survivors of the Hungarian uprising.

They are indeed the sorriest-looking bunch of folk I have ever seen and no wonder: most are penniless, some are recovering from wounds, all are stateless and homeless, and as in any war, there are many widows and orphans. Their gratitude for our meager donations sees no bounds. My arm aches from having my hand shaken, and Mam has been kissed more times than General de Gaulle liberating Paris.

In the midst of this cold war flotsam of humanity, I see a young girl like no other I'd ever seen. She has high cheekbones, dark eyes, black hair, and flawless white skin. I am reminded of the faces on the angels in St. Munchin's Church in Limerick, and let's face it, you never see an angel with red hair and freckles. She is holding a toy monkey that I have donated. I wave at her, but she looks away. I think she is shy.

As I'm boarding the truck to get a ride home, I look back to the rows of corrugated iron Nissen huts, and there she is, still hugging her monkey.

She smiles and shouts, "Dank yew!"

I feel like the risen Christ!

We later hear that despite everything, the Hungarians had a good Christmas after all and we are pleased. Ours was a little subdued, as you would expect, but Dad has a stroke of luck. He has been hired by the site manager to clean out some old storerooms that are full of junk.

"Just get rid of it all and sweep the place out. I don't care what you do with the crap." And crap there is, but buried under piles of old Leyden jar batteries, moldy books, and pigeon droppings is an army officer's personal traveling trunk..

This cornucopia of yesteryear is full to the brim with old photographs, personal letters, Victorian postage stamps, a silver-mounted hipflask (still containing red rum), a silver "Albert" for decorating a pocketwatch chain, and a Sam Browne belt complete with holster containing a .38 Webley revolver. Further investigation in the floor cavity produced twenty-four eight-ounce tins of army issue metal polish, three boxes of .303 rifle ammunition, and an ammo box full of hand grenades, all very saleable on the black market. Never ones to look a gift horse in the mouth, it seems that the year 1958 might be treating us more kindly than the previous one.

We have a handcart full of treasures to trundle along the cobbled pathway home. Turning up the cinder track to our part of the site, we bump into Mrs. Ayers. She is an old Shakespearean theater actress who long ago had hit the gin bottle and now thinks she is the reincarnation of Lady Fitzherbert.

"Isn't it a cold day, Mr. Wilkins?" says the old starlet.

"Watkins!" corrects my dad.

"What is? The day of course—damn cold, I said!"

"Have a drink!" says Dad, offering the ancient hip flask. She doesn't need a hearing aid this time!

"Thank you, Mr. Wilson, that is a lovely drop of stuff!" She smiles as she returns the rum and waddles away like an inebriate Queen of Sheba.

The new owners of the hall and its lands are the Allen family. The day they arrive I am sent down to open the big wrought-iron gates to let them in. To my astonishment, on a chill spring day, they drive up in an enormous white American Oldsmobile with the top down. I am black-affronted by this unexpected show of wealth and prestige. Damn it all, just who do these millionaires think they are?

"What's your name, kid?" says Mr. Allen, giving me a sixpenny tip.

"I'm Willy Watkins, and we're having SALMON sandwiches for tea!" That's shown them that they're not the only ones who live high on the hog.

The car speeds off in a cloud of dust toward the hall. I follow, pedaling furiously on my ancient bicycle. All the way down the long drive I thought I could hear the people in the Yankee car laughing. What's the big joke?

The Allens soon settle in and we become firm friends. They have three kids: Mark is a bit younger than me, Neil is a bit older, and John is very, very old, fourteen or something!

Mr. Allen is a big, leonine chap with a sense of humor. He isn't one of the landed gentry and that wrinkles a few noses amongst the country set. Wisely, he had sold his successful garage business in Birmingham and used the proceeds to buy the hall. This story isn't good enough for some of the busybodies on the caravan site who challenge its veracity. Rumors fly about that he is some sort of underworld gang boss who has retired from crime. Some say that he is a government agent sent to spy on them, and others have an even more outlandish theory. Before the outbreak of World War II, they allege that he took a risky gamble. When it was obvious that war was inevitable, he took the six new cars that he had in his showroom, greased them thoroughly, and wrapped them up in wax-soaked cotton sheets. He then secreted them in a barn in the Welsh mountains, far from the eyes of the military, who would surely commandeer all civilian vehicles. The begrudgers said that he would always get more than double his money back, in sterling or Reichsgeld, depending on the war's outcome. Mam's take on this was typical.

"If that's true, then good luck to him for having some foresight, and if it isn't, then some of those gossips down at Obnoxious Corner have more petty imagination than is good for them."

Mrs. Allen is a tall, thin lady called Edna. She is very nice to us ragamuffins and even sets up a television in the hall so that we can watch *Children's Hour.* The TV is the size of a chest of drawers and has but one black-and-white channel. It is an adventure just to watch the test-card transmission. We sit in the darkness waiting for the test-card to fade and the plummy Queen's English voice to announce:

"Theese is the BHEE BHEE SEE CHILDRAWNS HAAR! And NHAA we have the LEARN RAINJHA and TONTO!"

"HI! HO! SILVER . . . AWAAAY!!!" We all shout and make galloping movements sitting back to front on our chairs.

Mrs. Allen tells me that there is an odd coterie of people called high brows who can listen to the "William Tell Overture" and never once think of *The Lone Ranger.*"

On the way back up the hill I meet Dad; he has a bucket of paint and is furious.

"What's wrong, Dad? Where are you going with that paintbrush?"

"Come and see what some sick bastard has done to old Mr. Feidelman's caravan."

At the point where the cinder track turns sharply into the kitchen gardens, a little moss green wooden caravan stands covered with garish white Nazi swastikas. Across the side is scrawled "JUDEN RAUS!" Dad helps the owner to paint over the mess, but the color is a poor match.

"After six years of war, I thought we'd put an end to this load of bollocks once and for all! If I catch the bastard who did this—"

"What does that mean?" I point at the words now disappearing under the pea-green paint.

Old Mr. Feidelman looks at me sadly. "It means, Jews get out!"

The weather takes to the warm side, and I am able to venture farther afield in search of diversion. I take a notion to go fishing, and being surrounded by two rivers, a canal, and dozens of little lakes, there is no shortage of good spots. My first rod is a piece of willow branch broken straight off the tree. The tackle comes from the same source and consists of about fifteen feet of line, a float, three lead sinkers, and a hook—all salvaged from the branches, where some unlucky bugger had snagged it on a back cast.

"You'll never catch now't with that!" one of the weekend fishermen down from the big city says, laughing.

"Ah, you never know. What are you fishing for?"

"Perch," says his mate. "But I don't reckon there's any in here. We've been here all morning and caught just two roach and a skinny little gudgeon!"

"You never know your luck in a big town!" I sit about twenty feet away from them, catching four nice perch in the space of ten minutes. To make matters worse, I put them back upstream of the fishermen and all their fancy gear.

"There you are, boys, that will give you a chance at them!"

"He's taking the piss! Go on, get out of it, you scruffy little sod."

I laugh all the way home.

My horizons are to expand in more ways than one. I was always a bit of a daredevil and suffer from enough insatiable curiosity to fill the nine lives of a dozen cats.

Michael Waterson lives just around the corner from me and up a small hill. His caravan sits in a fork in the road and is hidden by trees. I never meet his dad; he is always away on business, which usually means in jail. His mum is very glamorous and a walking monument to Max Factor. I think her name is Trixie or something like that.

I like going up to Mike's place because there's never any parents around to chastise you for blaggarding or acting the goat.

He has a mandolin and is delighted when I get a tune out of it. I manage a ragged version of "Brian Boru's March," but I can't make much of a fist of it because the strings are so rusty. Mike, though, is thrilled. To him the tune is as magical and inaccessible as Elgar's *Enigma Variations.*

"Could you show me how to play that?" I try, but he has no ear.

"That's great!" He lays the instrument down. "Let's have a drink!"

A bottle of port and two glasses appear. "It's my dad's, he doesn't bother with it!"

Well, we bother with it all right—all afternoon, until it's empty!

The world has seemingly taken on an Alice in Wonderland quality and as I speed downhill home on my bike, I fancy that I'm riding through a mental kaleidoscope. The time comes to make the turn. I feel neither the power nor the will to do so. My trusty velocipede flattens the white picket fence and strikes a concrete lawn ornament. It stops dead. I don't, however, and fly like Flash Gordon toward a pea-green hardboard-built caravan. Mr. and Mrs. Feidelman had just finished their dinner when a large child going "Wheeee!" crashes headlong through the wall and lands squarely on the dinner table.

It is as well for me that the impact knocks me out for a while. My incoherent ramblings, on regaining consciousness, are put down to concussion. The truth is that I'm steaming drunk and can feel nothing.

The next day, lying in my bed, I can't find a part of me that doesn't hurt! Mam quizzes me suspiciously:

"When I picked you up, there was the smell of drink on you?"

"Yes, Mrs. Feidelman gave me a glass of brandy, or the like—to revive me!"

"I believe you, thousands wouldn't!"

"Is Mr. Feidelman really mad at me? Will we have to pay for his caravan?"

"No, he was pleased in the end. The old van was a mess after that graffiti business, and now he can get a new one with the insurance money."

"Oh, that's a bit of luck then!"

Later that day, when I try to stand, my luck runs out. I have managed to rupture myself during the crash and Mam has to take me to the doctor's. As I lie on the surgery table, I experience the worst pain

I have ever known, as the poor doctor, apologizing profusely, tries to push and probe my missing gonad back into its ancestral home.

For many weeks afterward, I have to wear a sort of cottonwool diaper with a little hole cut in it, for my toodle to hang out!

All this pain from one afternoon's drinking. What had I learned? Well, drinking and driving is not on, and drinking and flying is lethal—unless you want to sing soprano with the Treorchy Male Voice Choir.

School holidays provide the best opportunity for getting into trouble. I am in the shit whether I'm the perpetrator or not. The fact is, I suffer from a severe case of alliteration!

A broken window, a scratched car, a stolen bicycle, or a sudden outbreak of foot-and-mouth disease will all be, sooner or later, laid at my door by the simple tripping-off-the-tongue phrase "Willy Watkins did it!"

I'm no saint of course, but for me to accomplish half of what I'm blamed for, I'd have to work a 120-hour week.

My little bunch of ruffians spend most of our free time playing with all the army surplus uniforms and military equipment left lying around after the end of World War Two. Tin helmets, bayonets, webbing belts, even binoculars, and leather map cases are there for the taking, moldering in long-abandoned dumps. It is fun to dress up and play soldiers, but it can make for dangerous games.

Without thought of the consequences, we wilderness warriors throw handfuls of .22 bullets into the refuse dump bonfire to make our war games more realistic! The rubbish dump becomes the bullet-riddled Berlin bunker of a doomed Third Reich, its blazing ruins still crawling with S.S. storm troopers and Death's Head fanatics. In a brave attack on the burning tip, we engage our imaginary enemy with .22 rifles and BB guns, whilst the answering fire from the exploding bullets whizzes and whistles over our heads.

"Rocket Attack!" screams Michael Waterson, tossing a clip of moldy .303 rifle ammunition into the flames. This time the resultant explosions are a lot more spectacular. The bullets go off with a very loud series of reports, and it's quickly realized that our barricade of old cars and rusty kitchen appliances doesn't stop them. We run for our lives! Twenty yards away and in full retreat, I'm brought down by a .22 bullet that lodges in the back of my knee. I'm carried home on an ex-army stretcher. Fatty Roger drapes the Stars and Stripes over me, covering my face. My mother faints amongst the junk in the front garden. Dad takes great pleasure in removing the slug with a razor blade, without of course, any anesthetic.

"That will bloody teach you to play about with live ammunition, you stupid young prat! I hope you've learned your lesson?" He thrusts tweezers holding the small lead .22 almost up my nose.

"That bullet could have lodged in your fucking thick head!"

We later find out that another bullet had passed through the caravan belonging to old Mrs. Cheshire. It shattered a mirror and that, to us superstitious Celts, was an omen of bad luck. My pals and I resolve to play less dangerous games. There will be no more live rounds used in our war games. Had we fully learned our lesson? Hell, no!

It is the end of term when traditionally school's rigid regime relaxes a little. The headmistress feels confident enough to attend a teachers' conference in Blackpool. This leaves us in the affable hands of the calamitous Mr. Bury, who has come up with an idea. I think he must have read about "Show and Tell" in some American journal, for it is totally unheard of in our part of the world.

"Now, class, you must all bring something of interest into school tomorrow and tell us a little about it."

"What sort of thing, sir?"

"Anything at all! Pets, hobbies, weird objects, anything that you find interesting or unusual."

The next day, the classroom is alive with bizarre goings-on. Jean-Paul's French-speaking budgerigar has escaped and is being chased around the room by three kids and Katie Coughlin's cross-eyed cat. The poor bird screams Gallic blue murder in its panic, and the hubbub is increased by the antics of Paul Mead, who's shouting German-sounding gobbledygook and goose-steps up and down, wearing a Nazi tin helmet on his head and doing "Heil, Hitler" salutes each time he passes the wall mirror.

In the corner, someone's windup gramophone gives out a hiss-and-crackle rendition of Count John McCormack singing "Macusla,"—in concert with the screams of Mary O'Malley, whom Gypsy Paul is having great sport terrorizing with a shoe box containing a long, green grass snake! Nora Hedderman sits oblivious to all this, playing "Frère Jacques" on her recorder, whilst, in her element, naughty Elspeth O'Neill, wearing a tutu, is attempting to show the contents of her knickers to anyone who's interested. Saintly Joseph Ryan has been trying in vain to get someone into the stock cupboard to see his luminous Infant of Prague. Elspeth jumps at the chance and seconds later, young Joseph, with a face as red as a beetroot, erupts from the stockroom, shoots out of the door, and locks himself in the boys' toilet.

"What's wrong with ya, Joe?"

"Elspeth showed me her willy!"

"Girls don't have willies, Joe."

"I know that now!"

In the midst of the carry-on, Mr. Bury, telephone in hand, is trying to assure the absent Mrs. MacArthur that everything is under control.

"Yes, Head, yes, fine . . . that noise? Er . . . it's the wireless! Yes! OK, I'll see you after the holidays. Bye-bye!"

I sit at my table in the eye of the storm, between a stuffed owl and a model of Thor Heyerdahl's raft *Kon-Tiki* made completely out of lollipop sticks.

This is great! This is what school should be like all the time. I fondle my show-and-tell item, my pièce de résistance: a live hand grenade!

Mr. Bury has to resort to smacking the blackboard with a cane to restore order. Finally satisfied, he moves like a judge in a flower show amongst the tables, nodding approval, congratulating, and praising. He is enjoying himself—until he gets to me.

"What? What is that? What is that thing?" he says, pointing and backing off at the same time.

"It's a Mills bomb, sir, commonly called a hand grenade."

"It's disarmed though, isn't it, Watkins? Made safe, eh?"

"No, sir, it's still primed and armed. This is where the fuse screws in and here is where they pack the cordite. You hold this bit and pull out this pin and that plunger drops and BOOM!"

He goes white and begins muttering.

"Oh, my God! What to do? Call the police? Oh, my God! Oh, no, better not." He picks up the telephone, stares out of the window, and puts it down again.

"The gardener!" he shouts, finger raised in the air in triumph. He creeps over to my table and gingerly picks up the grenade as if it is going to bite him. Holding it at arm's length, he walks in slow motion to the book cupboard and places it softly on top. It is now way out of our reach.

"Don't you dare touch that!" Like a thing possessed, he tears out of the door in search of Mr. Giles, the school gardener and ex-soldier, who lives in a cottage at the back of the mill. I could have told him he wasn't there. I'd seen him this morning, all dressed up, waiting for the Stratford bus, off to the horse racing no doubt.

With Mr. Bury tear-arsing around the grounds, it is time for action.

"Come on, lads, give me a hand!"

Steven and Jerry rock the cupboard until the grenade does a little dance, then drops down. I catch it. To avoid any more trouble, I scarper off home, leaving the offending Mills bomb in a hollow tree by the river.

Later that evening, a small posse of us retrieves the grenade, and I resolve to destroy the evidence in the most spectacular way I can imagine.

Our little commando group sneaks through the undergrowth to where the languid river Alne runs through a small tree-lined gorge. Here, in a great show of bravado, I pull out the pin. With my thumb keeping the handle depressed, I show it around the semicircle of my friends. They are awestruck! I let go of the handle, which flies off into the gorge and with an overarm motion, I throw the grenade in a wide arc after it, John Wayne style. Nothing happens.

"It's a dud!" says Paul Mead, ever the pessimist.

Mike is pointing to something that is out of my view and is about to speak, when there is a tremendous explosion and a column of water shoots skyward. The echoes die away and the water crashes back down. Mike is spluttering!

"There was two fishermen down there!!!"

"Where? You're kidding me."

"Sitting on the pipe over the river. Look—there they are!!"

I move to where I can see farther upstream and sure enough, two bedraggled anglers are wading out of the water. Unseen, we melt back into the bushes and without further ado, disperse homeward.

My father tells me later of the two damp fishermen he met in the tap-room of the Bull's Head Tavern. They were still puzzling over the queer sight that they had witnessed.

An enormous pike, some hideous freak of nature that, through some odd biochemical chain reaction, had detonated itself with such force that the blast had killed a whole lot of lesser fish, decimated the pike, and blown them off the pipe and into the water. All that remained of the unstable leviathan was the head and tail, floating some eight feet apart, and by this they judged its size.

"Spontaneous combustion!?" offers my Dad.

No better explanation for the exploding fish is ever found, and thus it passes into local legend. I have no intention of setting the record straight.

There is, however, a bigger problem. Even though the summer holidays are eight weeks long, I fancy Mr. Bury's memory will match them. A word to Mrs. MacArthur about me and the disappearing grenade episode and I am doomed!

Deliverance comes in an unsuspecting way. The balmy breezes of June rustle the long vertical stalks of the osier beds as we three friends make our way through this ancient plantation of the old Celtic Britons.

Osier is a type of bog willow and grows dead-straight. Our ancestors used it for basket making, hurdle fencing, and ribs for coracles, the small Celtic one-man boats. We use it to fashion spears, which when tipped with lead make a handy javelin.

This day it is the river far beyond the osiery that is our destination. Gypsy Paul has it on good authority that fine bream have been caught there, and we are up to the chance.

We dawdle along on our bikes, going nowhere fast, and eventually we find the shade of the tree-lined river.

The gray-green water moves slowly, noiselessly spinning into eddy currents. Sweet the air is, suffused with the scent of wild garlic, and where the trees open to the sky, the river reflects every passing cloud above. Stretched out on the lush green sward, surrounded by trees and bushes, we are hidden from the world and especially the old water bailiff, who will fine us for fishing without a permit.

The afternoon sun drenches our golden glade, a delicious torpor envelopes us, and slowly, one by one, we fall asleep.

In my dream, I can see my fishing float jerk, dip twice, and then shoot away under the undulating stream. The end of my rod is whipping with tension. My arms strain to pull ashore the huge, flapping bream. *Splash! Splash!* It mocks, flailing the water and defying my efforts. *Splash! Splish splash!* I wake with a start to find Gypsy Paul pissing in the river about three feet away from my head.

"Get out of it, ya durty bugger!"

He raises a finger to his lips: "Shush!"

"What is it?"

"Listen!" He cocks his ever alert ear to the prevailing wind.

Mike sits up on his elbow. "What?" he mouths silently. I say nothing, but I can pick out a voice or a giggle or something.

Paul slips stealthily into the bushes, the blood of generations of clandestine poachers pulsating in his veins. In a twinkling he is back.

"What's your report number one?" I say, like Jack Hawkins in *The Cruel Sea*.

"It's crumpet, sir!" he smiles, picking up the theme.

"Bearing?"

"Green thirty, range two hundred yards."

"Rig for silent running," I whisper, and we all crouch low in our green oasis.

"Oooh!" says Mike dreamily. "Crumpet!"

Lying doggo, we choke in silent mirth, listening to the *cooeees!* and answering giggles as they move closer to us. Suddenly the shrubbery parts, and with a girlish laugh, a young woman springs into our midst.

"Oh, my goodness!" she says, trying to do up her blouse buttons. "I'm so sorry!" And with that she dives into the other side of the overgrowth and is gone.

We are just enjoying this spectacle when the bushes to our left begin thrashing about and a voice inquires, "Fufkin! Fufkin! Where are you?" Mike gets the giggles, causing the voice to report.

"I can hear you, Fufkin!"

"I've got you!" says the head as it thrusts out of the foliage.

"Good afternoon, Mr. Bury!!!" we cry out in almost perfect three-part harmony. The face first goes quite pale, then, as quickly as a chameleon, a fine ruby wine color.

"Er . . . em . . . I . . . I . . . am looking for my friend . . . er?"

"Fufkin!" I remind him with relish. "She went thataway," I say, pointing. He nods his head in thanks and disappears. We are helpless with merciless merriment.

"I know her," says Mike finally. "She teaches at the Church of England school in Henley. That's Miss Foster."

"Fufkin Foster," says Gypsy Paul in realization. "What a moniker!" We fall about laughing again.

"I can't wait to tell everyone at school."

"No, Mike, we must tell no one! It will be our little secret. This way he'll never mention the grenade business for fear we'll tell Mrs. Mack about him consorting with the enemy!" And so it turns out, a classic Mexican standoff.

Being eight is just the right age. You are glic enough to know most of what is going on roundabouts, but too young to have much responsibility foisted upon you.

An bliadhna d'ór—the golden years, as our old language has it.

Mam is getting fat and has started knitting again. I help her with hanking the yarn and she tries to teach me some simple stitches. I can't make a fist of it at all, but I'm good at unraveling the wool from old knitwear. I take great delight in tearing asunder my god-awful cream Aran sweater. The same one that made me tell lies and got Gypsy Paul the unwarranted beating at school, the time long ago.

"You never got much wear out of that! Sure it's shrunk now. 'Twould only fit Jim Hasset. Why did you take such a spite to that jumper anyway? It was lovely!"

"It stunk of old sheep and made my skin itchy, an' I didn't like the color, or them daft wiggly patterns in the stitch."

"Well, those sweaters are made for the fishermen of the Aran Islands and the sheep oil keeps out the sea spray and rain. The patterns have a special purpose, too, as every family on the Western Islands have their own distinctive weave. If someone is drowned, you can tell who they are by the cut of their jumper."

"Why not just look at their faces?"

"Because their faces get all eaten away by the fishes."

I was going to say, "Do you have a song about fishes eating your face off?" But Mam has already started:

> *With swelling sail, away! away!*
> *Our boat goes bounding o'er the bay*
> *Farewell, farewell, old Aranmore*
> *She curtseys, curtseys, to the shore.*
> *Farewell, fond wives and children dear*
> *From every danger, keep you clear*
> *Till through the surge, we stagger back*
> *As full of fish as we can pack.*

Mam places a pair of lemon-colored baby's booties in the seldom-opened drawer where she keeps little Keith's never-worn baby garments. She carefully places a layer of white tissue paper over the tiny clothes and sprinkles several miraculous medals on top of it. She whispers an ancient Irish prayer into the drawer before gently closing it:

> *If harm comes near thee, may the three greats in heaven,*
> *Who cast all evils into the sea, protect thee,*
> *And the seven angels of God, watch over thee. Amen.*

The big boys down at the Post Office corner are taunting me.

"Your mammy's a pregnant prostitute!" Derrick Davies shouts across.

"No, she's not—she's a Roman Catholic!" I shout back.

"Come over the road and I'll give you a bloody good hiding, you little bog trotter."

I go home and tell Mam what the older boys had said.

"That fat eejit Davies is right about one thing, I am having a baby in a few weeks. Now you keep away from that bunch of bullies. They're a bad lot, and you'll be led astray."

I need little encouragement to stay away from this gang. They go to the Church of England school, so I seldom see them and they don't hang around with us much, anyway.

The time comes and Mam departs in the taxi again. She takes her old battered brown suitcase, which somehow looks much smaller now. Through a cloud of cinder dust she waves at me and Dad.

Mam gives birth to a little girl who only lives for a few short minutes. The doctors know the baby has no chance, and Mam is seriously ill.

"What do you want to call the baby, Mrs. Watkins?"

"Mary," Mam breathes in a thin voice, her mind fixed on the Blessed Virgin.

"Any middle names?"

"No, just Mary."

Mam's life is draining away, and despite all efforts the doctors cannot stanch her hemorrhage. The priest is called with his oils and unctions to perform the last rites. Before I am taken to the hospital to say my last good-bye, I go alone into the woods to pray. Through my tears I see a small bunch of white snowdrops growing in a clearing. Plucking them up, I take them with me and the nurse puts them in a vase of water by Mam's bed. Mam manages a weak smile and closes her eyes.

"Mr. Watkins, the surgeon wants a word with you." A kindly nurse takes my hand.

"Come along now and let your mother sleep." Dad and I are taken to an office downstairs. The surgeon looks up from his notes; he is grave.

"Mr. Watkins, there's a new procedure I have been reading about in the British medical journal, *The Lancet*. It might work. Your wife will require a hysterectomy and if we can get it, a course of snake-venom co-agulant they've just devised in West Africa."

Dad looks doubtful.

"What have we got to lose? But if it's only available in Africa, how do we get hold of it in time?"

The surgeon picks up the telephone.

"Let's try the Royal Air Force!" he says, fingering his RAF ex-officer's necktie.

Later that day, an RAF Vulcan jet leaves Lagos, Nigeria, with the life-giving serum on board.

In the days that followed, Mam shows signs of improvement, her bleeding stops, but we are not out of the woods yet. She needs the hysterectomy.

"I can't have the operation without the permission of the Catholic Church, Reg. Don't you understand? I asked Father, but he won't sign the release form!" Mam starts to cry.

"H'm, I'll talk to him," says Dad.

On the way back, we stop in at the vestry and Dad argues with the priest. I am scared stiff that with Mam dying, God will strike my dad down for shouting in the church, and I'll be left on my own, with no one belonging to me.

"No! No, I won't sign! It's contraception, and that's no better than murder, so it is!" The priest is sweating and his eyes are darting around the room for some form of divine assistance.

"If you don't sign, she will die and what will that be?" asks my father.

"The will of God, that's what!"

My father stares long and hard at the perspiring cleric. He doesn't much care for "God botherers" as he calls them. He told me once of a fascist priest holed up with a rifle in the bell tower of his church during the Spanish Civil War.

"The bastard opened fire on the people sitting around the village fountain—his own parishioners!"

Dad went on to say that this so-called man of God had killed three women, an old man, and a child before he was flushed out by a group of volunteer Welsh miners from the Fifteenth International Brigade. His excuse was that he "thought his victims were communists!"

Dad said they tied the bell rope around his neck and threw him out of the tower. With grim satisfaction, they saw his head fly off!

My father is in no less a belligerent mood this day, and I fear the priest might meet a similar end if he doesn't put pen to paper. Heart thumping like an echo sounder, I stand in the corner, hiding my face in my hands and peeping through my fingers.

"You *will* sign!!!" Dad grasps the priest by the dog collar and draws his hamlike fist back slowly.

"I will not!"

Like the twang of a bow-string, my father lets fly a withering punch. The priest's knees sag, but to his credit, he recovers.

"I won't! I won't!"

Dad hits him again. This time, the priest's resolve caves in as fast as his nose, and in a very shaky hand, he signs the release form.

Later that day, we make the long journey back to the main hospital. Mam is seemingly much improved from the magic potion. Dad and I go in and gave her the crumpled paperwork. My mother looks at the brown spots surrounding the scrawled signature on the form.

"This looks like blood? Was this won under duress? You didn't hit the priest, did you? Jesus! Reg, you'll go to hell!"

"No, no, not at all," says Dad, looking as innocent as a lamb. "After I made my position clear to him, the priest couldn't wait to sign it!!!"

Mam looks at me and I close my eyes in panic. In my mind's eye I can see my father surrounded by fire and brimstone, holding the devil by the throat and drawing back his fist with relish.

My mother takes a long time to recover after her operation, and it is grand to have her home again. Mam tells me what it was like when she was dying. She said she flew back over home to Ireland and even had a chat with Grandda, who was long since dead. Sometimes she flew feet first toward a giant mouth that gaped open on her approach. She knew this was the point of no return and would scrunch up her toes and try to think of something else, something nice.

"What did you think of, Mammy?"

Mam smiles. "I thought of the snowdrops that you brought me and how I was too weak to say thank you."

My sister, Mary, is laid to rest in the same plot as my wee brother, Keith, together forever in the tiny nettle-filled graveyard behind our school chapel. The priest is very short with his service and stares at me over the sticking plaster across his nose. "Suffer little children to come unto me," he quotes, and gives me a menacing glance. He will make me suffer all right, if he gets the chance. It's just as well he's afraid of Dad.

It feel odd when I pass the little green bump that marks the grave of two of my lost siblings. Now when I kneel in the cold chapel my thoughts dwell on what might have been. Looking up I can see the faces of the angels staring down from the stained glass windows. There is Keith and over there is Mary, and here on my knees is me. The priest has the whole school praying, that some guy called John Fitzgerald Kennedy might become the next president of the United States of America.

Filing out of the mass, past their graves, I make the sign of the cross and think of Granddad Jim quoting a Rupert Brooke poem:

In that rich earth, a richer dust concealed.

✦ Chapter 9 ✦

MAM IS STILL RECUPERATING AT HOME AND I GET USED TO doing most of the household chores. I like having a go at cooking, and if I make a bollix of it, no one complains. Washing clothes is the hardest job, as I can't boil enough water on the stove to wet the really big things and I'm no good at rubbing them up and down the zinc washboard.

Mam takes short walks into the countryside. She never mentions her loss, but when I go to tidy out the baby clothes drawer, she tells me to leave it alone and not go near it. I ask my dad what I should do.

"Give her time, Willie, to mourn for the wee ones and she'll be fine."

Mam adopts a little abandoned tortoiseshell kitten that she calls Fluff. The purring ball of fur soon grows into a big strong cat and Mam's attentions to its welfare have been rewarded.

One day, out of the blue, she jumps up and takes to rubbing her nylon pinafore together with her hands. The friction produces a warble of tortuous, squeaking noises.

"Listen to the birds in Mummy's apron, puss! Listen to the birds!"

Both myself and the cat are caught unawares and regard my mother with mystified silence. She dances a jig around us, squeaking her pinny whilst entreating, "Listen to the birds in Mummy's apron!"

The cat's face becomes a row of blurry eyes as it shakes its head to dislodge the squealing noises from its ears. In a trice, Mam scoops the cat up in her arms and swirls around the kitchen, singing:

Pussycat, pussycat where have you been?
I've been to London to look at the Queen.
Pussycat, pussycat, what did you there?
I frightened a little mouse under the chair.

The dismayed cat scrambles free of Mam's clutches and darts under the bed. She grabs me instead and the waltz becomes a gavotte.

> *The thunder rolled, the lightning cracked*
> *And all the earth was shaken*
> *The little pig cocked up his tail*
> *And ran to save his bacon.*

The gavotte becomes a polka:

> *There was a little man and he had a little gun*
> *Up the mountain he did run*
> *With a belly full of fat and a big tall hat*
> *And a pancake stuck to his bum, bum, bum!*

Exhausted, we succumb to gravity in the middle of the red mat.

Mam's imagination, aided by a flowery nylon apron and some invisible birds, has made the long journey back from grief accompanied by a royalist pussycat, a paranoid pig, and a rotund, diminutive, armed mountaineer with no dress sense! This is much more like it! Mam's back to normal! She has walked out of the mist and is her old self again. This is a great boon to us all. In no time at all, she resumes her position as the head of the household and it feels good knowing Mam's hand is on the tiller, even though this ends my brief reign of freedom and I'm now accountable again.

"Willie, come here to me now and tell me this? What were you doing hanging around with those corner boys down at the post office again?"

"I wasn't doing anything, Mammy, just chatting."

"Well, I don't want you chattin' with them durty sods, always spitting on the floor and trying to look up under your clothes, filthy buggers. Anyway, what were you chattin' about?" Mam is eating tinned spaghetti in tomato sauce.

"Segs. We were talking about segs, that's all."

"What the bloody hell you mean, 'Sex, that's all?' What in the name of Christ the Almighty do you know about sex?" She stops eating, obviously intrigued by my tale.

"More than they do and that's a fact. Those older boys are always talking about segs, but not one of them has a clue. They're way off the mark. It's all to do with the way you walk. Now, I tend to walk hard down on my right heel and that wears the back of my shoe away at an angle, giving rise to the problem. So you must get a packet of segs. They work great in leather, but when I tried one in rubber, it kept falling out, until I hit it hard with the coal hammer and it went in fine. See . . . it's still there!"

I lift up the sole of my boot to show the crescent-shaped metal seg neatly hammered into my worn heel. "See? Dad had shown me how to use that wee three-legged anvil, called a cobbler's last. He says the last is the first thing a cobbler uses!"

Like a baby bird waiting to be fed, Mam sits open-mouthed. I never thought that an explanation of a wee bit of do-it-yourself shoe repair could be so spellbinding, but as I have previously observed, Mam is a woman of mysteries and best left to her own devices. She sits in a trance whilst white worms of spaghetti continue to uncoil from her motionless fork. Happy to be relieved of my duties as chief cook, bottle washer and handyman cobbler, I return to playing with my Dinkytoy fire engine on the little red hearthrug in front of the fire. Mam is back in command and makes me feel as secure as the segs in the soles of my hobnailed boots.

Motorcars are still quite a rarity in these parts, and a posh one arriving is always a cause for a crowd to gather. I liked cars, but preferred rural Ireland, where the horse and jaunting car still held sway.

"Come and get a load of this!" says Dad one Saturday afternoon. We walk into the courtyard and there stands a cream-colored Austin-Healy sports car.

"It belongs to Sabrina the film star!"

"Wow! Will you look at all that leather and chrome—what a monster!"

"I'll give you half a crown to wash and polish it," offers Dad. "All the stuff you need is over there in that bucket."

I don't need asking twice and am soon working up a good lather on myself as well as the car. Two shillings and sixpence is a half crown and could buy goodies beyond the dreams of avarice!

Dad disappears toward the bar, chuckling to himself. I later find out why. He had been given five shillings to clean the car and had subcontracted the donkeywork to me, thus earning the price of a good few pints of best bitter for very little effort on his part.

Sabrina becomes a regular weekend visitor to the hall, and the weekly ritual of Dad's so-called cleaning of the car is established. The young starlet, a busty peroxide blond, is a Marilyn Monroe look-alike who had a few small parts in some of the racy comedy films that were in vogue at that time. She certainly does turn men's heads, and her erstwhile mentor, the manager of the country club, takes a special interest in her development. She's very nice to me and one day gives me a wee trip up to the petrol station in her sports car. Unfortunately, none of my pals are there to see us, and next day they all call me a bloody liar.

Dogs, too, were a rarity on the caravan site. Most folk had cats as they were good for keeping down the rats and mice, and large dogs were discouraged by the site managers.

Mr. Allen, of course, owned the place and so had a huge black-and-white harlequin Great Dane. The monster dog was all bollix and no brains.

This day he's outside our caravan slobbering around Mrs. Ayers's Pekinese. I'm having great sport watching him trying to cock a leg over a tiny dog some three feet below him. The bitch wanders off uninterested, leaving the giant spotty hound in oblivious ecstasy, probing the gravel path with his raw-looking toodle. Mam appears.

"Jasus! What's wrong with that dog at all? Gowan, bugger off with ya! Get out of it, ya durty big eejit!"

She chucks a bowl of washing-up water over him and he stands there dripping, looking mystified, then with a heartfelt sigh he waddles off home.

"Durty bugger, that fella! Forever sniffing everyone's arse and making a spectacle of itself, with his old langer sticking out! Durty sod he is and thick as a brick too."

"Why is it the dogs are always sniffing at each other, Mam?"

"Ah well you see, some of the greatest minds in the world have tried to fathom out the riddle of that. Here's what I think:

'The dogs once held a meeting, they came from near and far
Some came by helicopter and others came by car
And so inside the city hall, no one dared to look
As each dog took its arsehole off and hung it on a hook.
There they were, sitting there father, son, and sire
Sitting round looking round, when someone shouted FIRE!
Up they got and out they ran, without no time to look
They snatched the nearest arsehole, from off the nearest hook
And so my friend sometimes you see your doggy leave his bone
To sniff another's arsehole, he's just trying to find his own.'"

It must be common enough that you think your parents are above criticism and can do little wrong. I take everything my mother says as verbatim. How is it that a simple poem I learn from my mam gets the arse leathered off me when I quote it during my weekly poetry class? Adults live in a strange world!

It's early morning and Mam is up with the lark and doing something very odd in the kitchen. Twisting herself into a queer contorted version of Aphrodite rising from the waves, she stands in an immodest state of undress in front of a large mirror. To the accompaniment of much wheezing and grunting, she draws long black lines up the back of her legs with an eyebrow pencil.

Now I'm not as naive as some of my pals. I knew that women did secret things, like the times when I would be sent to the shop with a note that I wasn't allowed to read. The shopman would read the note and wrap up something in a brown paper bag. "Take this home to your mam," he'd say, "and don't be peeking inside!" Well, bollocks to him and his rules! I had a good gander into the bag, but all it contained were long cottonwool pads with loops on the ends. Later, I asked my pals. Gypsy Paul, ever the worldly wise, responded first.

"My mam gets them, too, and so does my older sister. I think all the women have them." Mike Waterson nodded his head in mute assent, but I needed more information.

"But what are they?" Mike added what little he knew to the mystery.

"I don't know what they are, but I think they're called No-Nos.

Whenever I ask my mom to tell me what's in the bag, she says, 'No-No.'"

My father once told me to ask if I didn't know and he'd always try to give me an answer. I caught up with him on his way to work.

"Dad, what's them cloth things with the hoops that Mam sends me to the shop for every month?"

"Oh, that's one of women's secrets!"

"Well, if you tell me what they are, I'll keep it a secret from Mam!"

He was as good as his word and I was able to tell my astounded pals that they were hammocks for pet mice.

"But where do our moms keep the pet mice?"

"I don't know. Dad said that's a secret he hadn't discovered yet."

So I was aware that women were full of mysteries, but now my mother, seemingly content with the straightness of her pencil lines, is rubbing Bisto Gravy Browning powder all over her legs. I'm getting alarmed, thinking that she might be slipping away with the fairies.

"Mam! What are you doing?"

"Jasus, Willie! You gave me a fear! I thought you were still asleep!"

"But what are you doing with that food stuff?"

"Oh, I'm going for a job and I've no nylon stockings, so this is a trick we used to do in the war—see!" She pulls on her dress and sure enough it does look like she's wearing dark brown, seamed stockings. She wriggles into her high heels and admires her handiwork.

"American Tan, wouldn't you say? Very stylish!" Mam trips out the door.

"I'll see you later!" She waves. I go back to the land of nod.

I'm awoken by rain pounding on the aluminium roof of the tiny caravan. A short time later, I'm sitting drinking tea when the door opens and the bedraggled remains of my mother staggers into the kitchen.

"It's me that's wet!" she splutters, casting the remnants of an inside-out umbrella back out the door. Her best frock is ruined, and her white shoes stained brown from the gravy running down her legs. She rubs her face vigorously with a towel, smearing cherry-red lipstick and blue eye shadow in vivid arcs all over her face.

"Oooh, that's better," she says, oblivious to the effect. "Your dad should be home soon from the night shift."

"He *is* home!" I advise as my father enters the caravan.

Dad takes his cap off and stares at my dripping, multicolored mother with all the bemused expression of a man stepping into an empty elevator shaft.

"Dear God, Monica! You didn't have to dress up special for me!"

Mam gets the job, working back at the country club. I am lying in my bunk at home with the cat asleep on the quilt and my Eagle comic book recounting the tale of Captain Nemo and the Space Eels.

Mam enters, followed by my dad, who is dead drunk and falls asleep on the floor.

"Oh, Willie, you should have seen yer father tonight. He was marvelous!"

"What did he do?" I stare at the pile of father snoring by the stove. Normally Mam would be hopping cups off his head for coming in langers.

"What didn't he do? He came to walk me home from work an' when he comes into the club there's this gang of teddy boys all setting about the village policeman."

"Who? That big bloke, Copper Smith?"

"Yeah, well, yer dad pulls the one fella off the copper and puts his head through the wall. He gives the next one a fong in the bollocks that has the eyes pop out of his head and down he goes! Then the leader comes at your father with a cutthroat razor. Yer dad stands there, motionless like a statue. 'I hope you know how to use that, sonny?' he says, like Gary Cooper in *High Noon,* he was. The fella makes a swipe at your dad and Reg grabs the boy's arm and cracks it over his knee, then he gives him a dig with the flat of his hand into the throat, and the punk turns blue and falls down. The rest run like the beJasus, and your dad is dusting down Copper Smith, who was all cuts and bruises. If yer father hadn't have turned up when he did the policeman would be dead now, the kicking he got!"

"Me dad did all that fighting, in that state?"

"Notatall, he got free drinks till midnight off the manager, and I had a few myself—*hic!*"

Mam likes working as a barmaid at the club and sometimes sings there with a little five-piece band and the local skiffle group. I'm not so keen on it because it means I'm left alone often after dark when my dad's on night shift. But it's not too bad, I have my books and my crystal set, and if I do get scared, there's always the .22 rifle with two hundred rounds of long ammunition that Dad swapped for the .38 Webley revolver we found in the old trunk.

The next week when the postman comes around on his red bicycle, Dad receives a letter from the Warwickshire chief of police.

He opens it warily, as if it contains a bomb, but to his relief it is a commendation for bravery.

"Good!" says Dad. "I always sleep better when the coppers owe me a favor."

Dad's job on the railways has the yearly advantage that it provides two free return tickets to anywhere in Britain and Ireland. Mam and I decide to go over home for the summer holidays, and I am excited to see my family again. A few days before our departure, Dad comes home as drunk as a fiddler's bitch. He has been in the pub all day with his pal MacBride, who has won a "fistful on the gee-gees," as he would say. Celebrating the good luck, they have both got completely langers. Dad stotters up to the caravan and, looking quizzically at me, says, "I know what it is you need? A haircut. You look like a fuzzy-wuzzy!"

I didn't know my father could cut hair, but he rummages around in the kitchen drawer and comes out with a pair of hand-operated hair clippers that he'd sent away for from some mail-order catalogue or other.

With supreme confidence that my father can do anything, I sit as he hacks and chops at my flowing locks. Then he stops and blinks, swaying unsteadily.

"Oh, dear!" he says. "I've made a bit of an arse of it. Sorry, old chap!"

I look in the mirror and see that my once thick mop is reduced to a bald stubble with ragged tufts sprouting out at random, like a confused pineapple. Mam appears.

"Sweet Mother of Jesus! What have you done to the poor child?" She is not impressed by father's tonsorial expertise and quickly reaches melting point. "What do you think yer on, coming home and doing that to Willie just before his holidays! You're worse than a bloody kid, ya drunken sod!"

Mam marches me off to a real barber, who just shakes his head. He has no choice other than to cut off all my hair to make it even. I stare morosely at the baldy figure in the mirror. I look like a young, sad Humpty-Dumpty.

When we get home Dad has succumbed to an alcoholic haze and is in bed. Mam busies herself getting dinner ready, rattling pots and smashing pans on the cooker top as noisily as she can to spite him. It has no effect.

"Will ya look at him, drunken Thady, lying there farting and snoring like a warthog! I must of had shit in me eyes when I married that fella, Godforgiveme!"

I hate it when Dad comes home with a rake of drink taken and fills the tiny caravan with acrid blue smoke and stale beer fumes. Mam adds to the bad atmosphere by cursing Dad lying there, his bare chest covered in curly gray caterpillars of cigarette ash.

"Why *did* you marry him, Mam?"

"Ah now! Sure he was a handsome bloke in his day. I always thought he looked a bit like Robert Mitchum and sure wasn't he in uniform when I first saw him—very dashing he looked!" She stares dreamily out of the window.

Dad moans and rolls over in his stupor, noisily scratching his arse.

"Jeez, who'd of thought it, but all the girls were mad for him during the war, you wouldn't get a look in. They should see him now, beJasus, lying stinking in his pit!"

"How did you end up with him then?" Mam glances at me, sitting sorrowfully at the kitchen table, and laughs.

"I went out with some of the girls from the factory one night. All of a sudden, the air-raid sirens went off and Jerry started dropping bombs all over the place. Well, we couldn't find the shelter, so we ran into this little pub under a railway bridge. The place was packed and no one gave a bugger about the blitz outside. 'Live for today and sod tomorrow!' was the cry. I was making for the ladies loo, when I overheard this fella, common as shite he was, passing a durty remark behind my back."

"What did he say? Was it Dad?"

"No, no, he is standing next to your dad, he was another soldier. Anyroadup, he says, 'I bet she's had more pricks than a secondhand dartboard!' I turned to give him a look as good as a summons, just in time to see your father fetch him a belt in the gob for being disrespectful to a lady. Oh, very chivalrous, your dad, very gallant! Well, it was love at first smite—and Jasus, look at me now, living in the lap of luxury with Happy Harry there pissing his week's wages up the public house wall. Jasus Christus! Look at the gaatch of him? Robert Mitchum, me arse. You'd get more life out of Robert Emmet and he's long since dead! Ifeverawomansuffered!"

Dad didn't know that Mam called him "Happy Harry." It was our secret. Mam didn't know that Dad called her "The Dragon." That was Dad's and my secret. Being an only child could be a pain. Often, being piggy-in-the-middle during family disputes and rows, I learned that a good bit of tolerance and a huge amount of diplomacy could go a long way. My parents were like big kids themselves, either loving or hating each other and most often managing to do both at the same time. Both were consummate actors. Mam leans toward the melodramatic, whilst dad had a flair for comedy.

Father smiles in his torpor, blissfully unaware that Mam is pulling ghastly, gargoyle faces at him. She might be mad at him, but at least she sees the funny side of my predicament.

"Hey, Yul Brynner, I've got a riddle for you!"

A little white and round house,
and it is full of meat.
It has no doors and windows,
to let me in to eat!

"What is it then, Willie?"

"Is it an igloo?"

"No, no, to be sure, igloos have doors."

"Och, I don't know, I give up!"

"It's an egg!" she says, laughing, and taps me on the bald head with a spoon.

→ Chapter 10 ←

THE DAYLIGHT SEA CROSSING FROM THE PORT OF HOLYHEAD
is warm and calm. I discover to my great delight that the vessel's aft deck
contains a ship's wheel, a compass inside a brass binnacle, and a ship's
telegraph to relay commands down to the engine room: "Full Ahead!
All Stop! Astern!" There is no one around, so I play sea captain. "Ahoy
there! Splice the main brace! Avast behind!" I know these terms are nautical, but I don't know what a hoy is, or what a spliced main brace looks
like, and I was vexed to see the significance of somebody's vast behind.
Ah, but the sea is full of glorious mysteries!

There is a long cable going from a neat-looking, brass-dialed instrument affixed to the ship's stern rail. It trails off to sea in the wake of the
vessel. My curiosity gets the better of me and I reel in the yards of cable,
to find it is a brass, torpedo-shaped thing with little wiggly fins down
the sides. I let it fall to the deck for a closer inspection. As I kneel down
I am enveloped in the umbra of a large shadow.

"What the bloody hell do you think yer doing? Throw that thing
back overboard!" Terrified, I look up into the black shape of an angry
sailor, the flames of the afternoon sun flashing a coarse halo around his
hat.

"I'm sorry, mister, I didn't mean no harm. I just wanted to know
what it was. What is it?" The seaman laughs and, realizing I'm just a
curious kid, crouches down by my side and pokes the dripping instrument.

"This is the ship's tracking log. It records our speed in knots and how
far we have traveled in nautical miles, so you should have let it be."

"Yes, I'm sorry. What's a knot?"

"A knot is the way of reckoning speed at sea. One knot is the speed of one nautical mile per hour."

"How long is a nautical mile?"

"Six thousand and eighty feet, just a wee bit longer than a land mile, to compensate for the curvature of the earth." He picks up the log spinner and hurls it off into the ship's wake.

"There now, matey, no harm done and that's the log back into the oggin. Now don't be messing with the ship's equipment again, or we'll to have ye keel-hauled—*har-har!*"

By the time I get to Limerick a short velvet of hair has grown back across my bald pate, but hairstyles like that you only saw in American films or in magazines. My cousin Mikesy is the first to see me and the first to take the piss.

"Gee tonight! Look at the Yank!!" And so that becomes my nickname and it sticks for the rest of the summer.

And what a grand summer it is. We spend a lot of time in County Clare, mostly in Kilkee on the wild Atlantic coast.

"The next parish over is Boston," people would joke, pointing westward across the emerald green waves.

"And many's the thousands that joined that parish from hereabouts," someone would add.

"Where are you down from?" they ask.

"We're from up in Limerick."

"Sure the Limerick people are no good for Clare. They bring their own sandwiches with them!" The locals contend, trying to get the rise out of us.

I love eating dilsg, which is a form of red seaweed. "Full of iodine," Mam would say. Also winkles—I can't get enough of them. Just eating them is fun. They are small sea snails boiled in saltwater, and you have to pull them out of their shell with a pin. Hence the term "to winkle him out." Another delicacy is crubeens, which are boiled pig's trotters, These are Mam's favorite, whilst mine is pork pie, or pig's willy pie as they are known. Dad says that every part of the pig gets eaten except the squeak.

In summer you can buy all these tasty things from vendors' barrows as you walk along the circular harbor wall. Every second house in Kilkee is a pub, and they don't mind having kids in—if they behave themselves. I like the smell in these places. They have the aroma of times long past. You would know the smell of the right old pubs if ever you sniffed the inside of an old fiddle or an ancient piano.

We go up to the cliffs of Moher and peer cautiously over their brink to the thrashing ocean 668 feet below. We saunter along the strand to Spanish Point, where ships of the Spanish Armada were wrecked in 1588.

From the long white beach at Lahinch, I wade with my cousins into the Atlantic foam and try my hand at swimming. Unfortunately, like St. Columba before me, I step on a flounder buried in the sand and it shoots out from under my foot, turning me topsy-turvy in the surf. Spluttering under the waves, I guzzle more than my fair share of seawater and now understand why the good saint cursed the flounder to have both its eyes on the same side of its head, always looking up.

Back on shore, spitting sand and seaweed, I resolve never again to try to learn to swim. I realize that I'm never going to be amphibious, and like a cat, I don't like being wet anyway. There's something most unnatural being in the sea without the hull of a good boat around you.

I'll not be venturing into the water again without at least an aqualung to help me breathe. The same thought probably occurred to John P. Holland of the little village of Liscannor, about three miles away: in 1880 he astonished the world with his new invention—the first practical submarine!

There is a horse fair in Kilrush and we go along for the craic. The streets are teeming with horses and crammed with folk of every social stratum and walk of life.

> *The young the old,*
> *The meek the bold,*
> *The poet and musician—*
> *The relics of humanity*
> *In every known condition.*

I hear a queer noise and, turning a corner, I come face-to-face with a man playing an odd instrument. He has a box around his neck which is crisscrossed with fine wire strings. These he hits with two little leather thongs. It makes a lovely, tremulous, tinkling sound and I'd never seen or heard anything like it before. It is a hammer dulcimer.

In the alley by Crotty's pub, two ragged-arsed tinkers are rubbing brown shoe polish on the hind quarters of a venerable old horse. This serves to mask the gray and white hairs of the elderly beast. A young traveler lad is holding a bucket of oats and Guinness slops that the nag is slurping down with gusto.

Within the space of ten minutes a transformation takes place in the animal. Its belly starts to swell and the bony protruding ribs begin to disappear. Suddenly the old die-er is a young prancing pony again. The magic elixir of oatmeal and stout has transfused life into the creature's sagging frame, which now, as tight as a bow string, looks surprisingly youthful. Obviously enjoying the elation, the tipsy horse snorts and stamps its hooves, sending showers of tiny sparks up from the black cobbled road.

This display catches the attention of an English chap who is looking for a pony to give his daughter for her twenty-first birthday. After a lot of spitting on hands, bidding and bartering, the final hand shake is made and the deal is done.

The duped Englishman guides the frisking cuddy into a horse box, towed by a Land Rover. He gives it a playful slap on the rump and then stares incredulously at his sticky, brown stained hand. Lifting its tail, the horse lets off a string of beery farts and its ribs reappear! The mystified buyer looks around questioningly, but the tinkers are nowhere to be seen.

"Jayzus!" says a bystander. "That horse will be a sorry sight in the morning."

"A sorry sight with a hangover," adds another.

Buses are the great mode of transport. Everyone starts singing as soon as the bus is in motion. Not just on outings or mystery tours, but on regular commuter buses. It is a gas, right enough!

A common entertainment for us kids is to try and count the number of castles or ruined fortresses between Limerick and Kilkee. It comes to about thirty, I think.

Most of these represent the seat of some ancient clan chief, or king as they preferred to be known. At one time there were over two hundred and fifty small kings in Ireland, several queens, five regional big kings and an *Ard Rí*, or high king, presiding over the lot of them. It is no idle boast to say that even the humblest Irish person has royal blood—for all that's worth.

"Mam, did we have any royalty in our family years ago?"

"Oh, yes," she says. "Somewhere down the line, we're descendants of Aoibheal the fairy queen of Thomond!"

Good grief! A fairy queen on one side and Old King Cole on the other. It all seemed a bit nursery rhymish! After that revelation I give up on the royalty bit.

> *Imperial Caesar,*
> *Dead and turned to clay,*
> *Will plug a hole,*
> *To keep the wind away!*

"That's a good one, Mam!"

On the way back home on the bus, my die-hard Fianna Fáil nana is celebrating the results of the recent Irish election by singing:

> *Vote vote vote for De Valera,*
> *Vote vote vote for Fianna Fáil*
> *and we'll break the Union Jack*
> *Over Cosgrave's humpy back,*
> *and we'll crown De Valera*
> *King of Irrrrrrrrrrrrrreland!*

"A Spaniard will free Ireland," the old prophecy stated, and as far as Nana is concerned that can only mean Eamon De Valera. However, half the family think he's the biggest crook unhung, and there's always a good slagging match to be indulged in whenever his name comes up.

A spectacular event is taking place in Limerick. Uncle Seán hurries in with the news.

"Jeez! Sure the whole town is up in flames! Todd's store is burning out of control and the wind is spreading the fire all over the place—the city center's aflame!"

Sure enough! From the front garden of our house we can see the huge pall of black smoke climbing into the skies above King John's castle.

Excitedly we cross over the river bridge for a closer look. It seems like every fire engine in Munster is in attendance. The roads are a tangle of large canvas fire hoses, many of which are leaking at the big brass knuckle joints.

The corner of Todd's is gutted and the four-story blackened shell, windowless and roofless, is still steaming from the drenching it received from the hose.

The fire is raging farther up the block and has gotten as far as Lipton's tea shop. Behind the large street windows of the store, a curious gray fog has appeared that swirls about obscuring the goods inside. Two firemen in the street outside begin to run, leaving their hoses to snake about wildly, spraying everything but the conflagration. It isn't before time! A tiny point of yellow light glows for a split second in the center of the smoke, then mushrooms into a billowing red fireball that shatters the plate glass windows to smithereens. The crowd of gawkers, ourselves included, scream and flee to a safer vantage point. Some are wounded by flying glass splinters and are taken away to waiting ambulances.

Within minutes the roof caves in and a shower of sparks shoots skyward. These are joined by exploding bags of sugar, streaking and coursing through the smoky air, like distress-signal rockets.

Suddenly an eddy of wind sucks out the blazing contents of the shop and belches it into the molten sky. The whirlwind picks up pace and spreads the fire to the next block. The squads of firefighters run after the new threat and begin evacuating buildings in its path. The door of Teasey-Weasey's bursts open and a bevy of women with their hair in curlers, or crowned with cones of shampoo, flees the doomed salon, which is soon consumed by the holocaust. The brave teams of firemen play their battery of hoses on the buildings directly in line of travel to the fire. This tactic is proving successful until the note from the pump engines rises abruptly in scale and the water from the firehose nozzles is reduced to a piddling dribble.

The bewildered fire crews soon find out why. The water is being pumped directly out of the Shannon and the tide has gone out, leaving the syphon hoses high and dry, sucking air!

It takes several days for the fire to be completely terminated, by which time much of the area is in ruins. To us kids picking through the debris of the burned-out shops for treasures, it was a great hoot altogether, but the old ones said this was the greatest disaster to befall the city since the destruction brought by the civil war of 1922.

Fortunately, Limerick survives and is soon rebuilt. Living up to its tough motto carved into the rock of the Treaty Stone. "Urbs antiqua fuit studasque asperima belli"—An ancient city, well studied in the arts of war.

We are on the move again. Returning to Britain and this time no tears! It has been a great holiday and despite fire, brimstone, and near drowning, we've all had loads of fun, but I'm looking forward to going back to my little enclave of the Gael. People forget that Britain was once a Celtic country and still is—"In quiet places where the moss grows green," to quote a Scots poet.

The journey back is at night under a full moon. A harvest moon hangs like a ripe peach: *An Gealach*—the bright one, mirror of the Celtic soul, the Triple Goddess. She illuminates our voyage across the Irish Sea with warm honey-colored light. There is little wind, and the sea is a slab of black marble; the moonlight ripples through the surface like streaks of rose quartz. In the cabin, Mam sleeps like a baby.

I stay on deck absorbing every sight, sound, and smell that I can savor. The old sea shanty "Santa Anna" goes round and round in my head and I feel at home.

> *We'll sail across the river to Liverpool,*
> *Heave away, Santa Anna.*
> *Heave her up and away we'll go*
> *All around the bay of Mexico.*

I wonder if I have been a sailor in a previous existence.

No one in my family has gone to sea in nearly two hundred years, to my knowledge. The last one was the unfortunate Thomas Watkins, who had the temerity to speak out against the depravations and hardships of the Royal Navy and ended up swinging from the yardarm with a hemp necktie. Dad said he should have known that the King's Navy was built on three English principles: rum, sodomy, and the lash. He would have been better off in the Merchant Navy, which was more rum, bum, and concertina.

Wild and mysterious, the train journey from Holyhead to Birmingham is mighty and my mind is ablaze with its captured images. Everywhere red and green signal lanterns glow in the night, mixed with the white and amber lights of the point switches. We thunder through Angelsey, the Welsh teacup station my mother had shown me years ago; LLAN—BLUR—GOGGOG hurtles past the window.

Digedydee digedydaa digedydee digedydaa. The sound of the wheels become a hypnotic heartbeat broken only by *Digedydig dig Da dig dig dig,* as we clatter through sets of points before settling back into the incessant rhythm. Phantoms of flickering flashes spring from other passenger trains plunging past us in the opposite direction, probing our carriage with stark stroboscopes of filmlike montage. Somewhiles the shrill shriek of the steam whistle heralds the ear-popping vacuousness of an unexpected tunnel, from which we emerge moments later to see the soft moonlight spangle the midnight-dark Menai Strait in bands of quicksilver, and the jagged peaks of Snowdonia's mountains thrusting their quiet majesty into a silent star-washed sky.

The head of the train makes a long curve and looms into view. The glow from the footplate fire box is clearly visible, and the great steam-belching engine sends showers of hot cinders to join the plume of smoke in its wake.

Our friendly moon continues to keep us company, and while Mam sleeps in the darkened carriage, I rest my head against the window, watching the lunar visage play hide-and-seek with scurrying clouds, or dance along the transient telegraph wires until, swirling in steam, she is lost in the Conway tunnel.

Autumn is closing in and school is looming on the horizon. I make one of the last trips of the year to my favorite place—the rubbish dump. Quite often I find useful things, but this time I hit the jackpot and come home loaded down with books.

I was never conscious of learning to read; it just happened. Once I get started there is no stopping me. I will read anything, even the back of a sauce bottle. And trying to keep me supplied with good reading material keeps Mam busy. There is a small library at school, but they won't let you take books home. The county library in Stratford doesn't want our custom because we live on a caravan site, and so we are not only book thieves but probably murderers as well. Maybe the hours I spent with my granddad Jim triggered some osmosis. Anyway, my reading age is quite advanced and eclectic; even the school grudgingly acknowledges this when I win the prize for General Knowledge.

The books I have found are a godsend. Whereas the average school curriculum revolves around the well-known three R's: reading, 'riting, and 'rithmetic—we are encumbered by three more: religion, righteousness, and rubbish. With the aid of my booty of books, I can strive to transcend the guilt-ridden fetters of Rome.

These fabulous old tomes, all beautifully bound, deal with chemistry, physics, general science, botany, biology, geology, geography, anthropology, astronomy, French and Russian literature, English language, radio and TV engineering, and the Second World War!

How they came to be in a refuse tip is beyond me! Who would throw away a book? Well, people are odd, and odd people are even odder. These volumes become my constant companions. I do my best to suck the last kernel out of each one. Through their pages I journey to Peru in the time of the Incas, revolutionary Paris with its blood-spattered guillotine, the galvanic effect of electricity on a frog's legs and a universe burgeoning with facts, words, fantasies, ideas, and most of all stories of other folks' lives. "Give kids the love of books and they'll educate themselves," so said my granddad Jim, who ministered to me in that respect and grateful I am too. He would quote Kipling:

> Let us now praise famous men,
> Men of little showing . . .
> For their work continueth,
> And their work continueth,
> Broad and deep continueth,
> Greater than their knowing.

School starts up again, and to our relief Mr. Bury says nothing about the hand grenade business last term. He has probably forgotten all about it, as he told us he'd been on holiday in Greece most of the summer.

"What's it like in Greece, sir?" asks Nora.

"Well, after dinner we shall see. I've brought in some slides that I took!"

True to his word, after we eat, the curtains are drawn and Mr. Bury fumbles with the archaic brass slide projector.

There is a lot of giggling as we sit in the dark, waiting for something to happen. Then a shaft of stark white light, the shape of a playing card, hits the far wall, followed in glorious color by the appearance of a car on its roof with its wheels in the air next to an odd-looking policeman standing on his head!

"Damn thing's upside down!" the teacher murmurs to himself. After some pushing and pulling at the ancient mechanism, he manages to show us a picture of a Greek policeman standing next to his patrol car.

"Now," he asks, "has anyone heard of the Acropolis?" Two hands go up in the dingy light. "Well, Daly?"

Jerry looks hopeful. "Is it that new coffee bar in Stratford, sir?"

"Don't be daft, Daly. Cosgrave, tell him," our leader suggests with confidence.

"It's the horse fellas, sir, the four riders, *you* know! The four horsemen of the Acropolis, that's it!"

Mr. Bury chooses to ignore this dazzling display of ignorance and goes back to his slides.

"This is the Acropolis, the very citadel of the Greek capital. And this is the Parthenon, the temple of Athena, who gives her name to Athens. This is another shot of the temple showing the fine Doric columns . . . and here we have the view from the steps of the Parthenon showing the full extent of the Acropolis . . . !"

"The bloody place is in ruins!" whispers Gypsy Paul, unaware of its antiquity.

"I wouldn't go there if you paid me!"

"Shoosh!" I breathe, trying to stifle the giggles, but he won't shut up.

"Fancy going all that way to a dump like that—it's falling to bits!"

"It might have been in one piece when he got there and he wrecked it himself," says Steve O'Donnell. At this point I lose the ability to stifle my laughter and a stream of frothy orange juice comes out my nose and all down the front of my shirt.

"Pay attention there, whoever that is! Now this is the Aegean Sea named after Aegeus, the king of Athens and father of Theseus, and this is—"

"Mr. Bury's crumpet!" erupts Mike, as pandemonium breaks out at the sight of the young and lovely Fufkin Foster, stretched out on the beach in a two-piece swimsuit!

Mrs. MacArthur appears in a flash and calls out the names of those she thinks responsible for the cacophony.

"Daly, O'Donnell, Cosgrave, Dutton—report to me after school is over!"

I can't believe it! For once I'm not on the list!

"It wasn't them, miss."

"Who was it, Nora?"

"Willie Watkins, miss."

I don't even bother protesting my innocence. I know it is a waste of time. Nora has got her revenge from all those years ago when I hit her with the mallet.

From Mrs. Mack I receive the penance to write up a project of my choice as extra homework. Bugger! I'd rather have the cane and get it over with.

✦ Chapter 11 ✦

STRATFORD-UPON-AVON, JUST EIGHT MILES AWAY, IS A VERY ancient town. I decide to do my school project on it because of Shakespeare and everyone has heard of him. Also, it has two annual fun fairs, and this gives me the excuse to go. I start my research, first, on the name elements, and here Dad helps me. After that I'm on my own.

Stratford-upon-Avon.

Strat is from the Latin: Strata meaning a paved Roman road. Ford is from the Welsh: Fford corresponding to the English: way, or crossing place and Avon from the Gaelic Abhain, pronounced Avon, the word for river.

The town still has a medieval charm and a lot of black and white striped houses. Most of them would be familiar to Willie Wagglestaff, which was Shakespeare's real name before he joined the theatre. It is a market town and has a large cobble-stoned square and lots of pubs where Willie wrote plays in the afternoon.

Here you get the Stratford Mop every year. This is a traveling fair and was used to supply the wealthy folk with slaves. These were black women called Mrs. Mops because they were cleaners and skivvies. Some of the slaves escaped only to be recaptured and resold three weeks later when the fair returned. This is why the second fair is called the Runaway Mop.

Mrs. Mack said my history was very good and funny. She stuck a silver star onto my paper soul on the wall. It was the first one I'd ever had. It was the last one I ever got!

Mam is proud of the star and takes me to the Mop.

The fairs are now just carnivals, dodgem rides, big wheels, ox roasting, sideshows, cotton candy, toffee apples, and the smelly throb of diesel generators.

A thousand children lost in a maze of a million lightbulbs and me at the rifle-shooting gallery, winning a goldfish for Mam—four targets, three bull's-eyes, and an off center. After the first shot, I notice the rifle is sighted to fire high and left and compensate accordingly. The man gives me a quare look and a goldfish in a plastic bag.

The journey home on the Stratford Blue bus is fun. Mam and myself start to sing as if we are back home in Ireland. The locals frown at us and we don't care a bit:

> *Westering home with a song in the air,*
> *light in the eye and it's good-bye to care.*
> *Laughter of love, and a welcoming air,*
> *heart of my heart—my home land.*

"We need something to put the fish in. He can't live in there." Mam is staring into the caravan sink.

"How about this?" Dad has come up with a large pickled onion jar. "This should do!" He rinses out the jar with clean water and sniffs it. "Pooh! It still has a bit of a pen and ink about it. I hope he doesn't mind."

Mam is busy trying to catch the goldfish in her hands, accompanied by whoops of laughter.

"It tiddles when I try to grab him!" Mam giggles. Dad, ever the practical, scoops the wee fish up in a pint beer mug and pours it into the pickle jar.

"There you are, home sweet home, whatever your name is."

"Ooh! That's right. We haven't given him a name."

"How about Tiddles, Mam? You said he tiddles your hand."

"Yeah, that will do fine. Hello, Tiddles!"

"Now, Willie, people think goldfish lead a boring life, but someone once told me that they only have a tiny brain and can remember things for less than a second. If that's true, then each revolution would present them with an entirely new vista, as they can't remember the old view."

"Go'way, Reg, and leave the poor child alone. Ye'll have him puggled!"

"That's science, my dear wife. This is science I profess."

"Go'way with yer old guff. What are ye? Professor of Fermented Beverages?"

With the first frosts of winter, the air smells clean and crisp. The night sky hangs heavy with stars and bright planets traverse the heavens in elliptic excursions.

"That's the Milky Way, that long pale streak, and the W-shaped thing is the constellation of Cassiopeia. If you look down from the W, you see three stars equally spaced. Right at the end of the top one is a vague hazy blob. That's the spiraling Andromeda nebulae!"

Dad is giving us a lesson in astronomy and apart from the crick in my neck, I love it. Mam says she thinks she needs glasses.

"You see the three stars over there, about the same brightness? Well, that's the 'Belt of Orion.' Hanging down from the middle one are the three stars that make up his sword, and there's Rigel and Betelgeuse, and the two other stars, Ballatrix and Saiph, make up the famous Orion the Hunter."

"Who is this Orion, Dad, and what did he do to become so famous?"

"Ah!" says Dad. "I'm afraid you've got me there. I think he was a Greek."

"He was in his arse—he was Irish!"

"Glory be, woman! How in the name of the wee man do you make that out?"

She sings:

> O'Ryan is a mighty man
> Within the Irish nation,
> And hunting is his heart's delight
> And constant occupation.

She goes on to sing us an unlikely tale of O'Ryan the Hunter's encounter with a starving traveler who turned out to be St. Patrick. The hunter takes him in and feeds him on roast hare and Irish whiskey, which is called poteen. To repay this kindness, the saint promises O'Ryan a plethora of good hunting and sport in the afterlife:

Saint Pat—he supped the whiskey sweet
And says "Good luck attend ye,
And when you're in your winding-sheet
To the heavens I will send ye."

And so old Mick O'Ryan's might
Is famed throughout the nations,
You'll see him on a winter's night
Amongst the constellations.

"I tell you, Willie, that mother of yours is a walking encyclopedia of Irish bullshit!"

We are now in *An lathan dubh*—the dark days, as wintertime is known to the Gael. I arrive home from school and am walking down the path to our caravan, when something catches my eye. Mam often puts Tiddles outside for an airing and a change of scenery, but this time she has forgotten to bring him in and his water has frozen solid.

I pick up the pickle jar and gaze at my friend suspended in his frozen world. There is a loud *bang!* and I watch helplessly as the fish, still in its icy cocoon, smashes to the ground in a shower of glass. I go to pick up the spinning ice block containing its captive aquatic, but to my horror a large wedge-shaped piece of glass is sticking out of my wrist. My screams alert Mam, who wraps a tea towel around the wound, glass and all!

Mrs. Allen, who was an ambulance driver in the London blitz, drives at breakneck speed to get me to the casualty department at Stratford Hospital. There they remove the glass carefully, the sliver being just a fraction of an inch away from my main artery. The doctor says that it was the heat from my hands that caused the frozen glass to explode. He goes on to say that any attempt to yank out the glass would most likely have severed the artery and I would have bled to death. The removal of the glass and the subsequent stitches are administered without anesthetic, but I'm getting used to that. Still, it is bloody sore!

We get home, Tiddles is still lying where he has fallen, motionless in his glacial stasis. Mam picks up the block of ice and puts it in a sink full of cold water. Within the hour Tiddles is swimming and frolicking in the sink, none the worse for his experience.

And so my little pal—won at a slave auction, incarcerated in a vinegar-smelling jar, frozen by mistake, dropped by accident, spun by gravity, and defrosted by Mam—continues to live a full life with his circular window on the world, now illuminated by the first shafts of warm spring sunshine.

My parents buy a new caravan. This time it is a twenty-six-footer and affords me a room of my own. It seems enormous. There is a bathroom complete with a long plastic bath. My father, for reasons as mysterious as Stonehenge, rips out the bathtub and throws it into the garden. There it lies undisturbed for the next three years, in the midst of all the other junk, full of leaves and rainwater. The new trailer is very nice, but we still have no hookup to running water, no toilet, and now no bathtub either, not that it mattered a great deal to me!

Bathing takes place at a communal bathhouse in a section of the big hall that is reserved for washing clothes. There are coin slots on the doors of the three bathrooms, and it costs sixpence. I think it is a complete waste of money. Over home you could get six patsy pops for a tanner! I'm forced to have a bath once a month, whether I need it or not. I hate Mam scrubbing me with the hard black soap called Durback, which not only kills fleas and lice, but stings the eyes out of your skull. Still, it's better than breaking the ice on the water bucket, so's to rinse your bollocks down on a cold and frosty morning.

There are spiders up in the washhouse roof the size of dinner plates, and I would be feared one would fall off the ceiling and land on top of me. The two biggest black spiders, known as George and Georgina, have been there for centuries, producing millions of spidereens that migrate to every part of the known world.

Many spiders make the trek across to the whitewash and lead-piped realm of the public toilets, where they weave gossamer grids of fly-trapping thread over the dingy fanlights of grime-ridden windows. The lavatories are a long way from where we live, the nearest being at least a quarter of a mile away. Whereas you can pee around the back of the caravan, anything more exotic requires a long walk and sometimes a long wait at the other end if the khazzi is occupied. These facilities are not heated and going to the loo in the depths of winter puts enough iron in the soul to build a battleship. The lavatory walls are festooned with crude drawings of various male and female genitalia and lewd poems of the type described as limericks:

There was a young man from Clyde
Who fell down the toilet and died
Along came his brother who fell down another
And now they lie in-turd inside.

You're better off going for a shite in the woods. At least it don't stink, and Kilroy hasn't been scribbling his name all over the place.

Summer arrives with its attendant hordes of buzzing black flies and whirring swarms of iridescent bluebottles. These filth hounds of Hades congregate like a biblical pestilence, plaguing any visitor so brave as venture into ablutions. Even from a safe distance, the toilet buildings hum like electricity transformers, and the mixed smell of excrement and its Elsan Disinfectant antidote would be enough to make a tapeworm gag.

"Phew What A Scorcher!" says the headline in the local paper and then goes on to tell that factories and workplaces all over the country are closing down because of the heat wave. Anyone with any money heads to the seaside, where the fresh breezes and cool water calm the savage brow. We are of course stuck here in a caravan trailer as hot as a bread oven, with neither refrigerator nor ice box to keep milk from becoming a solid and butter from becoming a liquid. The only thing hotter than the weather is my mother's temper.

"Bad scran to you!" she says, throwing the last of the meat supplies out into dustbin.

"What's wrong with it, Mam?"

"It has the flyblow on it. The feckin' bluebottles are after laying their eggs all over your dad's pork chops, Godforgivemeforswearing. Curse this feckin' heat. We've nothing but tatties and vegetables for dinner. Your father will be raging. Ah, well, if the ouldfella doesn't like it, he can lump it! Being a vegetarian was good enough for great men like George Bernard Shaw and Mahatma Gandhi, so it better suit old baldy, too, or he'll get my boot up his hole!"

I leave my mam to her cursing and wander off around the corner to where the little Burmese woman, who'd told me how to get the shit out of the carpet, lives. She is out in the garden and her wee baby boy crawls around in the shrubbery, getting covered in shite and putting everything he finds into his mouth. She pays him no heed and bustles around the vegetable patch, clipping little green sprigs of herbs and uprooting quare-looking plants for their evening curry. Dad says the best way to preserve meat is to curry it; this makes Mam pull faces and say that curry gives you the skitters and that's why Indians and Pakistanis don't wear trousers. I decide to ask the Asian lady if what Dad says is true.

"Oh yes, yes, yes, spicy very good—make meat not go bad, not stinky stink. You watch, I show," she says, spreading spices and garlic over a large flat-topped boulder that grows out of the earth in front of her old hardboard caravan. The "Memsahib," as my dad calls her, then lays a piece of meat over the stone and pulverizes the living Jasus out of it with a big wooden club. Bits of flesh and peppercorns fly in all directions as she attempts to pound the raw steak into the cold cranium of the living rock beneath. It's a spectacular sight—like yer man wielding the jawbone of an ass in the Old Testament. Aromatic herbs and exotic flavors hang on the breeze, and soon the meat is diced and put into a large pot shaped rather like a cauldron.

"Must wait now for all to cook nice," she says, snatching up her little lad and making for the cool of the veranda.

"You come back later, I give you chipatti," she says, smiling, and closes the fly screen. Later, when I do return, she hands me a rolled pancake containing tangy, golden curry. I'm amazed at the taste and texture of it and, despite my mother's caution, discover that spicy food is wonderful and doesn't give me the runs either. I am glad to be friends with the Asian lady, with her great cooking and never to be forgotten advice: "Brush very hard, it is SHIT!"

The days continue sultry, sweltering affairs, made all the more irritating because bathing in the river has been declared out of bounds by the health ministry because of the great polio scare sweeping the nation. We are all vaccinated by the mobile hospital units that visit every town and village in Britain, but for some, it's already too late. The epidemic grows into a scourge which takes the lives of many and cripples even more. I'm glad when the summer finally fades and the sweaty sleepless nights give way to more tolerable circumstances.

It is a lovely autumnal day. With the onset of winter just around the corner, I think it is a good idea to get out and about while I still can. I am helping Dad down at the old piggeries where we are off-loading a pile of wooden lattice fence sections from the site manager's Jowett truck. The weight of these units is too much for me and, bandy-legged, I begin dropping my end.

"Jasus, Will, have ye no strength atall? Yer like a man made of smoke! I don't know why we bother feeding you. Put your back into it! I've seen more life in a tramp's underpants!"

"I'm doing my best, for the love of Mike! I'm nearly deaf with effort!" Wobbling most precariously, the entire load succumbs to gravity and slides majestically to the road.

"OK, let's take one at a time and stack them against the wall yonder."

"What are they for, Dad?"

"Well, the powers that be think that by fixing these trellises to the piggery walls and growing some Tudor roses up them, they can convert the pigsties into luxury weekend apartments for the city toffs and no one will ever know the difference."

"It seems a shame to turf the poor ould piggies out, just so some city slicker can play country squire for the weekend. I like feeding the wee pigs and scratching their backs for them—they're cute."

"Yes, I like pigs, too. D'you know they say that pigs can see the wind?"

"That's handy."

"No, really, they're amazing animals, almost human. It's reckoned that dogs look up to you, cats look down on you, but pigs treat you as equals! I think I might buy one of them when the auction comes."

"Where will we keep it, Dad?"

"With us in the caravan, of course!"

"What about the smell?"

"The pig will get used to it." Dad chuckles away to himself.

"Will they change the name? I mean, 'The Piggeries' doesn't sound much like a posh address, does it?"

"Yeah, Will, I believe they're going to rename it 'The Mews,' or some such nonsense, but it will still be the piggery to me." Dad stacks the last lattice against the pigsty wall as the incumbents within squeal with the expectancy of a good scratch.

"You know what Shakespeare said, Dad: 'A rose by any other name would smell the same.'"

"So would pig shit, my son."

We tarry with the porkers for a while, feeding them windfall autumn apples and rubbing their coarse hairy shoulders with sticks. The pigs whine and fret when we leave them to return the truck. Two weeks later they whine all the more as they're bundled off to Stratford market. The piggeries fall silent, until one day when a pig of a different kind appears, roaring at me and my friends.

"If I catch one of you scruffy gypsy bastards around here again, I'll have the hide off your backs! Especially you—I'll skin you alive, you little shit! Go on, Raus! Raus! Get out of here!" The old curmudgeon swings his knurled walking stick at my head. This is my first meeting with Grumpy, a nasty-tempered retired British army general who has become the self-appointed *Obergruppenführer* of the pastoral part of the trailer park. He acts like the emperor of this part of the site, which my mother has dubbed Obnoxious Corner.

This lace-curtain and rose water enclave of the bourgeoisie is infested with old military men, failed Conservative MPs, blue-rinse harridans of the "whip'em and hang'em brigade," empire loyalists, ex-Blackshirt fascists, and oddbods who think that "Herr Hitler wasn't such a bad chap, he was just a little misunderstood." To them we are anathema and represent the thing they fear most: tomorrow!

The big problem is that their citadel of refined reaction is directly adjacent to the two places we visit the most: the rubbish dump and the old livery stables. We constantly raid the refuse tip for raw materials, and the stables at the rear of the pigsties have been converted into garages and workshops where we can repair soapbox carts, bicycles, and help people mend their motorbikes. With the pigs gone, Grumpy has expanded his borders until these facilities lie within his self-proclaimed territory.

In the square courtyard of the piggeries there stands an old cast-iron hand pump that presumably drew water for the horses that were once stabled there before the pigs moved in. We resolve in the interests of physics to get it working—and we do! By priming it with tap water through a hole in the top, we are able for the first time in maybe a hundred years to pull up the water from the ancient well below. The handle, worked loose of its rust, swings free. With all the vigor of expectant youth, we pump like the mad apprentices of the biblical blacksmith Tubal-cain. There is a gurgling, sloshing, whooshing sound—with an eminence like a sperm whale blowing off. The entire apparatus erupts in a fountain of the foulest-smelling, rancidly stagnant water any of us has experienced since bath day. To us young scientists, it is a triumph; to Grumpy and his henchmen, it's another sign that educating the underclasses is fraught with danger and should therefore be a treasonable offense!

Before we are aware of it, a posse of the great like-minded descend upon us like the Spanish Inquisition and begin dealing out summary punishment. Some of my mates get an awful thrashing, but I am nimble and jump up onto the garage roof to run for my life. At a safe distance, I turn just in time to see Grumpy pick up my bicycle and throw it at the wall. It bounces back and lies, wheels spinning, on the cobblestones. With great glee, he leaps up and brings his considerable bulk down on the front wheel, which buckles beyond repair.

"Raus, you stinking Gypos! Raus!"

This *Raus* business is familiar. I remember Mr. Feidelman's caravan and begin to put two and two together. I don't get four carrots, I get a declaration of war!

"Right, lads! As my dad says, 'If you cross an Irishman with a pig, you'll get a pig that can hold a grudge for a thousand years!' We don't need that amount of time, we just need a good working plan!"

For the next few weeks, myself and my battered lieutenants conceive a dastardly counterattack that, in the fullness of time, is to prove devastating.

"What happened to your bike?" Dad asks, as I seek to replace the front wheel with another, two sizes too small.

"Er . . . nothing, just a stupid accident."

"That old Hooray-Henry of a general was down at the club last night, boasting that he'd worsted a gang of local hooligans? Dy'know anything about it, youngfella?"

"No," I says. I meant it, too. We had only received a cuffing, not a worsting, and we hadn't yet even replied to the challenge.

"Operation Moonstrike" goes into effect at the next full moon. We have three commando teams of two; each has a separate job. Every job is synchronized to the bells of the old Saxon church, which toll the hour, quarter, half, and three-quarters. This gives parameters of fifteen minutes for each phase.

We are well versed in this clandestine military stuff—we've just sat through two showings of *The Guns of Navarone* at Stratford Cinema.

It is 8 o'clock: Zero hour. The advance party moves forward to the corner of the piggeries and props a ladder against the garage roof nearest Grumpy's caravan.

8.15: The assault party climb the ladder with a large piece of turf, which they place over the caravan's chimney pipe.

8.30: The observation party monitors the buildup of smoke and the opening of doors and windows to let out same. An intelligence report confirms: *Grumpy cursing and waving smoke out of door with his hat.* Excellent!

8.45: The coup de grâce, the assault party removes turf and replaces it with a garden hose.

9.00: All rendezvous. Remove ladder, turn on water hose, and withdraw. The mission is complete!

This puts the kibosh on old Grumpy as far as we're concerned. He is left knee deep in soot and water, with "Nazis Raus!" painted on the roof of his caravan!

The next day our action is followed by a serendipitous event that places us kids beyond any repercussions that may occur.

A mysterious bearded bloke called Pikey, who for the last year has wandered around the caravan site wearing sandals and talking poetry to himself, pays Grumpy a visit, carrying a large metal container. Grumpy is on a ladder trying to scrub the graffiti from his roof.

"We have all, like, heard about what happened to you, general man, and have, like, taken up a collection, dig?" Grumpy smiles and the lanky beatnik throws the contents of an Elsan shit bucket all over him.

"Revenge is a dish best eaten cold," say the Sicilians, and as luck would have it, I have learned a lot about exotic dishes this year!

News of our part in the daring raid spreads around the web of intrigue that makes up the multistranded universe of the prepubescent. By some lapse of security or most likely a comrade's boast, made no doubt in the strictest confidence, the Bulldog Gang hears of it.

This unsavory outfit is the remote, but nevertheless, feared group of older boys who hang around the post office. They are mostly the sons of servicemen and live in a distant enclave of the caravan site. Their leader is the fat git called Derrick Davies who once called my mam a pregnant prostitute. He bears a remarkable resemblance to his pet: a squat, snarling, slobber of a bulldog from which they take their gang name.

Like most of my pals, I give these guys a wide berth when I can. They go to the Protestant school in Henley, and so are doomed anyway. If that isn't bad enough, they are all over twelve, and indeed some are fourteen! The main currency of their everyday conversation seems to be the esoteric world of masturbation, a presumed rite of passage at this time still alien to us in thought, word, and deed. The old air raid shelter at the back of the railway station is their headquarters, and to this den of dexterous depravity I am duly summoned by a pair of Derrick's hard-faced shock troops.

I enter the dingy shelter, festooned with pinup girls from *Parade* magazine and smelling heavily of stale spunk and mildew. In the half-light, surrounded by his faithful, *Obergrossenführer* Davies sprawls across a canvas-backed chair like a half-inflated zeppelin.

"So you want to join our gang, do you? We heard of the raid on Grumpy—good work!" Beside his master's chair, the drooling dog shakes its head, sending whiplashes of snot in a silvern arc about it.

"Who the hell has told him that?" I wonder, shuddering at the thought of joining this lot.

"Well, don't be a scaredy-cat! Do you want to join a real gang or keep hanging out with those little prats from the kitchen gardens? Can you fetch?"

"Fetch what?"

"Fetch your cock off? Have a wank? Shake the vinegar bottle? Come yer custard? For fuck's sake, give him the book, somebody!" At the flabby Führer's request, I am handed a stained, dog-eared copy of *Health and Efficiency* magazine, a monochrome tabloid of naked, beach-ball-throwing females, curiously devoid of any traces of pubic hair. My initial feeling of fear and trepidation is now approaching panic! What do they want me to do? If it's *that,* forget it! *That* is a mortal sin and I don't know how to do it anyway! The elbow-nudging storm troopers piss themselves laughing at my bewilderment amid cries of, "He's never done it!" "He hasn't got one!" "He needs two hands, one for the magnifying glass and one for the tweezers!"

The dirty book is slapped across my face and returned to the shelf. In the stinging silence that follows, I have a chance to reassess. What am I doing here? I don't want to be in this stupid gang of wankers!

Derrick is still pushing for my loyalty.

"If you want to join us, you must go though the initiation ceremony. First you must swear the oath of secrecy. Then you must cut your thumb with a razor blade and give it to the dog to lick. Then you must kiss the dog's dick!"

I stare around the ring of stern, cheerless faces, now all nodding approval to these arcane rituals. Tough, intimidating faces, eyes defiant and mouths set hard, mouths that, *mouths that*—oh! my Christ!—had kissed a dog's cock!

The tiny gene of the absurd that I have inherited from my mother causes me a convulsion of irrepressible mirth that not only drives away fear and foreboding, but makes me impervious to the blows of fists that rain down upon me. I am forcibly ejected into the clean crisp air of the countryside where, still being kicked and beaten, I jackknife my way home more aware of my ribs aching from hysterics than violence.

"Holy Jasus, child, what ails ye?" Mam is hanging up the washing as I reel into the yard, blood, snot, and merriment shining on my face. Still holding my splitting ribs, I recount to her the story of the dreaded dog's cock kissers.

"Durty fuckers!" says Mam. "Taking advantage of a poor dumb animal like that! It's little wonder they're always spitting on the pavement!" I commence back to roaring and howling with agonizing glee.

The Bulldog Gang never recover from their betrayed secret and subsequent crippling loss of face. No longer does this pack hang out at the post office corner, shouting obscenities at girls, smoking cigarettes, and gobbing on the street. They are only seen in shamefaced ones and twos, except when they march on Sundays with the Protestant Boy's Brigade troop. Then we cheer them on with *"Woof! Woof!"* noises combined with lip-licking kissy sounds.

Now with the opposition defeated and in disarray, we have the place to ourselves!

It is a great revelation when I find out that I won't be struck by a celestial lightning bolt when I dare go into a non-Catholic church. The truth is that most of the interesting ancient churches are Church of England or the like, and the Catholic ones are nearly all modern, some as recent as the 1890s.

There are many Saxon, Norman, Tudor, and Gothic buildings in everyday use all over the county, most within a good bike ride. I visit many such places and marvel at the tombs of crusaders, barons who knew Simon de Montfort, men-at-arms in stone chain mail, knights in armor with their feet resting on a lion to show they'd died in war or on a dog to signify that they met their demise at home, in time of peace.

Dad shows me how to take brass rubbings from the ancient tabloid effigies of long-dead knights of the realm, in the old churches. This process involves placing paper over the inscribed knightly representations and rubbing with a wax crayon or preferably a cobbler's heel-ball. The resulting image is very pleasing and educational. The unfortunate thing is that all of these old churches are now post Reformation and as a result Protestant!

Dad doesn't give a fling about this and neither do I—until I write a story about us going to an old Norman church in Alcester and rubbing the brasses.

My teachers are not amused.

"So you go into Protestant churches, do you? Do you know that's a mortal sin? What do you have to say for yourself?" I am not to be intimidated. My father has briefed me well.

"The brasses I rubbed were of good Catholics who had never heard of a Protestant. They were well dead long before Henry the Eighth, Cromwell, or any of them was pupped." I am very indignant! "And if they didn't think they were still Catholics, why did Cromwell's Iron-sides deface so many of the statues and old knights in these churches?"

Mrs. MacArthur looks at Mr. Bury, who in turn looks at Miss Hathaway. Miss Hathaway looks out of the window, and I look at her reflection and see her trying not to laugh.

They had been totally unprepared for such a vigorous defense. Mrs. Mack takes up the inquisition.

"Your father encouraged you to do this, isn't that right?"

"Yes, miss."

"He's not of the faith, is he?"

"No, miss."

"I've heard he's an atheist. Is that true?"

"I don't know, miss!"

"Well, does he go to church?"

"Only at Christmas, miss."

"Oh yes, I heard all about that. He doesn't have much love for our parish priest, does he?"

"I don't know, miss."

"Of course you know. He tells you everything. What's his opinion of our own holy father?"

"No different to how he sees the rest of the priesthood, miss."

"And what does he say about them, pray tell?"

"He says if priests wore their trousers around the same way as their collars, there would be fewer bastard children in the world."

There is a long silence. They are dumbfounded. It is decided more appropriate that the priest should confront my father with a list of my ill doings, and thus I would get my comeuppance at home. I am dismissed.

Weeks go by and nothing happens. I thought I'd gotten away with my outburst, and though I had seen the priest at church and at school, he had never made any attempt to converse with me, let alone give me a punishment. One day, however, the past catches up with me whilst I am playing with my toy soldiers on the kitchen table.

Dad has finished his rotating early shift and is having a kip on the settee, when there is a knock at the caravan door.

"See who that is, Will?" I open the door and there is a chap I vaguely knew, but who is he? A little ferret-face bloke with a familiar hunted look.

"Er, I'm Mr. Timmins. I work with Father. Can I have a word with your parents? If it's not too much trouble."

"Daaad?" I begin, but he is already up, pulling on his braces and looking suspiciously at the interloper.

"Who's this arsehole?" he says to me, ignoring the outstretched hand of the verger. "What does he want, waking me up in the middle of the bloody daytime?"

"Eh-hrm! I'm here on behalf of the priest to have a little chat with you about the behavior of your son."

"You're what?" says Dad, taking stock of the nervous stranger for the first time.

"Your son, he's bee . . . n . . ."

He trails off, aware that Dad is regarding him with jaundiced eye.

Dad cracks his knuckles with a sickening snap, before saying ,"*Listen you,* whoever you are! If that devil dodger wants to talk to me, he can come here his bleeding self! I don't parley with any bugger's fart catcher. I prefer to talk to the shovel, not the shit! Do you understand, lickspittal?"

"Yessyessyes!" agrees the poor verger, making his way back to his bicycle like a surreptitious sideywise crab.

"I will be going now—good-bye!" says the layman, throwing his leg over the crossbar and pedaling off, head tucked in, legs a-blur, down the cinder track road.

Dad is just about to close the door when a spark of recognition flashes in his eyes. He throws the door open wide.

"I remember you from last Christmas, ya shifty wee bastard!"

His words are lost on the fast-diminishing figure of the verger, who has sped away as swiftly as his 1930 three-geared Hercules Roadster can convey him.

"So what have you been up to that's pissed off the old sin bosun?"

"I told my teacher that you are an atheist and they called the priest about it."

"Well, it's no bloody business of theirs what I am—and anyway, I'm an agnostic!"

"What's that, Dad?"

"Well, when I joined the army, we had our first Sunday church parade and the regimental sergeant major has us all lined up in rank and file. *'Right, you 'orrible lot!'* he shouts. *'Catholics move to the left! Protestants move to the right! On my command, FALL OUT!'* This left myself and a long drink of water called Private Abel Goodman standing in the middle of the parade ground. The RSM goes to gangly Goodman and says, *'So what the bleedin' 'ell are you?'*

'I'm Jewish,' says Goodman.

'Hmm,' says the RSM, making his way over to me.

'So what are you, Private Watkins? Are you Jewish as well?'

'Erm, no, I'm an agnostic, Sergeant.'

'What in the name of buggery is an agnostic, Watkins?'

'Well, Sarge, I believe in a God of sorts, but I haven't made my mind up about what exactly it is yet!'

'WELL, NOW'S YOUR BLEEDING CHANCE! IT'S THAT LOT, THE OTHER LOT, OR THAT LANKY BASTARD OVER THERE! NOW GET FELL IN, YOU GODLESS LITTLE MAN!'"

✧ Chapter 12 ✦

DAD WALKS SLOWLY DOWN FROM HIS SIGNAL BOX AT HENLEY Station. It is two in the afternoon, and he has just been relieved by the second shift. Crossing the road by the Three Tuns public house, he roots in his greatcoat pocket and produces the grand sum of his wealth: a single copper penny bearing the head of Queen Victoria and on the reverse, Britannia sitting gazing at the ocean, shield and spear in hand.

"Not much good to man nor beast—well man anyway," he muses, popping the penny into a horse-shaped charity box labeled "The People's Dispensary for Sick Animals."

"Cast ye, your bread upon the waters and what shall ye receive in return? Soggy bread!" Dad begins the long walk home, but something catches his eye, fluttering like a small green woodpecker in a pile of brown autumn leaves. It is a one-pound note!

"Let joy be unconfined!" shouts Dad to the gray skies above. The smell of beer is enticing from the taproom of the Golden Cross Tavern.

"In for a penny, in for a pound!" Dad makes to venture over to the pub.

He pauses at the curbside. A lorry load of cattle breezes past and trundles down the High Street.

On the fulsome wind that follows its wake, a staccato voice drifts up from the offtrack betting shop. "Three minutes to go here at Newmarket before the Cesarewitch October Stakes is run. Here at this historic race, named after the czar of all the Russias, the field is as follows: Superfine, seven to four favorite; Hal's Lad, two to one; Continuous Wave, eleven to two; Lucky Note, ten to one; Bar, twelve to one. Two minutes to the off!"

"Lucky Note?" Dad stares at the pound in his hand and then back across to the alehouse. He tries to walk to the pub, but his legs take him into the bookie's.

"They're at the starters line here at Newmarket."

"Och! To hell with it. One pound, Lucky Note—to win!"

"And they're off!"

A big black car noses its way up the cinder track and stops outside our caravan.

"Willie, tell that fella to park somewhere else. If your dad comes home he'll have his guts for garters."

"Mam! Maaam! It *is* my dad!"

"Isn't she a beauty? I got her for ten quid."

"Ten pounds? Glory be, that's a week's wages! Where in the name of Christ did you get ten pounds?"

"It's a long story and you wouldn't believe me."

"Try me."

I inspect the sleek monster. It is black with big chrome headlights and looks like Al Capone had given it away to charity, a grand old rust bucket held together with holes.

Dad opens the bonnet and stares into the Medusa's head of coils, wires, and hoses.

"She's an Austin Ten, stoutly built. She's survived many's the long winter, and there's life in the old dog yet!" He slams the hood shut and the horn blares. He pulls at some wires and the horn never works again.

At the weekend we go on expeditions into the country. Off to the glorious west, Shropshire, Herefordshire, and over the border into the heartland of Wales.

Dad takes me to Bleddfa, the tiny hamlet where my grandfather was born and generations of Watkinses had farmed the lush pastures. The valleys of Powys are tree lined, verdant fingers, stretching in a fecund flourish from the Brecon Beacons over Offa's Dyke into the flatlands of Mercia. The air is rich and suffused with pine scent.

We still have kin living in mid-Wales and it always is a pleasure to visit and listen to them talking. Whether they speak English or Welsh, their voices have a musical quality that is sweet on the ear. They can make "Bugger off or I'll shoot your dog!" sound as pleasant as Dylan Thomas reading "A Child's Christmas in Wales."

My great-uncle, George Lloyd, is a bard of the old school, foremost in the art of Celtic storytelling and likewise the symbiotic Druidic craft of brewing. He talks in Welsh a lot with my father and calls him Rhienallt, the Welsh for Reginald. Me he refers to as Gwylym bach, little William.

Here in a little tumbledown house, behind Auntie Sis's post office in the village of Presteigne, he holds his impromptu Gorsedd court.

Shadowy figures, some of which are kin and some strangers, flit between fireside and ale barrel, like silent specters thirsting for the spoken word. In the focus of a concave arc of expectant faces, Old George is enthroned on a carved oak settle. In his left hand he nurses a glass of thick, home-brewed, Red-Rag cider, in the other a black briar pipe.

Master of intrigue, he knocks the dottle out of his pipe and lights the replenished bowl. The story does not begin until the pipe draws well and the room is silent except for the crackling of a log fire and the pendulous ticking of the longcase clock standing sentinel by the doorway. Pull your chair into the fire and listen to him now:

> Great-uncle Jack knew about horses, you see. He and generations before him had bred native Welsh ponies on the green hills of wild Wales. These stocky, sturdy little ponies are known to be good all-rounders; fine for working or carrying supplies in side panniers or maybe, when required, just right for riding. They can pull a medium-size barrel-top living wagon or a ladened flat cart and stay out on the mountain in all weathers. Strong and willful, they are the embodiment of the divine horse goddess, Epona, from which they take the name pony.
>
> The men and women that farmed these upland pastures are no less rugged and have clung on tenuously to the land of Cymru. They have defied famine, invasions, civil unrest, wars of all kinds, and even the pestilence of Palug's cat, who ate one hundred and eighty warriors before Cei ap Cynyr killed it on Ynys Môn, which is also called the Isle of Anglesey.
>
> It is the newly married Jack whom we see setting up

home with his wife just as the black ravens of war are gathering over Europe.

The king of England, the kaiser of Germany, and the czar of all the Russias are busy thumbing their royal noses at each other and spoiling for a fight. These three first cousins are in turn being watched by a score of second and third cousins, who make up the other crowned heads of Europe. Who will jump here? Who will jump there? Who will not jump at all when the battle royal commences?

It takes them four long years to finish their family feud. Eight million soldiers lie dead, and one of the fallen, whose name liveth forever on a Welsh village's war memorial, is the legendary great-uncle Jack.

It is 1916. The British army has lost so many men in the Battle of the Somme, nineteen thousand killed in one day alone, they feel they must introduce conscription.

Jack receives his call-up papers in the autumn of that year and grudgingly reports for duty in Cardiff. He doesn't approve of this imperialist war. If the English are seriously concerned about the freedom of small nations, why don't they pull out of Wales and leave it for the Welsh? Well, now, look you! If Jack must go, he wants to join a Welsh-speaking regiment. The British find out that he is a horse breeder and he is sent instead to the Royal Horse Artillery.

After his training as a horse gunner, he find himself in war-stricken France. He and his battery are sent to a small evacuated hamlet on the frontline. Their mission is to support a tiny detachment of dismounted French cavalry who are attempting to hold this part of the salient.

Horse units are still being sent forward by the generals at GHQ in Paris. Surely they must know they are useless against mud, barbed wire, and machine guns? Cavalry men are ill-equipped to fight on foot with their bright sabers, riding breeches, slim leather boots, and short-range saddle carbines. It is hoped that the presence of a few twenty-five-pounder field guns might discourage an attack at this weak point. It is not to be.

The first salvo of shells to leave the Allied battery gives away their position to the enemy spotters, and a withering fire is returned by the massed German heavy guns.

The German gunners are no beginners. They know well their trade. Their fire is meticulously accurate and sustained. In the first volley, Uncle Jack's field gun flies into the air like a toy and lands a hundred yards away, a crumpled wreck. A second shell rips into the ammunition carts parked next to their makeshift stables. In that one enormous explosion, all of the batteries' horses are blown to pieces, along with the British battery commander, the French colonel, and their entire staff.

Within minutes of the opening shots, every Allied field piece has been silenced. The gun crews lie around their posts where they have fallen. Jack has been blown clear off of his own gun and into a haystack, which catches fire. He dives for shelter into a ruined wine cellar until the first barrage ceases, then scurries to where the field headquarters had been established. There is nothing left but a smoking crater in the soft muddy earth. Not a single soul has survived the attack.

In the unearthly quiet following the deafening engagement, Jack hears the fall of hooves and cries of "Aller! Aller!" He jumps up and through the swirling dust he sees the remnants of the detachment of cuirassiers beating a hasty retreat on their mounts. He calls out to them, but they are out of earshot and riding hard.

There are but six of them left, and the last, in trying to clear a ruined wall, falls heavily from the saddle and lies still on the scattered stones.

Jack climbs over the piles of rubble to where the rider lies staring at the gray sky. He was a young captain who had previously won the Croix de Guerre. Now he is beyond all earthly help. Jack takes the man's papers from his top pocket. His name was Capitaine Jean-Baptiste Laurence. Jack will give these to the first casualty officer he meets. Then on a sudden impulse, he removes the medal, wraps it in its silken ribbon, and puts it in his own pocket. There is a *crump!* from the German lines and a single shell whistles over and falls in the pile of debris that once had been a farmhouse.

Jack makes his way back to his shelter, darting from cover to cover. Another solitary shell homes in and bursts behind him. "At least I'm going in the right direction!" he thinks, "away from the gunfire!" Diving like a rabbit into his sanctuary, he makes a bed out of a bale of straw and tries to sleep. All night long the desultory shelling continues and Jack has the wildest dreams.

Standing before him is the young cavalry officer, pale and deathly.

"Seek you the white Arab, lead him to safety, seek you the white Arab and save him. He is the last of his line. Restore the honor of my family and then I can rest."

In the dream Jack takes out the Croix de Guerre from his pocket and offers it to the pallid specter.

"No you must keep that. You will need it. Save the white Arab!"

Jack wakes, shivering as if ice water is running in his veins. The first fingers of the sun are probing the shadows and with the dawn he expects the counterattack that will have him killed or taken prisoner. It doesn't come! Maybe the Germans are still asleep or perhaps they fear a trap!

Emerging from his hidey-hole, he looks around. The visitation from the night before is now a distant memory in the melting warmth of morning. Way out in no-man's-land, he sees a stallion! A white stallion! A white Arab stallion! The poor horse is lost and confused, wandering amongst the barbed wire and shell holes, bloody and covered in mud.

Jack whistles and does his best to coax the charger over, but the horse is shy of him. Searching about in the remains of the orchard, he finds some apples and leaves them where the steed will smell them. This tactic works fine and soon he and the horse are pals. He is very relieved to discover that the bloodstains on the stallion are not the horse's but its unfortunate rider.

Staying holed up all day, Jack expects relief from the Allies or a German attack, but nothing occurs. Except for the horse, he is alone in a cellar, encompassed by the wastelands of futile Armageddon.

In fitful sleep, once again he is taunted by the ghost of the young officer. No words are spoken, but the officer takes the Arab's bridle and hands it to Jack. A ghostly finger points to the west. Go, the eyes of the Frenchman beckon. Go!

Jack wakes and lies in thought. The phantom is right! Enough of this war business. There's no glory here, just death—not only of iniquitous mankind but of beautiful innocent horses. What couldn't he do with an Arabian stud sire like this back home in Wales?

"Needs must when the devil rides!" Jack tells himself.

Jack ties a red neckerchief around his throat and looks at himself in the shattered mirror of a long abandoned bedroom dresser. "I could pass for a civilian!" he thinks, fingering the stubble on his unwashed chin. In the ruins of the farmhouse, he finds old clothes scattered where they had fallen during the hasty evacuation. Divesting himself of all traces of military garb, he dresses in a hotchpotch of civilian attire. A lone shell hums over his head and explodes beyond the poplar trees. Jack throws his army identification discs into the mangled morass where the first shell had fallen. The loose leaves of his army paybook flutter like butterflies over the stinking corpses.

"Now to disguise the horse!" An old blacksmith forge yields a large rasp file. This he uses to take off the French army brand, from the charger's right hoof. It works well and a good feed of apples will make up the difference in hoof horn.

The stallion is also branded on the lip. This seems a problem until Jack finds a tin of army metal polish. This he rubs into the brand, causing it to swell and blister until formation of a scab completely obscures the mark!

He fashions a bridle out of rope and replaces the French cavalry saddle with an old red velvet curtain, He mounts his mud-covered prize and slowly rides away from the insanity they call the First World War!

It takes Jack many weeks to thread his careful way across the French countryside. In the confusion of the front, he isn't even challenged. He's just another lost peasant refugee on the road to nowhere, mingling with the other dispossessed and evacuated. Horse and rider are of no interest to the army except as a bloody nuisance to be cleared rapidly out of the way.

His initial navigation relies on having the sound of the guns to his rear and joining the flow of other civilians fleeing the war zone. After which, he travels only at night and uses the stars for pointers. Early one morning, when he is many miles from the battle line, he runs into his first real trouble.

A platoon of recently arrived British soldiers is bivouacked across the road, and Jack, riding almost fast asleep, clatters straight into them.

"*Halt! Who goes there?*" challenges a London Cockney private, his rifle raised. "*Friend or foe?*"

"Bore da!" says Jack, in Welsh, just wishing the soldier a fine good morning. The sentry looks unsure and calls out, "*Sergeant! I think I've caught a German spy!*"

The sergeant runs up with two more armed soldiers. Pistol in hand, he orders, *"Hände hoch!"* Jack looks blankly from one to another. The sergeant tries again. *"Spreckenzee Deutsch, Fritz?"*

"Bore da!" says Jack, smiling and beginning to enjoy their discomfort.

"That's what he says to me, Sergeant!"

"Right, you, what's your game? Where do you come from? Who's your king?" The sergeant was trying a bit of psychology.

Jack, still staring down the muzzles of four guns, replies, "Beird byt barnant wyr o gallon, Diebyrth e gerth e gynghyr!" The poets of the world judge those to be men of valor, whose counsels are not revealed to slaves!

"There you are!" says the sergeant, "I knew it! He ain't no bloody German! He's a bloody Gypsy! Now get that Gypo bastard out of here before he steals something!"

To Jack's delight, he is given a British military escort through the camp and out into the open country beyond.

He passes unseen through the thickly hedged lanes of Normandy and into the Argoat, which is Breton for the Country of the Trees. Here in Brittany, he is amongst fellow Celts who speak his language and also have little love for the war. Many resented being conscripted into the army of France, who they considered to be an occupying force in their beloved Armorica. Uncle Jack can well understand that!

He and his horse are fed and watered by sympathetic families and guided from village to village. Within two days, they reach the coast at the tiny fishing port of Tréguier. Now only the sea stands between him and Wales.

Jack's helpers have informed him that fishing boats from Wales often call in to pick up sardines from the smaller Breton fishing smacks and that this is his best chance at getting across the Channel. His luck is holding.

In the small stone harbor is a French coaster about to set sail for Pembroke to pick up a flock of Cheviot sheep. Jack tries to secure passage by offering to work for his trip. The captain shakes his head. *"Have you no money?"* The captain pats Jack's coat pockets to emphasize the point.

"No, I have nothing." The skipper delves into the jacket pocket and draws forth a long blue, white, and red ribbon with its silver fourchée.

"My God! You have the Croix de Guerre! For that I will give you free passage and two bottles of apricot brandy!"

Jack and his Breton helpers drink a toast. Then he and his mount set sail for Wales.

No one takes the slightest notice of the scruffy, bearded figure leading his horse away from the bustling Welsh port. With an army to be fed in France, every coastal town is choked with livestock being loaded or penned up, waiting for ships. The streets are thronged with drovers, agents, farmers, and the other attendants that keep an army marching on its stomach.

All this Jack leaves behind and, mounting his steed, he turns for Powys and home.

Now Jack has to be careful, see? Because he is a deserter, which would get you shot, and also a horse thief, which would get you shot again! He makes his way to the cottage of a kinsman called Blind Old Harry, where he lies up for a while in secret.

Jack's poor wife has been notified by the war office that he has been killed in action. Old Harry gets word to Jack's grieving widow that there's an impediment in law about her ownership of the farm and will she come to Llandrindod Wells for a meeting. This she duly does, and waiting there for her is her bearded husband, Jack.

They say that she fainted clean away and thought he was an angel. Well, Jack might have been a lot of things you know, but he was no angel! They maintain a secret liaison until a respectable time is past. Then Uncle Jack marries the love of his life for the second time. They move to another part of Wales, and there, with the aid of the Arab stallion, who they named Captain Laurence of Arabia, they raise fine horses and four children. Black, white, gray, and piebald they were—the horses that is, not the children! And do you know? Until the day she died, Jack's wife received a war widow's pension from the English government. She donated it all to the People's Dispensary for Sick Animals.

He finishes his tale with a section from *The Gododdin,* the epic sixth-century war saga by the great Brythonic poet, Aneirin:

> *"Gredyf gwr oed gis*
> *Gwrhyt am dias*
> *Meirch mwth myngvras*
> *A dan vordwyt megyris.*
>
> *He is a man in mind, in years a youth*
> *And gallant in the din of war:*
> *fleet, thick-maned chargers*
> *Are ridden by this illustrious hero."*

The room fills with cheers and clapping. Old Uncle George motions me to join him outside.

"There be only one thing more thirsty work than telling a story and that be a-listening to it!" Uncle George contends and shuffles off into the outhouse, where he keeps his cider vats.

"Come and give me a hand, Gwylym bach, and we'll get these good folks a drink!"

The bottom of the oaken vats are covered with the bare bones of small animals which, bleached white, gleam through the murky cider.

"Was that story true, Uncle George?"

"Well, it all depends on what you want to believe!"

"Why do you put beasts into the cider, uncle?"

"It be to improve the flavor and give it body. Do ye want a flagon, young master?"

"I'm not old enough, uncle."

"Rubbish!" He scoops me up a pewter mug of the festering infusion. "I've been drinking this since I was a sprog, an' it ain't done me no harm either!"

There is no way out and I sup at the wizard's brew. The sensation of swallowing this stuff beggars belief, but once down, it gives a pleasing glow followed seconds later by a rush of blood to the brain that sends me reeling into the fresh air.

"Har, har, har! That's what happened to me when I was a sprog! It fetched me such a tightener. Har, har, har! It be like a red rag to a bull, that old zyder! I tell ye, Gwylym bach, our family be blessed by longevity here in the clean air of Wales. Aunt Sis is over a hundred herself and her father died, only after falling down an apple tree when he was one hundred and three years old. I'm telling you, it's that red rag cider that kept us young. Har, har, har!"

With trays filled with flowing pints of scrumpy, we rejoin the convocation. Uncle George taps out his pipe once more and that's the signal for quiet. When all is still, he recites:

Silver John is dead and gone,
and buried in Cole Harbor.

When I was a little boy, I remember the old men in the village talking about the events that were current when they were children the same age as me. People lived to be over a hundred, so could go back two hundred years of history in just two generations. Bonnie Prince Charlie and George Washington and Napoleon it was that were giving the English a run for their money around the world. Heroes they were to the old ones, who didn't care for the Saesneg.

One of my forebears, who didn't make it to quite such a ripe old age, was foully murdered whilst still a youth of seventy-four. His name was Dr. John Lloyd or Silver John, as he is better known. He was a traveling bonesetter and plied his trade through the highways and byways of mid-Wales and the border country beyond in the

1700s. His nickname came from the silver buttons on the great flared overcoat he liked to wear and the solid-silver buckles on his shoes. The unfortunate doctor is returning home one night from New Radnor, when he is attacked by a party of brigands. Although he tries to fight them off, they get the better of him and beat him senseless. His attackers strip the silver adornments from his clothes and then with great callousness push his unconscious body beneath the ice of the frozen Llyn Hielyn. "Murder will out," the old saying goes and sure enough it do! Under the ice his body lies until the spring thaw, when the lake boils and bubbles to the amazement of all and with a terrible eruption casts his body forth! They say the doctor's vengeful spirit still haunts the banks of the lake, seeking revenge on his murderers!

His assailants are never brought to justice, but it is said that to this day the grass never grows on the grave of Silver John.

One night, it was, when I was a sprog, I had been staying out too late and the sun had gone down quicker than I expected. Making my way back home, along the twilight filled lane that passes close by the shore of Llyn Hielyn, I begin to tremble.

A rustling noise dogs my footsteps from the other side of the hedgerow. It could only be *Silver John's Ghost!* I hasten my pace without trying to appear frightened. The accompanying footfalls take on speed, too. I stop, they stop. I creep forward, they creep forward! Finally I take off as fast as my legs can carry me, still paced by my invisible nemesis. At the end of the lane the hedgerow abruptly finishes and I clatter headlong into my phantom! A large saddle-backed pig it was, lying there with me in the mud. I'm up and running in my bare feet and the pig is calling after me, "Siors Lloyd, run hard, for a great storm approaches," and I run as fast as I can, for I know that pigs can see the wind. Lightning strikes the trees around me and great peels of thunder rend the air. The stones in the road sting my feet and hail the size of hen's eggs strikes the road behind me. "Take my shoes, Siors bach, and be fleet of foot!" I look down and a pair of black shoes with silver buckles appear on my feet, giving me new strength to outrun the storm. I gain the safety of my gate and run into the kitchen.

"Mam! Mam! Look at my feet!"

"I see them—they are a disgrace! You will go to bed without any supper!"

I look down and my feet are muddy and bare.

"But Mam—"

"There will be no buts. Wash those feet and off to bed, and it's sorry you'll be for missing supper! Your uncle killed his old saddle-backed pig this morning and brought us over a roast!"

There is a sigh from the assembly, the briar pipe is knocked out on the hearth of the old fireplace, and Uncle George drains the last of his pint.

"Tangnefedd fo gyda chwi, nos dawch a ffarwel!"

Peace go with you, good night and farewell!

We course through the night, our one headlight picking out the cat's eyes marking the median of the road.

"Are they real cat's eyes, Dad?"

"No, they were invented by a man who was out one night, when he saw a cat walking towards him, with its eyes reflecting his car lights. He made up similar reflectors out of glass and rubber."

"To help make the roads safer?"

"That's right! If the cat had been walking away from him, he would've probably invented the pencil sharpener!"

"Reg! That's enough of that filth in front of the child!"

"Do you believe in ghosts, Dad?'

"No."

"No, of course he doesn't, Willie. Yer father is what they call a daylight atheist. He doesn't believe in God unless he's at death's door, and then you should hear him. Oh, Jesus help me! Oh, my God! What is it they say?

> '*The devil was ill—the devil a monk would be.*
> *The monk got well—the monk a devil was he.*'"

"Well, at least I don't pray to some bug-whiskered old bollix up in the sky."

"No, you'd rather put your faith in trees an' stones an' cats an' dogs and them bunch of beauties you go boozing with down at the Bull's Head tavern!"

"You see, Will, though your mother doesn't credit it, most religions are like used car lots for the soul. Here the dealers—priests, vicars, rabbis, what have you—offer their best price on what you've got, provided you trade in your good sense, your free will, your obedience, and often all your money. Then you can drive away in their new model, which ultimately you hand in at the company headquarters. They check it over and if it's well kept, you're kitted out with something more luxurious that will last you for eternity! If you've thrashed it, then it's the scrap heap for you!"

"Listen to him and his lies! Your father is like the fella in the story, walking past the graveyard at night and shiting himself with fear. 'God is good!' he says out loud and feels better. A wee bit further on, an owl hoots and he is shiting it again, so he cries out, 'God is good!' Again he feels easier. Then he thinks to himself, what if the Devil is lurking around and hears me saying this? He might not be too pleased and he'll jump out and get me. So next time, he shouts, 'God is good, God is good—and the Devil ain't such a bad fella when you get to know him!'"

"I'm telling you this, wife. For all these buggers extolling the virtues of the next life, I've never found one in too much of a hurry to get there!"

"Goway, with you! What does it say in the Bible? 'Man who is born of woman has but a short time to live and is full of woe!'"

"Which I take to mean, Monica, Man has but a short time to live and is a miserable bastard!" Dad crosses himself in mock parody of the Catholic blessing. "Spectacles, testicles, wallet, and watch!"

"Reg, I'm warning you!"

He takes no heed other than to bless my mother with the sign of the cross.

"Ashes to ashes, lust to dust. If God don't take ye, the Devil must!"

"Reg, you're going too far!"

Between the solid rock of my mother's devout Catholic beliefs and the whirlpool of my father's paganism, I steer an erratic course. I'm put in mind of the child Taliesin tossed in his fragile Celtic coracle betwixt Scylla and Charybdis.

It is only then I realize that the Druidical circle of eternity encompassing the Christian crucifix gives us the Celtic cross. This fusion is something that both my parents can live with.

Despite my father's dislike of the church corporate, he does give the Welsh Protestant chapels the credit for preserving the ancient Cymric language. Without their insistence on using the Welsh Bible and singing hymns in the old tongue, it can be argued that English alone would be the dominant language nowadays. It would indeed be a tragic day when the Welsh phrase "Dim Saesneg" (I have no English) is heard for the last time in the hills of wild Wales, the land of my fathers.

> *Their Lord they shall praise,*
> *Their language they shall keep,*
> *Their land they shall lose*
> *Except wild Wales.*
> Taliesin, *Destiny of the Britons* (sixth-century)

Great-uncle George lives several years past his hundredth birthday. He dies peacefully and now sleeps in the ancient graveyard at Presteigne beneath a tall yew tree that will draw plenty of nourishment from his bones. Uncle George would like that.

✣ Chapter 13 ✣

A NARROW, DARK, TREE-SHROUDED LANE LEADS FROM THE
main road half a mile to the rear environs of Wootton Hall. Known as
Spook's Path, this eerie service way is surrounded entirely by evergreen
laurels, firs, and holly bushes. Its purpose was to obscure the everyday
traffic of servants, laborers, and lowly-born from the delicate sensibilities of the Georgian upper crust. Summer or winter, the peasants were
well hidden from the nobility promenading the broad main drive just a
mere hundred feet away. The lane terminates at the graveyard of the old
Saxon church in a thicket of ancient yew trees. Dad is looking for a likely
tree branch to cut and form into a longbow. He tells me the tale.

"These trees are only found in medieval graveyards on account of
their poisonous qualities when eaten by livestock. In the Middle Ages
there were few walled enclosures. Beasts grazed where they liked, with
the exception of walled burial grounds, where the intrusion of animals
would be considered profane. Here the yews could grow in safety. The
yew was one of the most important commodities in the economy of the
warring Normans because it yielded the springy wood for the English
longbow."

He goes on to tell me that this artifice of war was the most feared
instrument of battle known in its day. A master archer could fire off
three cloth-yard shafts before the first one hit its target, and this rapid-
fire technique proved devastating to the French armies on more than
one occasion during the Hundred Years War in the fourteenth century.

Dad continues: "These soldiers were so feared by the French that
when they captured an archer they would cut off the plucking fingers of
his bow-drawing hand. Without the means to fire an arrow, he was then
sent home as a pensionable drain on the English crown's war chest. By

medieval law the practice of archery each Sunday in Britain was compulsory. This formed a huge pool of likely recruits to fill the ranks, where they would wave their two intact fingers in the air in defiance of the enemy. This gave rise to the popular 'Up yours!' gesture, the one-fingered version of which our American cousins refer to as 'flipping the bird.' The old law is still on the statute books, but the practice of Sunday archery eventually evolved into the game of darts, which you play inside the tavern, not out in the pissing rain."

It takes Dad many weeks to manufacture the six-foot yew longbow, fashioned as per the descriptions in the old tales. Furthermore, he creates three cloth-yard arrows tipped with .303 rifle bullet ends. On a crisp Sunday morning, we test the bow and arrows in the safety of the wilderness.

Dad stands, legs spread apart for balance, one behind the other, with his shirt sleeves rolled up the elbows. He draws the bowstring back to the side of his mouth. There is a strange creaking sound akin to fingernails on a blackboard. Writhing muscles in my fathers forearm rise and twitch like electric sausages. His face contorts in a vile grin of effort, falling flaccid the instant the bow discharges and the arrow, with a screech of freedom, streaks away, thwacking straight through the walls of the old tar-paper pumping shed a hundred yards away.

"By Jove, that felt good! Do you want a shot, Will?"

He hands me the curve of tensioned yew and the keenly fletched arrow. I place the nock into the bowstring and draw back with all of my strength. To my chagrin, the bow hardly bends and I realize that the force required to pull the bow is far in excess of that keeping my sphincter in closed condition. On the verge of digestive disaster, I hand the weapon back to Dad with a half-apologetic smile.

"Och, no dishonor there, lad. It was all I could do to pull it myself. She's a tough one and no mistake!"

He shoots a second arrow up into the sky to test distance. It becomes a black dot that falls way out over the heron lake, where it disappears and is never found. I have visions of someone wearing it through their skull.

On the third firing the bowstring breaks.

"Oh, bugger! That was the strongest string the man in the shop had.

I think I'll have to trim some face wood off of the curve to ease the tension and make it more pliable."

That put an end to our archery caper, but it was fun while it lasted—even if I did nearly pooky my breeks. Dad is pleased with the experiment and sings an old ditty as we make our way home through the woods:

Here's to the bow,
The bow was made in England,
Of yew wood, of true wood,
The wood of English bows.

Directly over the road from the churchyard and down a little lane lies Finch's Fields. This is an undulating area of mysterious mounds, hillocks, and tumps. It has a quaint archaic feeling about it. A small tributary of the river Alne snakes through the rough green rises and its sandy banks are home to iridescent blue kingfishers, who build their tunneled nests in the soft earthen cliffs.

Fatty Roger and myself are convinced that one of these mounds contains a Viking longboat burial like the one discovered at Sutton Hoo, Suffolk, in 1939. This was thought to be the grave of King Raedwald of the East Angles, who died around A.D. 625.

We try unsuccessfully to excavate our mound; first into the top of it, then into the side, all to no avail. Alas, we know little about the sheer mass of impacted soil that required moving even to go down through one century in archaeological time line.

Though thwarted in our attempt, we still cling to the belief that there's something down there. And albeit this area is as far from the sea as you can get in Britain, we are sure it is a ship.

Summer comes and with it a posse of people in anoraks who divide up the field with wooden posts and lines of string. My father shows me a piece in the local paper. It reads: "Saxon burial ground discovered at Wootton Wawen!" There is no ship find, of course, but we have been vindicated in our conviction that this is indeed a tumulus. Roger and I go down to the dig and tell the attendant archaeologist that we have always known it was a burial site.

"Oh, yeah. Even the fool is wise after the event. What are you, psychics?"

"No, it's true! You can see where we tried to dig down over there!"

"Well, you could get into a lot of trouble, digging up archaeological sites without a permit. Now, bugger off! I've got work to do!"

"How did we know then, mister? A sixth sense maybe?"

"Listen, kids, that's a load of bollocks!"

"I don't care what you use to keep your ears apart, bollock brain!"

We run away giggling, but we were right! Perhaps we had absorbed some kind of feeling from the place. Maybe the knowledge was still in folk memory and we'd unwittingly picked up word of it from some idle overheard conversation or perhaps it was a lucky guess. I don't know. I ask my dad.

"You have a good point there, Will. I once heard author Laurie Lee talk about a tumulus near the village of Leonard Stanley in Gloucestershire. I think it was called Hetty Pegler's Tump. Lee asked his mother what it was and she told him, 'Oh, that's where the young prince is buried'. And sure enough, eventual archaeological investigation revealed the Bronze Age burial of a young warrior, who by his dress and grave goods must have been a nobleman or princeling some two thousand years before Christ. Yet that folk knowledge was handed down through some hundred and thirty-three generations, unmarred by time. A remarkable feat, indeed!"

"You're not kidding! But that university bloke down at the dig said we were talking bollocks, so he did!"

"Pay no heed to them geezers. You can have more degrees than a thermometer and still be as thick as shit! Mark my words."

Sitting at the kitchen table in the twilight of an amber setting sun, I study a Ordnance Survey map of the local area. Suddenly I realize that four of the ancient forts marked are in a dead straight line with each other.

"Hey, Dad, look at this! These old earthwork sites all line up! It's amazing!"

"Ah, ha! You've found a ley line! Just like Alfred Watkins, who wrote 'The Old Straight Track.' That's all about ley lines. You should read it!"

"Do we have that book, Dad?"

"No, we don't, but your granddad Jim had a copy. Maybe the library in Stratford might let you have one, if you lie about where you live."

"What are they, these ley lines?"

"Well, they seem to be ancient ways connecting significant points of the landscape—like standing stones, forts, tumuli, crossroads, and often churches that are built on old pagan sites like the one in Bleddfa."

"Oh, so people walked along from one landmark to another. But what are they looking for?"

"The folk years ago, for instance, had to travel to get salt, you know? It is a number one necessity and many people were paid in salt because it was so valuable. Hence the old terms 'To be worth your salt' or to 'Draw your salary.' Many of these ley lines terminate at a place called White Hill or Salt Hill because that's where the salt fairs are held at certain times of the Celtic year. Town names that end in *wich* are old salt sites, like Nantwich, Ipswich, Sandwich, and the like."

"Droitwich?"

"Yeah, that's the idea."

"So who was this Alfred Watkins? Was he a relative of some sorts? I've never heard tell of him before."

"Aye, he was a distant relation on your aunt Winnie's side, down in Hereford. A lovely part of the world. Great cider, the best! *Hhmm!*" Dad savors the thought before continuing. "They were the brewing side of the family and d'you know, the soldiers, on the eve of the Battle of Crécy in 1346, sang a fine old bawdy song called 'Watkins Ale'? Oh, yes! Watkins were the boys for making beer, all right. They had a brewery in Dublin, too, making stout! They sold it to Guinness in 1913, but it was destroyed by British shelling in the Easter Rising three years later."

"Aunt Winnie was in the last war, wasn't she?"

"Yes, she was a wireless operator with the Special Operations Executive, very hush-hush. Both she and her partner trained together so that they would always recognize the unique style of each other's Morse code."

"Why did they do that, then?" I try to get the creases of my map to fold in the right order.

"Well, this was very important, as one would be in Britain and the other parachuted behind enemy lines into occupied France working with the French resistance. If the operator and her code book were captured, the Germans might begin sending false information. The London-based operator could tell by the sound, or fist, as they call it, that the transmission was fraudulent. Every transmission had to contain a deliberate mistake, a Morse letter sent wrong, or the like. The Germans always tried to send perfectly. So if the fault wasn't there, the operators knew it was a fake transmission and sent back false information."

"I'd love to be a wireless operator and send Morse code like Auntie Winnie. She must have been very brave, don't you think?"

"She was and received a medal for it. What she was most proud of was being on Hitler's death list—here, give me that!" Dad takes my unruly map and folds it up like an expert.

"If you want to learn Morse code I can teach you myself. I did it in the army."

Fatty Roger and myself bike over to as many old forts and earth-works as we can find in the vicinity. Most are Celtic Iron Age hilltop forts from the period just before the Roman invasion. And sure enough, you can see the other forts way off in the distance in line of sight, some clear into Wales. At night, signal fires on these hilltops would be visible for miles, and, as a result, many such sites bear the name Beacon Hill.

I do my school project on local history.

> The castle mound at Beaudesert, in Henley-in-Arden, was hand built by the slave-labour of the Saxons, who had lost at the battle of Hastings in 1066. They were forced to erect a mote and bailey fortress for the famous Norman knight, Sir Simon de Montfort. He was very powerful and became the Earl of Leicester and leader of the Baron's parliament in London. All was well until he fell out with King Henry III whose ambitious son, Edward the first, killed him at the battle of Evesham in 1265. The Saxon word for slave-labour is graft and this word is still in common use today meaning, hard work.
>
> After the Norman invasion and the subjugation of

the Anglo-Saxons, two classes of English people emerge: the upper class; Barons, Earls, Knights, Lords and other gentry, and the peasant class; the once mighty Saxons now reduced to feudal bondage. The beasts of the field have Saxon names like; cows, sheep and pigs, but when killed and cooked for the table, become the Norman-French; beef, mutton and pork. The lesson is simple; the peasant class raise the animals, for the ruling class to eat.

Miss Hathaway loves my history project, but Mrs. Mack says that it sounds like *The Communist Manifesto*. I tell Dad this and he laughs his head off and says, "Good lad yourself!"

People were forever telling us to "Know your place!" and not to "Get above your station!" If you attempt to improve yourself in any way, you're told, "Don't ape your betters!" No doubt, this is a legacy of the bloody Magna Carta.

I hate to see old men doffing their caps when spoken to by one of the bigwigs.

My father treats the nobility with the same contempt as he does the royals and the clergy. "Nothing but a bunch of oxygen thieves and space wasters!"

One exception to Dad's "aristocrats to the guillotine" philosophy is old Lady Lucy. We first meet her when Dad gets a part-time job delivering soda pop to the outlying areas around Stratford-upon-Avon. I go along for the ride and it is a great way to see the lush green countryside. Miss Lucy lives in a massive ancient hall at Hampton Lucy and is a direct descendant of the Baron de Lucy, who came over from Normandy with William the Conqueror in 1066.

She has a beer ready for my dad and likes to chat with him. I think she admires his bluntness and total disregard for formality. I like to go to the hall with its wondrous expanse of gardens and wood-paneled rooms full of suits of armor. The kindly old lady tells me that she is the last of her line and when she dies the Lucy family name will die with her. She offers to adopt me and put the fear of beJasus into me.

Driving back home again in the old pickup truck, we pass through miles of orchards, their trees weighed down with apples. Dad begins reflecting on the many hundreds of apple varieties that have been lost since the Second World War with the shift to corporate farming policy.

"Potatoes, too. There were over four thousand species of the humble spud worldwide. Now some countries have whittled it down to a mere four or five kinds. I can remember one type of Scottish tattie called a Forfar, which was bright blue on the outside and a creamy yellow on the interior."

"It sounds a bit yucky to me! Blue and yellow mashed tatties? Ugh!"

"Naw lad, they were delicious! The same genetic destruction has happened to hops. Each town and village had its own brewery, you know? Likewise, its unique supply of hops. So as a result, each area of the country had a local type of beer, most likely differing from its near neighbors in texture, color, and taste. Marvelous it was! Both the local water supply and the indigenous ingredients would produce a singular brew that would be common to that region alone. And as the French wisely say, 'Vive la Différence!' " This last retort he shouts out of the window at a puzzled farmer as the ancient Bedford lorry hurtles through the Warwickshire countryside and disappears up a leafy lane.

The trip home is interrupted by a stop at the Dun Cow Inn just off the Stratford road near Wilmcote, a village of black-and-white half-timbered Tudor houses with elegant thatched roofs and tiny diamond-shaped, lead glass windows. This once was the home of the redoubtable Shakespeare, hence the name William's cote or William's hamlet.

The pub itself is contemporary with the Bard and was much frequented by him from all accounts. Near to the fireplace, a shallow depression has been worn in the ancient flagstone floor by the iron rings used in the game of quoits, a game rather like horseshoes. It's easy to imagine young Willie having a throw of quoits with his pals after a hard day of knocking out *Henry V,* part I, or *A Midsummer Night's Dream* and then wandering off to court my teacher's ancestor with his quill pen stuck nonchalantly behind his ear.

"No maiden has stole my heart, yet Anne Hath-a-way!" Dad mocks as he climbs into the cab and begins singing in a rich baritone:

Shakespeare was a very merry wit
And on his shirt tail was some sh . . . tea leaves

One day whilst walking by St. Paul's
A young girl grabbed him by his ba . . . shirt
Says he, "Young maid, you have a lot of pluck
Let's go round the back and have a fu . . . cup of tea."
This he did, then does a bunk
And leaves the young girl all covered in sp . . . tea leaves.

The green sunken lanes meander between soaring hedgerows studded with the lofty elm trees that almost obscure the sky. It's like driving through a leafy green tunnel.

"The old boreen. That's what your mam always says whenever we drive down one of these lanes."

"Talking of Mam, when are we going home?"

"Hang on, I think we're lost. Where in the name of the wee man are we?" Dad peers out of the cab of the battered lorry. The radiator hisses and sweats at the anonymous crossroads.

"I saw a sign back there, Dad, but it was overgrown with ivy and I couldn't read it."

"Yeah, I saw that too. We must be near Wellesbourn or somewhere round there—I have an idea!" He jumps down from the cab and puts his coat on inside out. He proceeds to walk three times clockwise around the truck, then jumps back in and speeds off down the left turn of the crossroads. Hardly two minutes pass when we break free from our prison of foliage onto the main road hard by Stratford horseracing track.

"What was all that about?" I ask as we pulled into the depot.

"The bloody fairies were leading us astray, Will! So I put my coat on inside out and by running sunwise around the truck, confused them so that they would leave us alone—and it worked!"

"What took you so long today, Reg?" the foreman asks, anxious to lock up the pop warehouse.

"We were away with the fairies, weren't we, Will?"

From the old Victorian railway station we take the train for our eight-mile trip to Wootton Wawen. I can see the horses limbering up for a run of some sorts. I ask Dad what they might be doing.

"Maybe there's a steeplechase on this weekend and they're training for it."

"Oh! Aren't they the old races they used to have between one town and another, over all the hedgerows, walls, and all that?"

"Yes, that's right. They raced between one town's church steeple and another, but now it's run over the hedge jumps and water jumps on the local racecourse. Your nana in Ireland is the one to talk horse racing with. I only bet on the Grand National apart from that day when I found the pound and bet on Lucky Note. Your nana likes to have a flutter every week!" Dad disappears behind his *Stratford Herald* newspaper.

This much I know. I remember asking Nana once how her horse had done in the big race at Leopardstown one Christmas.

"Jasus, that cripple—Godforgivemeforswearing! He was so far down the field he never saw so many arseholes in his life! Godhelpus! Sure he stopped to shit and he's shitting still!" She has a neat way with words, just like Mam.

"Ha ha ha!" I chuckle out loud at the thought of Nana's luck at the gee-gees. This involuntary machination coincides with the acidic pronouncement of one of two gossiping ladies who share our carriage.

"Men! They know nothing about pain, they don't, no! They have it easy, men do, yes! Yes! *Yes!* You may laugh, sir!" she intrudes, mistakenly aiming her remark at my innocent father. "You may laugh! But you have never endured the pain of childbirth, have you? Go on, admit it!"

"Very true," says Dad, folding his paper as the train pulls into Wootton station. "I have never experienced the pain of childbirth. However, you've never had to contend with a kick in the bollocks, have you, madam? Good day to you now!"

When we get back to the caravan Mam asks about our trip and I tell her about how we got lost and Dad doing the thing with his coat.

"Ah ha! An Seachdran na Si, the Fairy Straying. You were being fooled by the little people into getting yourselves lost. Jasus, it's a wonder they let you back! They could have kept hold of your father and turned him into an ogre. With an ugly puss like his, he'd be great for frightening the children at Halloween! Away with the fairies, eh? It used to happen a lot to my father when he drove the milk lorry for Cleaves's Creamery in Limerick—usually after a couple of glasses of the whiskey, so I hear!"

"Hey, Mam, while we were gone, Dad taught me a song"
"Oh, that's nice! Sing us a stave or two of it?"

Shakespeare was a very merry wit
And on his shirt tail he had some sh—

"Reg!"
Mam has her hand clamped tightly over my mouth.

✦ Chapter 14 ✦

A POLICEMAN IS STANDING AT THE CARAVAN DOOR.

"Can I speak to your dad?"

"Daaad?"

"Reg, your relief signal man has been killed in a line accident. Can you go in quick? There's no one on duty in the signal box."

"Oh, my God! The poor wee bugger. Yes, of course. I'll grab my coat." Dad looks at his pocketwatch. "Jasus! We'd better hurry. The Cornishman Express is due through in fifteen minutes and if the loop points aren't changed, she'll wreck!"

"Right, Reg, let's go. I can run you there in the squad car."

Bell trilling and blue lights flashing, the Wolsley six-eighty police car disappears up the track in a pall of cinder dust. Heart in my mouth, I count the minutes until, from a distance of two miles, I hear the Cornishman's steam whistle scream through Wootton Wawen station unscathed. Dad had saved the day and unbeknownst to driver and passengers alike, the West Country Express darts safely across the Midland plains to the high moors of Devon.

Dad has to work double shifts until a replacement can be found for the young chap who had been killed by the train.

"I'm on all over Christmas and New Year, too. You and Willie might as well go to Ireland, as I won't be seeing much of you."

"OK, we will, if you can get free passes in time."

"That won't be a problem with me getting the company out of a hole."

Later that week, I wave to my dad as the train passes the signal box. Dad waves back and pulls a daft face.

At Liverpool docks the wind is blowing sleet sideways into our faces. The sailing timetable carries the message "Morning sailing canceled due to bad weather." We have eight hours to kill before the night boat sails.

The wind is at our backs as we walk up Water Street, trying to find a decent restaurant to get breakfast. We stop at a neat little corner café called the Khardoma.

Mam watches the office girls shuffling through the rainy streets on their way to work. They are all dressed in the same drab way.

"Just look at us! We need a bloody good shake-up! The war has been over for fifteen years and you'd hardly know it. The fashions are almost unchanged since the nineteen thirties. This country needs a good fong up the arse to get it going, a bit of vigor, a bit of zest!"

We spend a few hours in the news theater watching *Casper the Friendly Ghost* and *Bugs Bunny*. Pathé News is showing the pictures of Mr. Kennedy, who is to become president of the United States in January. We eat ice cream and snooze in the dark cinema. The program repeats and we leave to take a wander around T. J. Hughes's department store.

"Do you want to see Father Christmas, Willie?"

"No, I don't. That's just for wee kids, Mam—I'm nearly eleven!"

"Oh, my, we are grown up. That Kennedy's a handsome bloke, isn't he? I could go for him m'self!"

"D'you know the priest came to our school and told us that right until the last minute it was neck and neck between Kennedy and the shifty-looking fella with the long face, and it was only our prayers that made the difference and that's how he won!"

"Maybe Father was right?"

"Well, I told Dad and he said the priest was full of shit!"

"Jesus! Willie, there's no need for language like that. Never mind what that pagan of a father says to you."

"What, the holy father?"

"No, the unholy one!"

We walk back downhill toward the docks, the wind hard against us. An icy squall slashes sleet in our eyes and we take shelter in a warehouse doorway while it blows through. Mam reads the event poster pasted to the door:

The Cavern Club Presents
THE SILVER BEATLES

"Jasus, fancy calling a pop group an ugly thing like that. Silver-beetles—makes them sound like a bunch of cockroaches! Jeeezus, creepy crawly things! They should change their name to something a wee bit nicer."

Somewhere out in the Toxteth area of Liverpool, John, Paul, George, and Ringo heed similar advice and a legend is born.

We sail out of the Mersey estuary into a fierce gale. Mam is taken bad and I get her some Lucozade to sip. It is very rough and the ship pitches and rolls. I doze off and am awakened by the ship's hooter. Alarm bells are ringing and crew members are hurrying on deck from all quarters.

"What's happening? Are we sinking?"

"You lie there and I'll find out, Mam."

I run on deck. Searchlights clip the waves in wide arcs about us. A lifeboat is being lowered, and I am scared for Mam, who's feeling so ill.

"Are we going down?"

"No, son, but some other poor bugger is!"

Officers are shouting from the bridge. "Clear the boats! Clear the boats!"

The door of the radio room is open. I peep in.

"Mayday relay! Mayday relay! Mayday relay! Steam ship *Irish Prince* sinking eight nautical miles west south west of the Skerries Light! All vessels please assist!"

The wireless man is talking into a microphone.

"Mayday relay! Mayday relay! This is the MV *Leinster*. We are at the scene and holding station. Boats are away for survivors. MV *Leinster* listening out."

The great ship is turning off the wind to keep the stricken vessel in her lee. I see red, green, and white lights flickering out in the heaving black swell. Ships of all shapes and sizes form a huge circle scanning the waves with their lee lights.

There are men in the water. Our boats are pulling them onboard. A full lifeboat returns to the ship, and figures, more dead than alive, are helped onto the deck, where they lie like drowned rats. Passengers and crew members get blankets around the shoulders of the survivors and help them in out of the wind. I bring cups of warm cocoa from the galley and give it to the steward who tends to the bedraggled men. I get hot coffee for the crew and another glucose drink for my ailing mother. When I get back to Mam's seat, she is being comforted by a dapper-looking chap with a transatlantic accent. I take him for a priest and go back on deck.

A gray dawn reveals the scene of the disaster. The sea is empty now except for a long slick of oil and some bobbing clumps of flotsam. The *Irish Prince* has gone down.

One by one the rescue ships break station, leaving the cold sea to digest its prey.

Mam and I spend the next day in Dublin. She says that she can't face the long train journey just yet, so we get a chance to explore. O'Connell Street is very wide and teeming with bicycles, green buses, horse-drawn carts of every size and cargo, and a few private motorcars. In the middle of the street, a policeman stands in a black-and-white pagoda, directing the milling traffic by means of a whistle, a nightstick, and a string of verbal abuse that would shame the demons of hell. The sidewalks, broad as they are, cannot contain the press of people surging through the capital city. At each street corner and intersection, human waves of fleet-footed pedestrians break over the vehicular traffic, bringing all motorized movement to a horn-honking halt. Henry Street and Moore Street are awash with shoppers threading their way through wheelbarrow stalls of open-air markets that haven't changed much since the days when Molly Malone sold her "cockles and mussels, alive alive-o." Here the din of car horns gives way to the clatter of horse hooves and the strident cries of street traders roaring from their market carts.

"Luvelly payers, tuppence a pownd! Appuls, payers, banawnas, pick yer own fer a shillin' a bag!" The costermonger's cry gives way to the greengrocer's chant from the next stall along . . .

"Padayshaws, tomayshaws, ingons an' leeks, get yer veggies here now, missus! Grand green cabbawges, finer never grew, cawleyflowers, carrots, an' kale, get yer King Edwards, luvelly spuds, great fer chippin', sixpence a pownd!"

Tinker kids and other street urchins dive under the cart wheels to retrieve fallen vegetables and discarded bruised fruit. These they share with the tired-looking donkeys and cart horses tethered down the side streets awaiting the long pull home.

Two hundred and twelve feet above the hubbub, Admiral Lord Nelson's one good eye surveys the chaotic scene from his lofty stone column. His statue, identical to the one in London, marks the last remnant of the British occupation of Ireland.

Mam buys a punnet of fresh strawberries and we make our way back up to the main street to the bullet-scarred general post office building in the city center.

"This is where Patrick Pearse read the Proclamation of Independence in 1916."

"They shot him, didn't they?"

"They did—BloodyEnglish!"

Mam describes the Rising of 1916, when fifteen hundred poorly armed men and women rose in revolt against the might of the British Empire.

"The GPO was the first building the rebels seized. They made it their headquarters. The rest of the Irish Volunteers and Citizen Army were scattered in little units all around Dublin. They fought all week until the British shelled every building in the city and the GPO was burning around their ears. Then Pearse and James Connolly surrendered to save further loss of life."

"What happened then?"

"The British took them to Kilmainham jail and shot them for treason." She recites:

> The beauty of this world hath made me sad
> This beauty that will pass
> Sometimes my heart hath shaken with great joy
> To see a leaping squirrel in a tree
> Or a red ladybird upon a stalk

Or little rabbits in a field at evening
Lit by a slanting sun.

"That's a beautiful poem, Mam. Whose is it?"

"They are the last lines of Patrick Pearse, written on the eve of his execution."

"Oh, what a shame."

Mam sees my sad face and makes to cheer me up. At the Rainbow Café she buys me some pop called 7-Up. I've never heard of it before and when it comes, there is a large scoop of vanilla ice cream floating in it, which is very strange, but nice. Over the foaming glass I quiz my mother.

"Why did the rebels take over the post office? Surely the castle would be a better headquarters?"

"Well, the rebels tried to capture the castle, but were beaten back by the British. The GPO was a very important target, with its telephones and telegraph. It was the crossroads of communication for the whole country. In the olden days, people out in the country would stand at the crossroads for hours, waiting for travelers to come along with word of what was happening elsewhere. Since the roads went north, east, west, and south, the information they picked up was called 'news.' I bet you didn't know that, did you, Willie?" I have to admit that I didn't, but my father's oft-used call of "Encyclopedia Bullshitus Hibernicus" echoes in the back of my mind.

Leaving the café, we head west from O'Connell Bridge into a setting sun. Under an orange sky, streaked with mackerel clouds, we stroll down Bachelor's Walk and along the length of Ormond Quay. Brewery tugs pull barges stacked high with wooden barrels of Guinness under the gray wrought iron arch of the ha'penny bridge and down to the docks beyond. Bathed in the honey-hued gloaming of an Irish sunset, the great green dome of the shrapnel-pocked Four Courts shimmers up from the surface of the turgid, dark waters of the rolling river Liffey. Our walk up to Kingsbridge rail terminus is pleasant and unhurried. The train doesn't leave until six-thirty and the Angelus bell has still not called the faithful to six o'clock prayer.

At the newspaper kiosk in the railway station, an *Irish Independent* banner headline proclaims: "President Kennedy to Visit Ireland." Mam nudges me.

"Lookit! The first Christian president of the United States of America and he's coming home to the Ould Sod. Isn't that grand?"

"How is he the first Christian? I thought the others were Christians, too."

"Hmm! They were all Protestants! Nothing but pagans, so they were, except Abraham Lincoln. I think he might have been a Jew, with the beard and the big hat an' all."

"Could my dad be president of the USA? He's a pagan and you call him an old sod?"

"That's different. Yer dad can't be president because he's not an American, and anyway, he's going bald and the Yanks like their leaders to have a fine head of hair!"

"Eisenhower doesn't have much hair."

"That's his military haircut. Anyway, he was a soldier and wore a peaked cap."

"My dad has a peaked cap."

"HolyJasusWillie! Would ye ever stop yer nonsense? Ye'll have me worn out. Come on, there's our train." We board and lo and behold—

"Hello, Monica! How are you feeling? Good. This must be Liam. We never got a chance to say hi, with you helping out with the rescue an' all."

It's the American bloke from the boat and he's no priest! He hangs on my mother like an old coat. This makes me jealous and I keep mentioning my dad. Eventually the interloper feels obliged to say something.

"You're very proud of your dad, ain't you, young fella?"

"Yes, I am, and if he wasn't a bald, godless pagan, he could be your next president!"

The Limerick Express speeds into the evening shadows spreading stealthily across the Curragh of Kildare. My mother is flattered by the attentions of the American gentleman and as it's his first trip to Ireland, she fills him in on odd bits of history, mostly from her own "Irish Encyclopedia." He asks us if we want a drink, as the buffet car is now open. Mam says she would like a gin and tonic, and I ask for a Canada Dry with ice. Whether the man misheard me, or the order is placed wrong, I don't know. He brings me back a double Canadian rye whiskey on the rocks. I duly drink it down, and by the time we get to Limerick Junction, I'm half langers.

Mam's friend changes trains here and says good-bye. I give a half-hearted wave out of the window.

"Oh, Willie! Stop being a prat. I wasn't flirting with him. We were just passing the time of day. Mind you, he was a handsome bloke and he must have plenty of money. He said he was in oil!"

"What was he, a bloody sardine?"

"Willie!"

I sleep for a long while at Nana's house. When I rise on the second day, my family are all there just as before. Nana, Seán, and Frances look as I remember, but the room has somehow shrunk. The kitchen light switch is at eye level and my green spindle-backed chair looks too tiny to have ever flown me through the First World War. In the garden shed, my *Captain Biggles* comic lies on the bench, tattered and yellowed by time. I feel a lump in my throat.

Across the road, the Shannon still courses its boiling flood, and the seagulls spin above me watching my every hand movement to see if I have scraps for them. I do have a lump in my throat and it's sore, too. Inside the house I stare at the little gray gas meter, whilst Mam flattens my tongue with a lollipop stick and pronounces, "Your throat is swollen up. We'd better get the doctor."

I have the mumps.

"Live horse and you'll get grass!" Mam sits on the end of my bed while I try to eat a bowl of strawberries and ice cream. The coldness feels great on my throat and helps ease the throbbing pain. The smell of the Christmas dinner that is to be denied me wafts up the stairs. I nod off to sleep.

"Oh my sainted aunt! Will ye ever look at poor Willie?" Mam is holding up the bedclothes and with me lying there bollick naked, everyone is getting a look at my willie!

"Jasus! He's covered from head to foot with red blotches!" All my family have their own diagnosis.

"It's the scarlet fever!"

"'Tis the measles, so it is!"

"I've had the measles."

"It's the German measles!"

"I've had the German measles, too."

"It's the Irish measles, then!"

"Go'way with your measles! It's obvious—he's allergic to strawberries."

This is the first indication I'd had that strawberries are bad for me. Uncle Seán is right. When my mumps have gone away, I try some strawberries again and come up in spots within the hour.

Christmas passes without me. New Year comes and goes, but with Grandda gone there are no music sessions in the tiny kitchen. I find the end piece of his wooden flute in amongst the slabs of turf in the peat store.

"Where's the rest of it?"

"I dunno, probably burned."

Sadly I remember how lovingly Grandda looked after his blackthorn flute. How he would talk to it, and put it to bed wrapped in a red cloth, and pour Guinness into the barrel of it to sweeten the tone, and the fluttering flurries of soft notes falling gentle on the ear—jig, reel, slip-jig, and slide. Majestic march, noble air, mournful lament—all gone, gone forever.

I am ill for a long time and miss a fair bit of schooling, but eventually Mam pronounces me "as fit as a butcher's dog" and says it's time to go back to Wootton and see how Happy Harry is getting on without us. We have a last family outing to the Thomond Cinema to see *The Mask of Zorro,* and it's a great laugh as usual. People sit chewing on boiled pig's feet wrapped in newspaper and shout warnings and encouragement to the hero on the silver screen.

"Don't come in—he's behind the door!"

"Kick his head in!"

"Look out, Zorro—he's got a knife!"

"Shoot the buggers!"

And when the fighting is done and the masked marauder sweeps the girl into his arms, "Get awayoutadat, ya durty ould sod. Sure she's not old enough to leave her mother!"

Or alternatively, "Give her a tongue in the lung for me, Zorro!"

✦ Chapter 15 ✦

THE YEAR OF OUR LORD 1961 IS A GOLDEN YEAR BECAUSE, like 1001, 1111, 1691, and 1881, it reads the same upside down. It is a special year for me, too, as I have to take the eleven-plus examination. This compulsory exam decides your future at the absurdly early age of eleven, just when you're catching every bug and disease in the devil's armory. I've lost so much school that I have as much chance of doing well as a fart on a windy day.

Should I pass, I could go on to grammar school, college, and maybe even university, but if I fail, I'll have to go to secondary school until I'm fifteen and eligible for a dead-end job in some factory, or, if I'm lucky, an apprenticeship to a tradesman. Mam does a novena to St. Jude, he of lost causes, but he's still at enmity with me over finding the threepenny bits that time and cocks a deaf ear to Mother's pleas. Ah, but junior school can be boring anyway, and there are mighty things happening in the world.

Two important walls are built in this historic year: the first in Berlin, where President Kennedy, who only got elected because we prayed for him, will cry out in Cold War defiance, "Ich bin ein Berliner!" which to the crowds of puzzled Germans listening means, "I am a doughnut!" The second and more notable wall is built by my father and his pal, "Dustbin Tom," around the newly opened Sabrina Gardens annex of the trailer park.

This masterpiece of medieval engineering is two dustbins high and two hundred dustbins long. It contains twenty-five dustbins full of cement and countless dustbins full of rough field stone.

Like Laurel and Hardy before them, Dad and Dustbin Tom work on the tried and tested principle of "When I nod my head, you hit it!" It's a rare delight for us kids to watch the antics of these pair of eejits, clowning around in their Herculean labors for our amusement.

Dustbin Tom's only form of measurement is the dustbin. Even the scaffolding takes the form of two wooden planks laid across two galvanized metal dustbins. Unlike its more famous German predecessor, this wall is welcomed by all and stands as a great memorial to good old-fashioned shoddy workmanship and sacred measurement.

On a silvery moonlit night, not long after the completion of the mighty wall, I dress as Zorro in a mask and cape and for sheer devilment climb up to lie in hiding along the top of the dustbin wall.

My plan is to leap down and "Zorro" the first person to walk past by making a Z shape in the air with my car antenna rapier.

The problem is, nobody comes. I am just about to give up, when I hear hesitant footsteps coming down the path from the direction of the Country Club bar.

Perfect! An old drunk!

As the footfalls come right under my hiding place, I leap down, shrieking, "The mark of Zorro!" My rapier makes a Z in the air.

My unfortunate victim is not the reeling drunkard I was expecting, but the refinedly inebriated and elderly ex-actress, Mrs. Ayers. In her fright, she lets out a high warbling sound and, in a fit of the vapors, faints clean away! I take to my heels and don't stop until I get safely away and out of my Zorro garb.

The poor woman, on regaining her wits, is helped back to the bar, where she is plied with several double gin and tonics as she tells the incredulous customers that she has been attacked by "The Laughing Cavalier."

For the next few weeks I lie low as groups of vigilantes comb the night for prowlers, thieves, and footpads. My voluntary incarceration yields unsuspected benefits. Instead of roaming the caravan site looking for mischief, I spend the evenings working on household projects with my dad.

"This," says Dad, holding up a glass tube with three wires coming out of it, "is an EY51 EHT rectifier valve and it's buggered!" I am on all fours, staring into the back of an ancient television set.

"How do you know that's what's wrong with this thing, Dad?"

"Well, if this was all right, we would have a very high voltage on the tube anode—and we haven't, have we?"

We'd never had a TV of our own, but relied on Dad fixing one for a neighbor and us holding on to it for a few days to soak test it!

Later that day, Dad comes back from Stratford with a new tube, which we solder in, and the old TV set that I've dragged back from the rubbish tip bursts into life.

"A TV for three and six. That's a good price and no mistake!" Mam is pleased.

I find an old radio set at the rubbish dump and marvel at the pretty little multicolored bands on the resistors and the funny wee wax things called capacitors.

Dad comes in from the pub while I'm playing with it.

"Willie, what is a microfarad?"

"I don't know, Dad."

"Find out and tell me tomorrow."

I do and I'm able to tell him it is a unit of electrical capacitance. He is very pleased.

Dad, true to his word, builds a small one-tube practice oscillator from spare parts given up from the old radio and teaches me to send and receive Morse code.

I take on a fierce bent for anything scientific. Mam presents me with a belated Christmas present, a small microscope. I have great fun studying leaves, crystals, fleas, and the like.

Dad's Christmas bonus helps buy a power × 45 refracting telescope. With the aid of this beautiful instrument, I am at last able to transport myself way past this solar system and into the galaxies beyond. Nebulae, star clusters, planets, and lunar craters all become familiar as I spend night after night out in the frosty darkness seeking the rings of Saturn or Jupiter's moons.

My parents now have me looking into two cosmos at once, the macro and the micro, each as fascinating as the other and strangely similar in design.

In the daytime I turn the kitchen of our little caravan into a makeshift laboratory, where I conduct experiments with my chemistry set. My father says it is like living with Doctor Frankenstein, but I think they enjoy having a son who seems interested in the whys and wherefores of the physical world.

He laughs and quotes Kipling:

I keep six honest serving men,
They taught me all I knew.
There names are What? and Why?
And When? and Where? and How? And Who?

If necessity is the mother of invention, then I'm its bastard child! What started out as a small toddler taking his tin toys to bits with a spoon has become a series of full-scale operations. The motorbike engines, TV chassis, gramophones, telephones, and car gearboxes all give up their secrets, as the mounting piles of junk outside our caravan will attest. I drive my poor mother to the edge of distraction.

"For God's sake, Willie, you've used up all the margarine getting that grease off your hands and you've wiped the mess on a clean towel."

"Sorry, Mam. I'll give you a hand!"

I try to help tidy up and accidentally spill potassium permanganate all over the kitchen table, turning the starched white tablecloth a brilliant purple. Meanwhile my experiment bubbling on the stove produces hydrogen sulfide, the bad egg gas, stinking the entire place out. In an attempt to clear the atmosphere, I plug in an electrical fan that I'd found in the rubbish dump. This blows the fuses and plunges the caravan into darkness.

"OUT! Out, ya demon! Out before you kill us all with yer nonsense!"

Nothing, however, is impossible to the mind of the alchemist as I transmute my intellect from its base form into sublimation. I once make an egg custard pudding disappear from the oven, but I'm not sure how I did that! Ah, the quintessence of it all 'twould get the rise out of a dead man. It is grand to be young!

With spring comes the urge to venture back out into world of wickedness that I had shunned throughout the long winter nights. The game was afoot.

Neil Allen would be just in his early teens when his dad gives him an old wrecked car to play about in. It is an Austin 7 and, though it can only boast of two gears, one of which is reverse, it is a lot of fun and we all get our first shot at driving.

Most of our weekend games are precipitated by what we see at the cinema or increasingly on the television. This week we have been exposed for the first time to the American gangster series *The Roaring Twenties*.

We had all seen Edward G. Robinson in *Little Caesar* and George Raft and Humphery Bogart doing their tough-guy stuff. My favorite is James Cagney. I love all his films! "I'm on top of the world, Ma!"

Parents' closets are raided for trilby hats or fedoras and anything resembling a zoot suit. Our little mob, who last weekend had been ridding the local trees of Japanese snipers after seeing John Wayne in *The Sands of Iwo Jima,* having been demobilized into civilian life have immediately taken to a career of crime.

We cut a bizarre picture dressed in our oversized suits with wide-brimmed hats that obscure our faces. We chew imaginary gum.

"Hiya, Mack, how ya doin'!"

"Aw, it's been tough. I'm getting rubbed up the wrong way by the Feds."

We adopted new names. There is Scarface, Bugsy, Lefty, Dutch, and Dillinger. I am Dillinger. Sasha Dutton doesn't want to play as the only hoodlum names left are Pretty-Boy Floyd and Baby-Face Nelson, both of which he thought soppy.

"I can't be a gangster with a poof's name!"

"Let me fix him, Boss! I'll mess him up good! He won't need a name!!"

"Nah, nah, Lefty! We'll get some udder shmuck ta do da doity woik. Maybe we'll tell the mob on the east side that he's a stool pigeon for the cops!"

"Ah, come on, guys, I only want a proper gangster name!"

"OK, you can be . . . Hitler!"

"Hitler wasn't a bloody gangster!"

"Well, he was a bad guy anyway! So do you want to play or not?"

"OK, Hitler it is. Anything's better than Baby-Face!"

History turns on its head as Adolf Hitler becomes the latest member of the Chicago mobsters underworld.

We next check our stock of shooters. I have my trusty .22 rifle loaded with blanks, Neil has brought a .410 single and a 12-gauge double-barreled shotgun with six dressed cartridges each, "Dutch" Dutton has his Webley air pistol, and "Lefty" is carrying a wartime souvenir German Luger that mercifully has no ammunition for it.

After the incident in the woods, some time ago, we had stopped using live rounds when playing about with guns. Shotgun shells are rendered almost harmless by "dressing" open the ends and removing the lead shot, but you can still get a sting from the wadding.

We don't want to hurt anyone, though. Our sole object is to look mean and make a lot of noise, and this, like the little hoodlums we are, we achieve!

The ancient prewar automobile is a total heap and has no exhaust pipe. Its one remaining headlamp is permanently on and the under-inflation of its bald tires gives it the appearance that it waddles along rather than glides. We are supposed to drive it only in the fields or on the back roads of the trailer park, but it runs better on the paved roads and temptation is readily succumbed to by our fearless mob of outlaws.

After tearing around at fifteen miles an hour with the engine screaming for release, the radiator boils over and we are obliged to stop for a while to let it cool down.

It is then that we hear the church bells.

"Hey, O'Donnell! What's going on over at the chapel?"

"Oh, that's a wedding! They asked me to be an altar boy. I told them to stick it."

"Yeah, they asked me, too! But we're too tough to be altar boys, eh, lads?"

"Yeaah!" We spit on the ground and suck on pieces of fennel stalk like they're cigarettes.

There are times in one's life when some inner demon takes complete control of the good sensibilities of the human condition. This is to be one such occasion.

The radiator has stopped hissing, and at last we speed off on our lurching way, down Spook's Path to the old church.

The wedding party is just out of the service and is lining up between the front of the church and a large tripod camera. Here they are going to record their day to remember.

Birds sing in the yew trees, and the sun pours down on the happy couple.

"Watch the birdie!" says the photographer, as he vanishes in under his black-cloaked box camera.

The rows of teeth frozen in cheesy smiles melt into looks of astonishment as a battered car full of 1920s gangsters flies round the corner and screeches to a halt, blocking the church drive and sending a black cloud of rooks squawking from the yew trees above.

"YOU BIN ASKING FOR DIS, YOU DURTY RATS!!!"

A sustained volley of deafening gunshots rings out over the quiet serenity of the Warwickshire countryside.

To our absolute joy the entire wedding party is routed at the first broadside.

In their haste to gain the sanctuary of the moss green gravestones, members of the wedding leave top hats, high-heeled shoes, flowers, wedding gifts, and invitations scattered like confetti all over the green church lawn.

"That guy there's a G-man—let him have it, boys!"

All guns turn on the verger. We blast a parting salvo in the direction of the cowardly Timmins, who throws up his arms as if he's been hit. He drops behind an old ivy-covered tomb, whilst his pebble-like glasses curve a glinting arc in the dappled light.

"Call the police!! Someone call the police!"

"Let's get the hell out of here!"

We jerk the car around in a wide circle, decimating Timmins's bicycle in the process, and blaze off in the same direction from which we have come.

This is to be my last hurrah! We have been a nuisance far too long and what little sympathy we have amongst the site dwellers after the Grumpy episode has long since dissipated. It is decided, by the powers that be, that the time has come to bell the cat!

The village policeman, Copper Smith, rounds us up. We are disarmed and told if ever we are caught with weapons again, we will all be sent to the local Borstal prison institution for young offenders. To the great satisfaction of the wedding guests, we are lined up in the hall car park and publicly flogged. It is a barbaric but bloody effective punishment, and we vow to keep our noses clean, for a wee while anyway!

Neil, being the oldest and the ringleader, gets the worst of it and we don't see him for the rest of the summer. Poor "Hitler," even though he took no part in the actual shooting, got a licking just for being along for the ride.

"If this had gone to court, it would have been very bad for you idiots. Having a serious incident on your record at your age is no good thing, especially when it concerns firearms!" The cops get into their car and leave. Maybe Dad has picked up on his long-outstanding favor from the police, I don't know.

I inch my way painfully out of the car park, the red weals of the cane cut like the furrows of a horse-plowed field across the horizon of my arse. Paul catches up with me, mournfully holding his backside.

"God's teeth, that was a rough old paggering!"

"Too damn right, but what was worse was seeing that wee shite Timmins gloating! He blooming well fainted with fright back at the church!"

"Yeah, I saw him smirking all over his kisser. Mind you, he's probably not seen his bicycle yet!" I almost laugh.

There is an age-old saying, "If things don't alter, they'll remain as they are." The first news comes in the post. I have failed my eleven-plus with flying colors, mostly because of my inability to grasp the mathematics of the vegetable kingdom. The second and more surprising announcement comes from Mrs. MacArthur.

"Our school will close this summer and will not reopen. You will all be transferred to a nice modern Catholic school in Henley-in-Arden that is being newly built—all except you eleven-year-olds, who will be going on to a high school or a grammar school, depending on your exam results. It has been a pleasure teaching you all. Good luck, everyone, and God bless you!"

That is it. Later in the summer, just before the holidays, Mr. Bury presides over the destruction of the school's property. It is every child's dream to burn his or her school's contents. Now we were doing it under the supervision of the staff. Out-of-date books, out-of-fashion teaching papers, and out-of-the-Ark blackboard easels feed the conflagration as the enormous bonfire in the playground consumes all that has been so familiar to us. There is kind of a carnival atmosphere and everyone is very elated. I feel odd, seemingly heavy in the heart. At one point, I catch the eye of the headmistress, Mrs. Mack. She looks over to me and smiles. Somehow I know at that moment, we both have the same feeling of loss. There is a tear running down her cheek. Maybe she wasn't so tough after all.

So it comes to pass that our four-hundred-year-old school ceases to be a quaint anachronism in the brave new world. The little academy, which has seen Henry the Eighth ax the monastery and convert the flour store into a schoolhouse, is lost and gone forever.

Concrete-and-steel brutalism is to be the future of secondary schools.

As I say good-bye to Miss Hathaway, I notice for the first time how frail she is and wonder if she was always like that.

I go to shake hands with Mrs. MacArthur, but she gives me a hug.

"It's three o'clock. School's over, you can go home now."

"Will you teach at the new school, miss?"

"No, we ladies are both retiring. It won't be the same without hearing the cry, 'Willie Watkins did it!' Will it, Miss Hathaway?"

"Indeed not, Head."

I turn to the now unemployed, hapless, and harmless Mr. Bury. I feel melancholy and slightly guilty that we have taunted this poor chap, whose only sin was to try and ease some erudition into our thick heads. Guilt? Melancholy? Quare types of feelings for a young lad to entertain surely, but the history of this place hangs as heavy in the air as the smoke from the bonfire. We shake hands. I feel this is an opportunity to apologize for some of my past misdemeanors, but decide instead to pull his leg one last time.

"What will you do, sir?"

"I don't know yet. Maybe I'll apply for a job at the new school in Henley or maybe go and teach abroad for a while."

"Oh, like in Greece, maybe? I hear a lot of young teachers go over there." He shoots a nervous look at the headmistress. She doesn't take any notice. I give him a friendly thumbs-up and venture inside for a last look.

I stand for a while in the empty halls that were once filled with the hoots and stampedes of Scottish country dancing. Gone now, the swish of the bamboo cane. Silent, the cries of anguish from punished children. Hushed, the hysterical laughter at Mr. Bury's madcap antics, and stilled forever, the buzz of learning.

Certainly, I won't miss the waffling of the old parish priest droning on like a frustrated bumblebee about impure thoughts and about our parents not giving enough to the Sunday collection plate. I've finished with that load of bollocks.

Standing on a rickety old stool, I unpin my motley paper soul from the wall and inspect the blots of my past misdemeanors.

"Hm, not too bad. There's still a wee bit of white showing up there in the top righthand corner! I can't be such a bad chap after all! Sure didn't I steal *The Secret of the Old Mill* and keep the book for three weeks to see if God would strike me down—and then put it back when nothing happened! Maybe I didn't keep it long enough? Or more likely, God knew I was going to give it back anyway, so couldn't be arsed punishing me."

I wander into the infants' room and marvel at the tiny desks and the wee chairs where once we struggled with adding carrots and dividing apples.

Crossing the threshold into the daylight, dreamily aware of the other threshold I'm crossing, I stand for the last time in the tree-lined playground. Either way, I am certain of one thing: that old school bell would never ring again.

Walking past my school chums, I put my soul on the embers of the bonfire and watch it smolder, spin skyward and flutter, sparking over the beech trees and into the river. Then without further ado, shouting a general farewell to all, I leave the little medieval school and the Catholic education system forever.

✦ Chapter 16 ✦

"COME ON, INSIDE WILLIE! YOUR FATHER AND I WANT A SERIOUS talk with you."

"Oh, Jasus! They're putting me up for adoption!"

"Am I in trouble?"

"No more than usual," says Dad smiling. He continues: "The Warwickshire County Council are offering to rehouse us in a proper house. They're trying to relocate people off of these caravan sites and into new homes with modern amenities. There would be hot water, a bathroom with a toilet, your own bedroom, and a real kitchen with a cooker, a washing boiler, and everything."

I try to tell them that I'm happy where I am, but their minds are made up and they have convinced themselves it's all for my own good.

"When will we be going?" I tremble at the reply, thinking of my friends and the wonderful life of nonsense and childish pranks that I would be leaving behind.

"Oh, not for ages yet."

"Good!" I says, and skipping out of the door I promptly forget all about it.

I spy Mike and Paul, two of my erstwhile confederates, lurking about by the service entrance to the big Georgian hall.

"What are youse lot up to?"

"Shoosh!" They are listening at the window of the site office.

"What's going on?"

Paul takes me conspiratorially aside. "I was in the office with my mum this morning, to pay the site rent. Anyway there's these three geezers in there talking to old Mr. Rice about *ghosts!* So I starts to *ear-*

wig and it turns out they're from the Sigh-kick Phenomenal Society and they're coming here to investigate the ghost of Lady Fitzherbert, better known as the Gray Lady."

"Oooh, there's great possibilities of a good wheeze looming large here! When are they coming?"

"Friday night, and they're staying for the weekend."

I give Mike, still listening at the window, the thumbs-up and add, "We must think of a good ruse to fool the Hun."

"We will, by crikey! We haven't had a good wheeze since we got the flogging."

Now, I know the Georgian hall inside and out. I have many times sat daydreaming on the elegant great oak stairway, waiting for my pal Mark to come out of his parents' apartment to play. I've always felt curiously at home in this Mecca of silk tapestries, marble fireplaces, Greek urns, and gilt-framed masters. Alone in the richness of the mahogany-paneled rooms, I have watched the sunlight dappling through the huge stained-glass staircase windows in a million prismatic fingers, savored the smell of the old beeswax-polished edifices, and I drink deep from the chalice of antiquity.

I have never seen the Gray Lady and no credible person to my knowledge has. "But she's there!" we are told by the old ones in hushed tones.

"Dad, do you believe in ghosts and the like?"

"You worry about the buggers who walk around this earth on two feet and don't be bothering yer head about any old spooks or such nonsense!"

Well, that is good enough for me. The plot thins. If my dad thinks there is nothing to be scared about, then we can enter into our dastardly plan unfettered by fear of the hereafter. "From ghosties and ghoulies and long-leggedy beasties and things that go bump in the night, may the Good Lord deliver us!" sayeth the ould Scottish prayer.

Once more the game is afoot!

Lady Maria Anne Fitzherbert had a secret—and so does the ancient, ivy-wreathed hall. Although she and the Protestant Prince of Wales, later to be Gearge IV, were secretly married, the union was illegal under the Royal Marriage Act of 1772, and Maria Anne was shunted to the sidelines when George made a legal marriage in 1795.

Wootton Hall, like so many stately homes of the eighteenth century, has a priest hole! This contrivance manifests itself in a secret underground passage from the hall to the old church. By means of this, the priest can give the banned sacraments to the Catholics in the household, under the very noses of the king's militia. Also, if caught in attendance on the papist sympathizers, he can make his ecumenical escape through the tunnel, just like a rat up a drainpipe.

This priest hole, we think would be the epicenter of the psychics' endeavors, and so we prepare to lay a trap.

I know the layout in the labyrinthine maze of underground passageways that make up the service basement of the old mansion. Oftentimes I have accompanied my dad as he stokes the main boiler when the caretaker is on holiday. Forearmed with this intelligence, we will wait until the ghost hunters are set up and then creep in and give them a fright to remember!

I have an old McMichael valve wireless that suffers from incurable I.F. instability. The frequency-changer tube has an internal short that, as it warms up, causes the entire radio set to oscillate in a most ghoulishly entertaining fashion. The resultant unearthly screeches, wails, and screams would put the heart crossways in the pope himself.

Our simple ruse is to preposition this old radio in the priest hole tunnel with a long length of twin flex running back to a mains outlet. Here, at the crucial time, when they call out "Is there anybody there?" we can switch on the caterwauling apparatus and run away giggling.

It is time to do a reccy. We need firsthand intelligence of where and what our prospective dupes will be doing. Unnoticed, our little team of Paul, Mike, and myself slips quietly into the service door of the great hall and presses forward to the inner basement door. Down into the dark abyss of the cellars we slowly ingress, like three souls descending into Anwyn, the Celtic underworld.

There is a long, dank passageway to the right that leads to the priest's hole. We turn the corner, and miraculously a light comes on. I look around, but none of us has touched a switch. There is none to be seen anywhere. We walk on through the ancient asbestos-lagged perplexity of heating pipes and archaic overhead electrical wiring. Reaching the old well, still full to the brim and incalculably deep, we hesitate. For a second we think we can hear the sound of whispers, and not too far off either! Inching forward along the wall, hardly breathing through a bristling silence so profound that the relieved sigh of a defecating rat would be clearly audible, we make our snail-like progression toward the door of the priest's hole.

"This is it!" I whisper, swallowing hard. My saliva seems to taste like frothy lemonade, and my ears are hissing with the crackling excitement of it all. Paul's huge brown eyes look like dinner plates, and Mike has a face as white as a ghost's arse! Lighting our bicycle lamps, we swing open the iron door, which replies with a spine-shuddering creak.

We step over the threshold into the rank smell of decayed soil and the lifeless humors of a long-dead tunnel. Much to my surprise, there's already a wire running along the dirt-strewn floor! As we creep nearer, I see a thing that I recognized to be a microphone sitting on a tripod. I reach out to touch it—

"Aaaaagh! Aaaaaagh! Aaaagggh!" Mike is screaming, his face completely enveloped in a giant spider's web whose disgruntled owner is still at home and biting.

Paul is already running for the exit, emitting a high warbling whimper. This all put the dread of the Devil into me, and fearing the loss of my immortal soul, I lapse into the old Latin and blurt out, "Pater noster, qui es in coelis: santificétur nomen tuum . . ." My teeth-chattering chant fades as I flee the accursed tunnel with my terrified companions. With a rush like a hot spring's geyser, we erupt into the daylight and stand in a trembling triangle staring at each other. For several minutes we drink in enormous drafts of cold clean air, then without a word, shamefacedly, make our way home. This almost became the ruse that never was, but fate had a trick up her sleeve.

"Well, there's a thing!" Dad is reading the local paper. "Do you remember those loonies from the big city who were looking for spooks here a while back? Well, they reckon they may have found proof of a murder of a young woman by a Catholic priest!"

"Go'way! Lemme see!" says Mam, peering over his shoulder with interest.

"It says that the microphone they left secretly in the priest's hole recorded footsteps and weird muffled whispers, then the old rusty door opening, and a woman's horrible screams mixed with whimpering like a lost soul—and to cap it all, the definite voice of a Catholic priest or old monk chanting away to himself in Latin! Maybe there's something in it after all?"

"Do you believe in ghosts now, Dad?"

"There are more things in heaven and earth, Horatio, than were ever dreamed of in your philosophy!" Dad replies mysteriously, and, as usual, I have little idea what he is talking about. He throws the *Stratford Herald* onto the table.

Mam picks up the paper; on page three there's a picture of the pope.

"Oh, that's a shame. It says here that the Vatican is to do away with the Latin mass. The service will be in the language of the country. That's a scandal so it is, a downright shame!"

"And why would that be, woman?"

"Because it will be in bloodyEnglish and God won't understand a word of it, that's why. Sure, he only speaks Latin—and Gaelic of course!"

"Of course!" Dad raises his eyes to the home of the bilingual God.

"I learn Latin at school, Dad."

"And a fat lot of good it will do you this day an' age. You're hardly likely to bump into a passing Roman centurion, are you? But if you do, be sure to say 'Quo Vadis!'"

"That means where are you going, doesn't it, Dad?"

"It do! So if he doesn't know where he's going, tell him. Nil desperandum et nil carborundum illegitimi."

"I've never heard that phrase. What's it mean, Dad?"

"It means, 'Despair not and don't let the bastards grind you down.'"

"Reg! Stop poisoning the child's mind with your pagan nonsense and your filthy language. All I said was, that it will be a shame when the Tridentine mass is no longer celebrated, that's all."

"Why is it called the Tridentine mass, Mam?"

"Ask your clever bollix of a father!"

"Well, Will, it's because most of the silly old sods in the congregation only have three teeth between the lot of them."

"Jasus, Reg! I'll have no more of this—get out of here before I scatter you, by Christ, you spawn of Beelzebub. Out, out, you bloody heathen!"

Mam beats my father around the table and out the door with the rolled-up newspaper. Dad runs shrieking into the night with several inky images of the Holy Father indelibly stamped on his bald head.

It's Sunday morning and Dad is sitting on the front step rubbing brown stinky dubbing into his winter boots to make them waterproof before polishing them. I sit in beside him and have at my own wee boots.

"Be careful with that stuff, you don't want to get any on your clothes. It smells like the devil's armpit and sticks like shit to a blanket."

"I'll be careful. Where's Mam? She never got me up for mass."

"No, she went away up the church, ages ago. A posse of the local witches came around for her. They're having some black mass about the Third World War or something!"

"Oh, yes! It's the women's novena for world peace today."

"Well, it must be working. I'm having a very relaxing day without your mother nagging my earholes off. Your mam praying for world peace, that's a good one! She could cause a fight in an empty house. Do you know, Will, that your mother can assemble a machine gun faster than a British army weapons instructor?"

"You're kidding me!"

"No, it's true. When I was still in the army, before we were married, mind? Your mam came down to visit me at my camp. Well, she was a little early and myself and the sergeant instructor were still putting the raw recruits through the dismantling, cleaning, and reassembly of the Bren light machine gun. This sergeant was a big-headed sod and prided himself on how fast he could put the gun together from stripped. He liked to impress the rookies with this display of old bullshit, and within a few minutes the gun was assembled, much to the awe of the young lads who had been struggling with it all morning.

"That's what you call 'putting the gun together in double-quick time!' he says. The audience lets out a gasp and the sergeant stands, preening himself with a smile on his kisser like the cat that got the cream.

"'Double-quick time, my aunt Fanny!' says yer mother. 'Sure even a mere woman like myself could do it in half the time!'

"'Well, miss, perhaps you'd like a go?' he laughs, stripping the weapon back to parts. Well, yer mam walked down to the table, picked up two wrong pieces, and with a puzzled look, tried to fit them together. The sergeant was grinning like a Cheshire cat, when suddenly, with the time nearly up, yer mam snapped that Bren together like greased lightning and pointed the barrel at him. She pulled the trigger—*click!*

"'Bang! You're dead!' says your mother, with a wicked grin, and all the squaddies are cheering your mam and catcalling at the sergeant instructor.

"'How the hell did you learn to do that?' asks the sergeant, mystified, like!

"'Ah now, wouldn't you like to know, Tommy?' says yer mam in a conspiratorial Irish accent!"

"Gee! But where did she learn, Dad?"

"She worked at the BSA during the war, of course. She made thousands of Bren guns on the assembly line."

"But I thought the BSA made motorcycles?"

"They do, but it still means Birmingham Small Arms! Hmm! Remarkable woman, your mother." says Dad, staring at his reflection in a spit-and-polished toe-cap.

World peace doesn't come, but fall does and we soon need the rain-proofed boots, especially when I go for a long walk in the wilderness with my father. It is cold and the curled brown leaves of autumn lay thick and crunchy with frost. A thin, pale, wintry-looking sun floats above the lines of silver birch trees like a runny fried egg. Great deciduous giants of oak and chestnut, having shed their summer finery, slumber, swaying gently, their creaking arms communing their spirits skyward to heaven. From where the river cuts a swatch through the forest, a filmy white mist is swirling upward in the eddies of an easterly breeze.

I know Dad has wanted to talk with me for some time, and I am terrified it is going to be about "the birds and the bees." I don't know too much on the subject of S.E.X. and that suits me just fine—for the moment anyway!

Instead, my Dad tells me how he'd fallen out with two of his brothers years before the argument about Granddad's Masonic trunk, over, of all things, a wee bag of sweets! They wouldn't share with him and he told them to stick the sweets up their arses. This happened when they were little kids and they are still at enmity about it. I think this is very sad, but many bitter things have been said over the years and the hatred of brothers is said to be the most galling.

He speaks to me about greed and loss, not as father to son, but as man to man. It makes me feel very important.

"Of all the vices, greed is the worst—I reckon anyway. It makes people do crazy things. It causes wars, and murders and the like. Show me a money-grabbing man who's at peace with himself. You can't! The greed that makes people do anything to acquire riches is a hunger that can never be satisfied, a thirst that a pint of the best bitter beer cannot slake. I shudder at the unholy thought!"

We walk on, with Dad still edifying the beJasus out of me.

"We collect firewood from the forest, right? Now we only take what we need, OK? No man in his right mind would possibly take away more wood than he can use, of course not. But someone who suffers that curse of greed will chop down all the trees, whether he can use them or not, and be too mean to let you take a few bits home. He's the fella old Jesus is talking about when he says, 'What does it profit a man if he gain the whole world and suffer the loss of his own soul?' Well, avoid those buggers in your life. They are a sorry lot and bring misery to all around them, like that mangy old Blackshirt Grumpy, as you call him. If he was a ghost, he would be too mean to give you a fright. Do you see what I'm getting at?"

"I think so," I says, wondering where this is all going.

Dad takes up the charge again.

"In order to gain something, the soul must lose something first, since it must always weigh the same. The loss of your loved ones is hard, but the soul gains an understanding that in life there is death and in death there is renewal. That can be comforting in times of sorrow." I try to nod my head in the right places. He continues his theme.

"You see, it's like this. Me and your mam have tried to give you a decent upbringing, but stuck out here in the country we don't have the opportunities we would have in the big city. So . . . so . . . we're leaving for our new house next weekend!"

So *that's* what this was all about. I knew already! Mam had told me yesterday, but I don't let on because it is nice having a ramble and talking with Dad.

We stroll back to the cosiness of our little blue-and-white caravan, from which a long silver-gray plume of wood smoke issues, suffused with the yeasty aroma of fresh-baked bread.

Yet again in my short life, I am about to leave everything I have ever known and go on to new adventures and new pals.

The Irish have a saying: "A child that is not brought up in the country has only had half a childhood." I have had a fine feast of a rearing in our little Celtic enclave in the wilds of Warwickshire.

> *Is buaine port ná glór na n-éan*
> *Is buaine focal ná toice an tsaoil.*
>
> *A tune is more precious than the song of birds*
> *And a tale more precious than the wealth of the world.*

→ Chapter 17 ←

PULLING OUT IS A COMPLICATED BUSINESS AS WE ONLY HAVE the old Austin motorcar to move our belongings. With the car stuffed with boxes and a mattress tied to the roof, we drive like hillbillies along the twenty-eight miles of country road to the new house. Dad navigates by the only landmarks he knows: pubs and gas stations.

We arrive in Lower Beeches Road, Northfield, Birmingham. I am on the lookout for a quaint little detached house. I'm disappointed to discover that the address fits one of a number of new monolithic brick-built tower blocks. It looks more like a drab suburb of East Berlin than the outskirts of an English city.

The high-rise apartments are jerry-built monstrosities—shoddy mushrooms sprouting all over Britain, ill-designed by architects who eventually go to jail for negligence. These tower blocks are made of the cheapest materials and the flat roofs usually leak, in contrast to the ground floors, which suck up the dreaded damp like a bath sponge. The middle floors have little in the way of sound deadening and neighbors are constantly fighting over noise problems. The tower at Ronan Point in London collapses, killing many of the residents. Blocks in Yorkshire are stripped of their roofing by North Sea gales. And an old gypsy relocated in the block opposite us is ejected for keeping goats in his front room. The authorities have his goats put down and the poor sod goes insane.

Stress becomes a part of daily life in many of these hen coops. Depression and suicide are common. The one elevator in our block seldom works, and the staircase invariably smells of piss. To a flat on the sixth floor of this earthly paradise, we move our few items of old furniture and settle in as best we can. I hate the damn place.

"I have an important announcement to make!" My folks look at each other and then back at me. "Henceforth, I wish to be called Bill, like my uncle Bill. No one knows me here and I don't want a anymore of that 'Willie Watkins did it!' business. It's been the bane of my life."

"OK, Willie . . . er . . . Billy . . . er . . . Bill. Sure you can be who you want here. Make a new start. That's what I did when I came over from Ireland, so I did."

"What, changed your name, Mam?"

"Certainly not! Just the color of my hair." She flicks her blond curls.

"What color was it before you came over?"

"'Twas auburn, so it was."

"What color is that?"

"A sort of russet red."

"Did you not like it that color?"

"Well, you know what they say about redheaded women?"

"No."

"Ask yer father. Go on, Reg, tell him."

"Well, Will, it's best explained like this. A fella goes to the doctor and finds out he's only six months to live. He asks the doctor what he should do.

"The doc says, 'Go and marry a redhaired Irish woman.'

"Yer man says, 'Will I live longer?'

"He says, 'No, it will just seem longer!' D'ya get it?"

"No."

"You will one day!"

We do one more trip to Wootton Wawen. Making a last walk around the caravan site, armed with an ancient Kodak 620 box camera, I snap a handful of photographs of the people and places that have been so dear to me.

Sitting later in my lofty prison, I gaze at the circle of smiling faces that once were my childhood pals, captured forever in that last sad hour of leaving, each elfin visage brimming with mischief and merriment, now pressed like wildflowers between the pages of time, a treasury of the age of innocence. I never see any of my friends from that day forward. By the time I'm old enough to make the long trek back to the caravan site on my own, they have all left or moved off on the road, gone like leaves in the wind.

The only good thing about this bloody apartment is the view. From the living room window we can see westward clear into Wales, across open fields and woodlands. One night we hear a distant explosion, and Dad stabs the air with a clenched fist.

"The boys are at it again—Cymru am Byth! Wales forever! Up the FWA!"

"Who's the FWA?"

"They're the Free Wales Army, and they're blowing up the water pipeline that steals Welsh water from the Elan Valley to feed Birmingham's reservoirs."

This at least brings some diversion to our new isolation, and we fill the bath with drinking water as we know the taps will be dry for a few days.

My folks take jobs in the city, nine miles away. It makes for a long bus trip each day. Dad works in a factory, making car batteries, and Mam becomes a barmaid at a pub in the city center. I have to go to school, but the nearest is called Tinker's Farm and the education department deems it inappropriate that a child from a caravan site should attend a school named after gypsies. I'm sent to Colmer's Farm school, a good three miles away across country. It never occurred to me that you need to lock a bicycle. It's soon stolen and I have to walk to school. I make no friends locally, and being shy about a protruding incisor that has grown over a stubborn milk tooth, I stop smiling.

Dad is in a similar plight: the old car dies and leaves him thinking that moving here was probably a big mistake, as the local pub is both a noisy dump and a long walk away. Like myself, he misses his pals and spends his nights painting in oils, reading, and helping me build working wireless sets out of army surplus junk. We try to make the best of it.

Only Mam seems content with our new existence. Being brought up during the lean years of depression, she loves the hurly-burly of a brightly lit city enjoying the first wave of economic boom heralded by the prime minister's announcement: "You've never had it so good!"

Like W. B. Yeats exiled in the tower of Thoor Ballylee, I become a disenchanted recluse with just an old cat for company and a hand full of memories. I brood over my fate and think of the happy times, now so distant. A homemade ham radio is my only window on the world. Night after night, I put on the headphones and drift away beyond the brick walls of this citadel of solitude. Aloft on the magic ether of the wireless waves, I tune about, visiting "HCJB, the Voice of the Andes"; "FK8AZ, calling from New Caledonia in the Pacific"; "G5SS Birmingham, calling on the 160-meter band"; "Ici Radio Canada." I am on the point of dozing off to sleep when through the static-filled ionosphere crackles a sound I've heard before: "Mayday! Mayday! Mayday! This is Dutch coaster PXCC . . . PXCC, Schevening Radio! Do you read? Over!" There is no reply except the hypnotic noise of an atmospheric storm, hissing and spitting like bacon frying in a pan. I jerk awake! I remember the *Irish Prince* and know that somewhere out in the dark of the cold North Sea other men are nearing their death.

"Mayday! Mayday! All stations, all stations! Do you read PXCC . . . PXCC! Mayday! Over." I detune my transmitter from 1,900 to 2,182 kilocycles per second. Distress frequency. I know this is breaking the law, but it's obvious that the electrical storm is blacking out radio links and no one else can hear them!

"PXCC . . . PXCC! This is amateur radio station G10924 calling you! Over?"

"G10924 . . . G10924! We are sinking three miles off the Tershcelling Bank! We require immediate assistance. Please Mayday relay! Over."

"Roger PXCC. Mayday relay! Mayday relay! Dutch coaster PXCC sinking off Terschelling Bank. All stations report." There is no reply. I try several more times until in desperation I run down the fifteen flights of stairs and across the road to the telephone box on the corner.

"999 Emergency, which service please? Police, fire, or ambulance?"

"Hello! Can you get me the North Sea Coast Guard, please?"

"I'm sorry, caller. It is an offense to make nuisance 999 calls. Please hang up."

"Listen, lady, I'm a ham radio operator and I've picked up a distress signal from a sinking ship. This is not a joke. Please get me the nearest Coast Guard! Please?"

"Just one moment." *Click!* "Hello, North Foreland Coast Guard here, what can I do for you?"

"Dutch ship, call sign PXCC, aground and sinking three miles off the Tershcelling Bank. They've been calling Mayday for ages and I'm the only one they've been able to contact. I'm just a ham operator."

"What's your call sign, sir?"

"G10924. Now hurry please!"

Back at my wireless, I hear the North Foreland radio station, GNF, make contact with the coaster at the third attempt and I breathe a sigh of relief. Dad comes home and listens to the drama play out as the crew is evacuated by Dutch and British rescue vessels. As the signal for Mayday stand down is given, a voice out in the ether says, "Thanks, G10924, good job. All PXCC crew are safe." Dad hears the message too and smiles as he pats me on the shoulder.

"I'm proud of you, son!"

My interest in shortwave radio causes me to read Thor Heyerdahl's, *Kon-Tiki Expedition*. He had two radio hams on his crew, and LI2B was the call sign of the balsa wood raft he sailed across the Pacific on. This book engages me in the story of ethnic Polynesian migration, and I read more of his books. The local library becomes my second home, but on my first visit there, I ask for Heyerdahl's enormous tome, *American Indians in the Pacific*. The librarian refuses my request point blank, saying, "You kids always want the biggest books in the place, and I'm fed up with it!"

I have to explain that I am seriously interested in Polynesian ethnology, not weight lifting, and grudgingly I'm given the huge volume to take home with me.

Dad takes an interest in the subject, too, and draws parallels between the dispersion of the seafaring South Sea islanders and the Celtic sea peoples.

"The sea was always a highway to the ancients. There were no natural barriers like impassable mountain chains or deep rushing rivers, dangerous forests, or swamps to impede the progress of migration. They could sail where they wanted as long as the prevailing wind and currents were kind. On land, they might meet hostile tribes barring their way, but at sea, there were only the elements to overcome. In this way, the prehistoric travelers populated the farthest corners of the earth."

Dad sees similarities in the method of erecting the giant statues of Easter Island and the huge trilithons that make up the circles of Stonehenge.

"Levers, rollers, and ropes, that's how they moved those bloody big stones—that and a good eye to science."

"So why were the Easter Island statues erected, Dad?"

"No one knows. We know more about Stonehenge, although we don't know who built it."

"Wasn't Stonehenge just a place for the Druids to make human sacrifices?"

"No, no, it was there long before the Druids, who never indulged in human sacrifice either. That's just a load of shite dreamed up by Julius Caesar to give the Celts a bad name. Stonehenge was a clock for predicting winter and summer solstice, a calendar by which ancient farmers could read the seasons and know when to plant their crops."

A noise in the front hall brings an end to the lesson. The post has arrived and Mam comes in with a manila envelope bearing the legend: On Her Majesty's Service.

"Ooh, Billy, this is for you. It's from the government. I bet it's a commendation like your dad got from the police that time long ago."

I tear open the official looking envelope and read:

Dear Mr. Watkins,

Operating an Amateur radio transmitter without a full licence is an offence under the Wireless Telegraphy Act of 1949.

Operating an unauthorised transmitter on a Maritime Distress frequency is an offence under the above Act and also the International Maritime Treaty Piracy Laws.

Due to the nature of this offence and your age, we have decided to limit our proceedings to an official *caution*. Any reoccurrence or future offences on your part will be prosecuted to the very letter of the law.

The punishment for such misdemeanors is a fine of one thousand pounds, six months imprisonment or both. Plus the confiscation of all transmitting equipment.

The Home Office.

I let the letter drop from my hand. Mam picks it up. "BloodyEnglish."

I make a few friends at the new school and in due course some enemies.

The school bullyboy finally notices my presence. He is an ugly-looking bollix with a shock of carrot-colored hair and a face like a freshly smacked arse. He's about fifteen and has an IQ of roughly the same. I think his name is Spencer.

"Come here, you!" He grunts at me in a guttural Brummy accent. "I'm the cock of the school—the best fighter!"

"You look more like the prick to me!" One or two of my attendant classmates laugh nervously, but most draw in an audible breath and move away. It takes several seconds for this unexpected rejoinder to sink into his cartilage-filled skull, and a dilatory look of puzzlement comes over his face. Then slowly, like the sunrise over the mountains, he has it. He'd been insulted by a mere twelve-year-old student!

I'm still laughing when he hits me full in the mouth. The force of the punch dislodges my rogue incisor, which firmly imbeds itself in his hamlike knuckle joint.

Although I'm in some pain, I am delighted. That goddamn ugly tooth is gone! "Good man! Good man! Thanks a bunch!" I shake his injured hand furiously. In agony and bewilderment, he's led away to the school nurse, who sends him to hospital. He requires surgery to remove the tooth. By the time he had been operated on and gets back the use of his hand, he has left school, so I never see him again. Now I have a straight row of teeth, and I smile at everybody!

The fact that I hospitalized the school bully and laughed after he punched my tooth out spreads around the school like a measles epidemic. It offers me great kudos and I am never molested again.

The red brick and plate glass school is home to an odd complement of teaching staff. Mr. Hobbs, our wonderfully gay art teacher, is great fun to work with and his art room is a no-go area for stuffy authority. If you don't feel like drawing or painting you can make coffee and talk about art, politics, pop music, or who won the 4:15 race at Doncaster. To him all expression is art!

The aquatic-looking "Froggy" Palmer is the mathematics master. Here I stumble and fall as before. More bloody allegory!

"A farmer plants 800 potato plants, 6 out of 10 die. What has he got, Watkins?"

"Colorado beetle, sir!"

Mr. Palmer has a particularly nasty punishment for wayward students. He sends me to the washroom to soak his blackboard-cleaning rag. When I sit back at my desk he hurls it into my face with unerring accuracy. If you duck, the punishment is repeated.

At first sight, the science master, Mr. Druce, cuts a strange figure. Dressed in moss-green tweeds, he affects a wide-brimmed cowboy hat of the same color and white gloves. Sprigs of snowy hair jut out from under his sombrero and he wears thick tortoiseshell spectacles. I discover he is an albino and allergic to sunlight.

His junior in the science block is young Mr. Shaw, who seemingly is from the same school as Mr. Bury. He gives a lesson in biology and attempts a jocular aside.

"All cells must have a nucleus, just like we—all must have a belly button!"

"I have no belly button, sir!" says moon-faced Edward Hall.

"Don't be stupid, Hall. Everyone has a navel, even a worm like you!"

"I have no belly button!"

"Rubbish, of course you do!"

"I have *no* belly button, I tell you!"

"Right, smart arse, get out here!"

Edward strolls out to the front of the class and up onto the podium. Mr. Shaw spins him around toward us and whisks up his shirt.

"This is your belly butt . . ." Mr. Shaw's words trail off as he realizes he is pointing at a smooth round belly totally devoid of any trace of a navel! Edward is triumphant and afterward tells me his secret. When he was born his navel developed an infection and was operated on. When the stitches were later removed, the scar healed up, belly button and all. Mr. Shaw, however, is kept in the dark!

I like "Mad Gary" Hedges the English teacher, not just because of his projecting "Eraser Head" haircut and eyes that flicker to and fro a hundred times a minute, but also because of his unconventional taste in literature. Blaggards like us fall eerily silent when he reads aloud horror stories like, "The Forest of Fear," by Lurhendorf, a terrifying tale of being lost in the Amazon jungle. Or the sinister, futuristic politico-nightmare embodied in George Orwell's *1984*. He struts at the front of the classroom, red hair flaming skyward like a struck match, reading from banned books, uncensored books, and everything that isn't on the approved reading list. We love him for it!

An American poetry teacher arrives for a year's exchange and, with great enthusiasm, introduces me to the sacred arts of imagery, metaphor, and onomatopoeia. I spend a lot of after-school time talking to him about poetry. He is fascinated that I can remember epic Irish poems, recitations, and other gleanings of Celtic oral tradition. He writes these down with the old songs and sayings that I know. He makes copious notes.

"You could make a living singing these ancient songs and reciting this beautiful poetry."

"No one is interested in it, sir. It's all too old fashioned."

"They will be one day, Bill, you wait and see!"

"Why did you come all the way over from the U.S.A. to work here?"

"Oh, that was almost too easy! I was teaching at this university in New England, and I fancied a change of career. For a bit of divine guidance I opened a compendium of verse and read, 'Oh to be in England now that April's there.' I thought, Hello, this is a good omen, and so moved over on a teacher's swap program!"

"My grandda used to say that there is great guidance in poetry, a sacred thing to the Celts!"

The day he leaves, he gives me my first-ever book of selected poems by William Butler Yeats. I open it and there on page three is the same poem that I had heard on the wireless during my days as an infant fighter pilot.

"An Irish Airman Foresees His Death." As I read the text, the intervening years telescope and there I am in my mind's eye, still flying my spindle-backed chair through the wild blue yonder of Ireland. It makes me miss the old country terribly and I yearn to go back home.

I have no fellow countrymen worth a toss here in the big city. The kids with Irish names are more English than the English themselves. I am lonely for the ways of the Celt.

The biggest bugbear at school is the quaint preoccupation with sport, in all its torturous forms. I find this to be a right royal pain in the arse.

Soccer is compulsory, as are rugby, cricket, basketball, and field and track events. All this with the promise of nice cold showers afterward and the big eejits laughing at your willie! To avoid any future compliance in these arcane endeavors, I effect a grand *ruse de guerre* by way of which, although appearing to be exerting myself to the maximum, my total incompetence causes groans of exasperation from my teammates and appeals to the sports master to send me off. This he invariably does, and the punishment for being a duffer is to be sent to the school library.

They must think it a great agony for me to sit reading in a warm library on a freezing winter's morning, witnessing the other lads turn blue with cold whilst getting slaps in the face with icy leather footballs. 'Tis a quare castigation to be reading *National Geographic* with your feet up a throbbing radiator.

My ruse held, and eventually, after constantly own-goaling at football, running the wrong way in cricket, and throwing a javelin through the changing-hut window, I am excused from team games altogether.

"God almighty, boy! Didn't you play football where you come from, Watkins?"

"No, sir!" This was true. I'd always found more entertaining ways to expend my excess energy than running around a muddy field chasing a pig's bladder.

"Well, what games have you played in the bogs of Ireland then?"

"Only hurley, sir! It's the only one I know!" I'm on safe ground here.

"Good God, lad! That's a game for bloody barbarians! People get maimed, killed even, playing that!"

"Yes, sir, it's an ancient Celtic game from the Bronze Age, a game for warriors. It won't suit you civilized folk at all!"

"Sarcasm is the lowest form of wit, Watkins!"

"'Tis when you're dealing with the lowest form of life!" I mutter under my breath.

"Don't get smart with me, Watkins, or I'll whip the skin off your backside. Now go on, get out!"

That was easy! Now how do I get out of cross-country running? Fate lends a helping hand.

They show me the five-mile course. This leaves the back of the school and follows the same route that I take home every day. I pace myself until, neither with the keen bunch of athletes in the lead nor the wheezing desperadoes in the rear, I find myself alone. As I jog past the back of my apartment block, I swerve into the rear door and up to my flat. This gives me a twenty-five-minute break. From the living room window, with a cup of tea and sandwich in hand, I watch the true sons of Britannia run to the top of the distant Frankley-Beeches hill and turn about. Fifteen minutes later they pass my back door and I join the gap once more, usually arriving back at the finish in seventeenth place out of thirty-six.

"William is not a natural athlete—but tries hard!" my report card reads. I have always liked the idea of being seventeenth and find the concept of any person wishing to be number one rather vulgar. The seventeenth best gunslinger in town, for instance, would be ideally suited as the sixteen above him would scarcely stoop so low as to challenge him, and the ones below him, would be so inept as to pose little threat. I begin to look upon seventeen as my lucky number, and I'm very pleased when I discover that it is the sacred number of the Druids.

From the tower of my brick Bastille I gaze on the world beyond. Through my telescope I spy a pretty young girl at the end of the street. Sadly I discover that she's one of the Kirby clan, who are the number one terrors in the neighborhood, and as lovely as she is, old man Kirby is a villain and puts me in mind of the song "Riley's Daughter." I keep well away from her.

Riley has a murderous way,
Riley has a mind to murder and slaughter,
Riley has one big red eye,
And he keeps his eye on his lovely daughter.

I'm still rather shy of girls, especially the city ones, who, with the exception of Elspeth O'Neill, seem a lot more forward than I'm used to. The sap is rising and I endeavor to overcome my coyness with the lassies. I am granted luck from an unsuspected quarter. My school is Church of England, and since I am a Catholic I'm not obliged to join in the morning assembly for prayers and hymn practice. Instead, along with the Muslims, Jews, Sikhs, and divers denominations, I am given other school duties.

The one I enjoy is late monitor. I sit inside the main entrance and take down the names of any tardy stragglers in the late book. Three consecutive bookings lead to a punishment, so I change the names of constant recidivists to give them a break.

One such offender is a pretty young lass called Sue Lloyd, and, despite living directly across the road from the school gates, she is always late.

Each day I have ample time to talk with her as the assembly meetings are forty-five minutes long and longer, if Welshman and chorister Mr. Davies gets the *Hwyl* or the Welsh religious fervor and carries the hymn singing to dizzier heights than normal.

Soon teachers and pupils alike think she's just another non-Protestant late monitor, doing her secular duty, and that is fine by us. One day I ask can I walk her home.

She laughs and says, "What, across the road? Are you nuts?" Nuts or not, I eventually do, however, and the walk usually takes at least an hour.

She is my first girlfriend.

At home, I get a marvelous picture on the old black-and-white television I'd retrieved from the dump that time. Now, plugged into the big antenna high on the roof of the building, we are able to tune in all sorts of queer transmissions, including, under certain atmospheric conditions, *The Beverly Hillbillies* in Spanish!

That year the big news in television is the forthcoming world heavy-weight title fight between Sonny Liston and Floyd Patterson, but what I want to see again are those four Liverpool guys who had been on the BBC's *Tonight Programme,* singing a song called "Love Me Do." They have a fresh new sound and mops of long hair. The stage set was a build-ing site scene, and on the corrugated iron fence next to the band are spray-painted the words "The Beatles."

For several days I have been monitoring the shortwave broadcasts from Voice of America, Radio Moscow, and Radio Havana. The United States is convinced that the Russians have developed ICBM missiles and is not having any of them stationed in Cuba.

The great Kennedy versus Khruschev showdown is *High Noon* for real, and for three days we teeter on the brink of nuclear war. To make matters worse, coincidentally, the number one record in the top 10 is "Don't They Know It's the End of the World?"

The door of my classroom opens and a runner hands the teacher a note.

"Class, I have a notice here from the headmaster. It states that the war has indeed started. The factories are closing, and your parents will be bussed here to pick you up!"

God knows where this rumor had sprung from, but it was current all over the Midlands of England. There is no panic, just a slow sad res-ignation; like the Jews who knew their fate, stoically lining up for the gas chambers.

Our teachers tell us to line up in the playground class by class. All of the factories shut down and people are told to go home and prepare to die. Suddenly there are my folks amongst the worried throng of parents streaming off the buses. On a beautiful afternoon, I walk westward home down the country lane, hand in hand with my mum and dad. I have no fear of dying, I just feel cheated. Here's me on the brink of growing up and these loonies are going to end it all. We don't say much, but as I walk into the sunset with my folks, I wonder if this will be the last time I'd see the sun go down.

No one in Britain has fallout shelters except the rich, the government, and the royal family. The Civil Defense tells us that we are protected by a four-minute early warning system; radar detects the incoming missiles and we have time to hide under the kitchen table from the fifty-megaton blasts. We are urged to take off all of the doors in the house and stack them around the table for protection. My dad says he couldn't even find a screwdriver in that short time, but on the plus side, there are some athletes in the country who can run a mile in four minutes! Grim times bring on grim humor.

So this is it, the big one, and I am going to die as I was born—a damn virgin!

At home we listen on the shortwave radio to the to-ing and fro-ing of the standoff. For once, good sense prevails and the threat of annihilation is diverted. It has not been the disaster it might have been, even though Dad has drank all of his stock of home brew.

In the days that follow, a curious anger spreads amongst the populace. Most people are disgusted with the superpowers who've almost killed us, with our own government who afford us no protection, and with themselves, who have so calmly accepted the thought that we are all going home to be fried in our beds.

This wave of revulsion sweeps the country in the aftermath of the Cuban missile crisis and I commit my first political act. I join the Campaign for Nuclear Disarmament, the CND.

At the invitation of the school metalwork teacher, who is also in CND, I do my first gig as a musician. It's a benefit for a new branch of the burgeoning organization, a concert of song and poetry, located in the parochial hall. I am very pleased and honored to do it.

To say that I am nervous would be like describing the Marquis de Sade as a little eccentric. Minutes before going on stage, I am a leading contender in the brown-trouser Olympics! Total amnesia sets in, and I am convinced that my guitar's out of tune.

"Got a wee bit of stage fright?" asks my teacher.

"No!" I lie, my voice two octaves above normal. Suddenly, I think it wise to visit the lavatory. I open the toilet door and a wild-eyed bearded figure, dressed completely in black, thrusts a handful of papers into my face.

"The eagle of death sits on my head and shits down the back of my neck!"

"Oh . . . er, that's nice for you. Are you performing?"

"I do not perform, I transfigure! I am the great Kropotkin! The finest poet in the world—nay, the universe!" He thrills in a mock Russian accent, holding his sheaf of papers aloft, like the torch of a demented Statue of Liberty.

"Who in the name of Jasus is that?" I say to my teacher, as the demonic poet flits past us, black cape akimbo.

"Oh, that's Dave Patton, the awful poet. He's as mad as a hatter!"

"Well, he has me feeling much relieved! Whatever happens I won't be the worst of the night's offerings."

"Och, you'll be fine!"

Two brothers are on in front of me, and they are very good, singing in tight harmony, a bit like the Everly Brothers.

Finally I hear my name announced and I walk on stage. After a shaky start I get into the swing and I'm away. I start with an Irish song called "The Spinning Wheel," which I'd learned from Nana. Then, Ewan MacColl's, "Dirty Old Town," and I finish with a song I'd heard a lot on the American shortwave stations called "Blowing in the Wind." I announce it as "written by a chap called Tom Dillon." No one corrected me. Bob Dylan was not yet a household name!

I leave the stage and the dazzling lights to a pleasing ripple of applause. It is all over. I have done it and survived!

I feel elated. The pretty girl I'd seen earlier passing out leaflets smiles at me and says, "That was lovely! Is this your first gig? You are very good, don't you think?"

I'm suddenly a bag of nerves again. I try to nod my head no to her last question and say, "Yes" to her second question at the same time. This gives me the appearance of a badly operated string puppet with a red face. As I blush, stammer, and splutter I feel her squeeze something into my hand. My heart flutters like the leaves of the Holy Jasus Bible in a gale. *It must be her phone number or the like!* But when I look down I find I am only holding a leaflet stating "Ten Good Reasons Why We All Should Say—BAN THE BOMB."

"Bugger the bomb!"

Back home Dad is carving a wooden Tiki figure like the ones on Easter Island.

"How was your gig, Will?"

" 'Twas grand! I sang a few old songs that went down well, but I was a might nervous!"

"Good lad!"

"Dad, with the Second World War over and fascism defeated, why do we need so many armies and weapons?"

"Oh, Billy boy, if it was only that simple."

"What d'you mean?"

"Well, we only got rid of Hitler and Mussolini. Half of the world is still under dictatorship. Franco rules Spain, Salazar in Portugal, apartheid in South Africa, the white racist regime in Rhodesia, not to mention Stalinism behind the iron curtain, segregation in the U.S.A. and in Northern Ireland, the war in Indo-China, the Belgian Congo, and Israel! Every bloody eejit in East and West seems to be glaring at each other! The same tired old politicians are telling everyone to 'Tighten your belt and take less money for more work!' If all jobs were based on productivity, where would these buggers be in the league tables, I wonder."

"Reg, for Jasus' sake, look at the poor child! He came home all happy and now you've depressed the hell out of him with your fascists and fat-shits and God knows what else! Jasus, what do you think yer on!"

"I fought with Monty, woman!"

"I thought it was supposed to be the Germans you were fighting? Mind you, Willie, your father could cause a fight in an empty house!"

"That's what he says about you, Mam!"

"Go to bed, Willie!"

President Kennedy is shot. We cry. He was our man. We'd prayed for him, so he was ours! Now the TV brings his death right into the heart of our home. The world has gone mad, and now, even more so, I fear a nuclear war.

The electrifying events of these months of turmoil produce a couple of odd side effects: the folk music revival and the protest movement.

There begins a series of antinuclear folk concerts at Birmingham Town Hall with some great singers and musicians turning up for them. The anchor band are the Ian Campbell Folk Group, with the incomparable Dave Swarbrick on fiddle. Their guests include Ian and Sylvia Tyson from Canada, Guy Carawan, Pete and Mike Seeger, Buffy St.-Marie, Judy Collins, and Joan Baez, from the United States. British singers are represented by Martin Carthy, Ray and Archie Fisher, Nadia Catouse, Alex Campbell, Ewan MacColl, and the Scottish group the Corries. My dad knows Ian Campbell, and Ian introduces me to some of the performers. It's a great school for a lad like myself. I am very lucky to play and sing with some of these artists. From Joan Baez I learn to play the syncopated style of clawhammer picking that she excels at, and hearing Judy Collins singing Gordon Lightfoot's fine song, "In The Early Morning Rain," moves me to tears. One Saturday I sit and swap songs all afternoon with Phil Ochs.

Ian Campbell and my father are buddies from the Spanish Civil War. They both hate fascism, the destruction of which will seemingly be attained by consuming vast amounts of gargle and singing durty songs about General Franco.

Back home in Castle Doom, Dad, enlivened by several more bottles of Nut Brown Ale, continues to wax revolutionary.

"Fascism is like a nettle, laddie. You must grasp it firmly by the throat!"

"What about nationalism? Doesn't that lead to fascism, like National Socialism?"

"Not necessarily. A little of each can work together. To be an internationalist you need a nation, and the struggle of small nations to be free is the very cornerstone of the Celtic evangel." He begins to sing:

> It is England that bade our "Wild Geese" go
> That small nations might be free.
> And their lonely graves are by Suvla's waves
> Or the fringe of the great North Sea.

"Do you know, Willie, that throughout history, Irishmen, Welshmen, and Scots have joined in the liberation of subjugated nations all over the globe? The United States of America's Declaration of Independence was referred to by King George III as 'that damned Welsh document!' More people in General George Washington's army spoke Gaelic than English! Chile, freed from Spanish rule by Juan MacKenna.

The storming of the Bastille, led by Seamus Blackwell, a cobbler from Leitrim! Celts have always been to the fore! Bernado O'Higgins, chief of staff in Simon Bolívar's liberation army, hero of Latin America. Ernesto 'Che' Guevara de la Serna-Lynch, an Argentinean-Irishman, helped Fidel Castro overthrow the Cuban dictator, Batista, in 1959!"

"Reg, stop filling the child's mind with your old commie nonsense. Ye'll have him as daft as yerself!"

"Bollocks, madame!" He uses the interlude to open another beer.

"Now where was I, before I was *rudely* interrupted? Ah, yes! The Celts have long been known to be a querulous and pugnacious race, and this is seen by some to be just pure love of conflict. Standing up for your rights and beliefs can't possibly be misconstrued as bellicose, can it, young man? Hell no, indeed! The BloodyEnglish have invaded almost every country on the face of the earth, yet they still pretend to deal in fair play. A likely bloody story! Look what they did in China—got the Chinese hooked on opium and then invaded and stole every bloody thing that wasn't nailed down. Disgraceful! The British Empire was built on drug money and slavery and murder. That's why the Union Jack is known as the Butcher's Apron!"

"Well, why do they think that it's all right to have empires, Dad?"

"I touched earlier on the difference in the Celtic and Anglo-Saxon psyche and that reminds me of the time when we kept chickens. The hens wandered around the yard, pecking here and there, wherever they wished, they were no problem. Then a mate of mine gave us some ducks. Now these wee buggers have a structured order of behavior and a well-developed hierarchy. Every morning the ducks would come out of the coop and line up in a row. The leader would then take position at the front of the file and nod its head up and down. This is the cue for the line of ducks to obediently do likewise, and when they have all nodded enough, they would waddle in single file down to the pond. The problem was, if you let the free-spirited hens out first, the ducks would get hysterical trying to make the hens line up, pay homage, and toe the line. It is a comical sight, but it seems to me to be a powerful cultural analogy with overtones of Aesop's fables. It's a great pity the so-called political experts, waxing lyrical on the Anglo-Irish problem, don't keep poultry. They'd get a better idea of what they're talking about! Pour me another beer, Will. My throat's as dry as a pharaoh's sock."

Well, I'm one chicken who isn't about to be walking in a straight line anyway! My school chums leave for jobs in one of the many Austin Motor Company factories that take up most of the available land around the school. If you are smart and stay on to do fifth- and sixth-year studies you can expect a job in the drawing office or the administration block. However, if you leave at fifteen, you're a grunt, "doomed to the broom," as they say. A life of sweeping up and waiting for a grease-monkey job to open on the vehicle assembly line. Bollocks to all that!

The largest part of the school is the metalworking shops. The many full-size machines bear the legend "Kindly donated by the Austin Motor Co." Here you are taught drilling, tempering, center-grinding, capstan-lathe operating, tool and pattern making, and all the other skills you need for a life of car making. I would rather poke a pencil in my eye than go to that sausage machine existence.

My school careers officer asks me what I want to be. I answer cheek-ily that I'd like to be a merchant navy wireless operator or a folk singer. He says, "Why not do both?"

My schoolwork is going to shit. It never recovers from the Cuban missile scare. Algebra, logarithms, Thomas Hardy, and the bloody Magna Carta all seem so puerile in the shadow of the valley of death. What I learn, I learn at home. Dad teaches me many crafts. He shows me how to paint in oils and work in metal, wood, and stone. I study hard at my radio manuals and pass the Postmaster General's certificate of wireless proficiency.

In the long winter's evenings, Dad teaches me to play chess, drink Woodpecker cider, and hold an intelligent conversation all at the same time! This is my dad's way to get me to use my faculties—even when I might be just a wee bit tiddly!

✦ Chapter 18 ✦

"HOW OLD ARE YOU NOW, WILL?"

"I'm fourteen, Dad."

"Hmm." He stares at me as if he's measuring me up for a suit. The air about his bald pate seems electrostatically charged, and I sense one of his philosophical eruptions about to happen. I had become quite adept at recognizing the seismology of my father's periodic volcanic outflows, but it was still an unnerving spectacle.

He paces the floor, leaving plumes of blue cigarette smoke marking the quadrants of his traverse. For a while his theme eludes him; his muse is timorous. Then, suddenly illuminated, he's off, invoking the spirit within the poetry of Taliesin, the Welsh bard:

> *I was a drop in the shower,*
> *I was a torrent on the slope,*
> *I was a salmon in the pool,*
> *I was a sword in the hand-grip,*
> *I was a cry in battle,*
> *I was a bubble in the beer,*
> *For a year and a half I was the pin in a pair of tongs!*
> *I was a buck,*
> *I was a wizard,*
> *I am Taliesin. Come, ye learned Druids, and prophesy unto*
> *Arthur!*

"Don't you see, Willie? This is what it's all about! Metamorphosis, shape changing, the essence of the Celtic soul. We are born in one form and throughout our existence transmute into other levels of being, each of which is like a new skin or shape. Some changes are dynamic, like when you become seven years old and enter the age of reason. That was a sad year for you with all the death in the family. Twice seven years brings you up to the age of logical thinking and you're a fourteen-year-old coming to terms with the postnuclear world after Cuba. Thrice seven years is the supposed age of majority, the key of the door! Twenty-one. What folks forget is that the key is for unlocking the door behind which knowledge and wisdom lie. Other changes are daunting, you can find yourself between the hammer and the anvil—very unpleasant! But from the dull, raw iron is formed the pure bright steel! This is the spiritual rebirth that you hear about in almost all of the major religions of the world. We are made of atoms. The *dust* of the Bible stories. We are a carbon-based life form, and just as carbon can materialize in the appearance of coal, soft graphite, or the hardest of known rocks, the diamond, we can appear in the myriads of shapes, colors, sizes, and demeanors that are all around us. Are you following me intelligently?"

"Don't you mean that all the races are the same, Dad?"

"Yes, all mankind is basically the same. We can look different, one from another, but that's how we have evolved to suit our individual climates, locations, and diverse environments."

"So there's no point at all in racism, is there?"

"No, none at all. It doesn't bother dogs what shape or size or color they are, they treat each other as what nature intended them to be—dogs!"

"Then how is it that we think the Celts are better than other people?"

"We aren't better or worse than anyone! We are all flowers in the same garden and all have the same right to be here. It's the buggers who think they are the chosen people or the master race that cause all the problems. Never walk that path! No, no, the difference with us is purely spiritual. That, if anything, makes us a little odd. Do you know what atavism is?"

"No, Dad, I don't. What might it be?"

"It's having thoughts and remembrances that you cannot possibly have experienced in this life, flashbacks to another time, a previous existence!"

"Oh, like déjà vu, that sort of thing?"

"More like the second sight of the Gael or the *Hwyl hudoliaeth* of the Welsh. All of us only have a very thin veneer of so-called civilization, and in some folk, just below the surface, there is still the genetic memory of the ancient hunter-gatherer waiting to manifest itself. For us Celts, it comes out in our art, music, and poetry. These traits are amongst the few things we can be truly proud of, and some aspects of these wise arts are unique to our people. A practitioner of the wise arts is called, as a result, a wiz-art or Wizard! This same sense of otherworldliness is found in the ancient Druid religion, the central point of which is the transmigration of the soul. Natural phenomena become objects of worship. The wind, springs, the trees, rocks—all take on deities, and through this world the soul must travel to find its path to rebirth in a higher spiritual form."

"It sounds a bit like Buddha or the Tao."

"It isn't all that different, but our culture has suffered severely at the hands of our Anglo-Saxon neighbors, and its light has been almost extinguished. It is up to your generation to take up the challenge and rebuild the glory of the Gael. You are the rebirth of King Arthur!"

"Me? I'm the reincarnation of King Arthur?"

"Not you personally, but your generation, growing up in the first period of relative peace in God knows how long. It is up to you to build the Camelot of the mind and be the *Rex quondam, Rex-que futurus*—the once and future King. This is the start of a new golden age for the Gael, you mark my words. Strive for that which is honorable and noble, and you shall be the once and future Celts! Now give me over that bottle of beer and two glasses and I'll show you something!"

My father pours out the beer and stares into the side of the glass.

"Look at the bubbles. Where do they come from? What's their point of origin? We don't know. They start from nothing in the tiniest form imaginable and grow larger on their way to the surface, where they disappear—*pop!* This is analogous to the human existence and why Taliesin says, 'I am a bubble in the beer!' Now drink up your lesson and here's to Taliesin, the chief of the bards!"

I down my glass of Flower's Best Bitter with relish. Bubbles, lesson, and all flow sweetly down my throat.

"Who was Taliesin? I know he was a Druid and a poet in King

Arthur's court, but what else can you tell me about him? How did he come to be so powerful?"

"Well, now . . . There was a witch called Ceridwen, who had a son so ugly that he was called Morfran Y Fagddu, Great Crow in Utter Darkness. She sets a cauldron of magic herbs to boil for a year and a day from whence it will produce three drops of divine fluid. These she will give to her gruesome son and he will receive great beauty and the gift of wizardry. She makes an orphan boy called Gwion Bach stir the pot, but at the moment of sublimation, she has fallen asleep and the divine droplets leap from the cauldron and land on Gwion Bach instead. The cauldron cracks with a scream and spills poison all over the land. Ceridwen wakes and, seeing her son unchanged, realizes that Gwion Bach has taken the powers. She flies at him to tear him asunder, but now he is wise to her and turns himself into a hare and escapes. The witch takes on the shape of a greyhound and gives chase. He jumps into the river and becomes a fish. She becomes an otter. The boy speeds out of the water in the form of a bird. Ceridwen follows as a hawk, but Gwion Bach flies into a barn and becomes one of a pile of wheat grains on the floor. The witch turns herself into a chicken and eats up all the grain before becoming a woman again. And guess what?"

"What, what?"

"Now she's pregnant and in due course gives birth to a child of such beauty that she cannot bring herself to destroy him, so she casts him afloat in a coracle upon the Irish Sea. The small boat eventually is washed ashore at Cored Wyddno, the weir of Gwyddno near Conway, and is found by a poor but kindly nobleman called Elphin. He looks at the child wrapped up in the coracle and proclaims, 'Behold the radiant forehead'—*Tal iesin* in Welsh. Gwion Bach replies, 'Tal-iesin it shall be,' and the nobleman is amazed at the beautiful baby, who can speak words and prophecies, and raises him up as his own. Taliesin becomes the foremost Celtic bard in Britain.

I was revealed in the land of the trinity
I was moved through the entire universe
I shall remain till doomsday upon the face of the earth
No one knows what my flesh be, meat or fish?

> *I was nearly nine months in the womb of Ceridwen*
> *I was formerly Gwion Bach,*
> *But now I am Taliesin.'"*

"Drink up your ale, Will—Iechyd da!"

"Good health to you, too, Dad!"

It is pleasant to have a wee drink with my dad, but I also mind what my mam says: "A hangover is a poor friend and makes for a rotten master."

The biggest disaster that befalls me through using too much alcohol happens in the kitchen. Dad is teaching me the rudiments of cookery, and I am the sorcerer's apprentice.

"The secret art is in knowing how much salt to put in and to always use an onion!" His fabled advice is great for stews and soups, but is total disaster when it comes to making custard, puddings, or cakes.

"We will make a Polish casserole with this." Dad holds up a small flat-sided bottle with a red label. Polish Spirit 212 proof. He has been given this fierce distillation by a Polski mate at work, along with the recipe for a vodka-based beef stroganoff–type dish. The chunks of beef are sautéed in garlic and cayenne pepper, to which Dad adds a good measure of the spirits. While this is suppurating, we both try a glass of the firewater.

"In the name of the wee man! That'll put hairs on a whale's back. Holy moly, I think me teeth have dissolved!" Goggle-eyed and wheezing, Dad regards the bottle as if it contained nitroglycerin.

I am unable to speak at all. The searing liquor has set my throat aflame and cauterized my vocal cords. I've only taken a wee sip and I will take no more! When Dad isn't looking I pour the remainder into the Pyrex casserole dish.

The gas oven is heating up to working temperature. Meanwhile, Dad stirs the vodka-infused meat and garlic, and sniffs the resultant concoction with trepidation.

"I'll give it another shot of this rocket fuel. God knows how the Poles can drink this stuff. It's little wonder they're always dancing and flinging glasses into the fireplace—pheew!" The bottle is emptied into the dish and carrots, celery, and tomatoes added to the pungent potion.

"There now, give that a couple of hours of slow cooking and it will be fit for a feast. Open a couple of bottles of beer, Will. I need to see if my taste buds still work—oh, Jasus! Put the telly on quick! The wrestling just started!"

This is our Saturday routine while Mam is away at work. We would cook the dinner and settle down to the afternoon of televised grappling matches with commentator Kent Walton. A fearsome grudge match is in progress between Jackie "Mr. TV" Pallo and the sinister Mick MacManus in his black leotard. The crowd jeers and boos as bad boy Mick picks pretty boy Jackie up above his head for a body slam. As the wrestler's back hits the canvas, a deafening explosion resounds from the kitchen behind us! Dad and me stare at each other for a split second, then dive next door. The kitchen is in ruins. flying food has spattered the walls and windows, and the oven door lies smoking in the corner. Dad scrapes a piece of beef from the doorjamb and tastes it.

"Hmm, very good! Try some, but look out for bits of broken glass."

It takes a lot of cursing and elbow grease to get the shrapnel from Dad's Polish vodka bomb from the kitchen walls and even longer to rehang the oven door. We are tidied up when Mam comes home at midnight.

"So what's for dinner?" she says, not noticing anything out of the ordinary. Dad looks sheepish. In our haste to square up the place, we have forgotten about eating altogether, and Mam's dinner had self-destructed in the oven.

"Oh, I get it! Muggins here is out at work all day while you pair of idle prats sit on your fat arses watching the bloody goggle-box and drinking Polish piss water!" She throws the empty vodka bottle into the rubbish bin and storms off to bed.

The next day is spent in a frenzy of painting to cover up the remains of the evidence of our culinary catastrophe.

"At least we didn't get found out!" says Dad, running a paint roller across the kitchen ceiling, while I paint the door panels.

"Yeah, we are lucky! If Mam had seen the mess, she would've put the house out through the window and murdered the pair of us!"

Dad smiles a satisfied smile at the newly painted kitchen.

"There now, that will please yer mam!" And it does—until three weeks later, when Dad comes home drunk, puts two pork chops under the grill, and dozes off in the armchair. He is still snoring when Mam and I come home. The chops are burnt to a cinder, the grill top has melted, and the freshly decorated walls are black with greasy soot.

Mam swears at him for over half an hour and never repeats herself once.

Whenever Dad is short of a latch lifter, which he called the price of a pint of beer, we take my guitar up to the local pub and do a bit of busking. I sing some sad old Irish songs for the many laborers from the Emerald Isle, who are temporally exiled on some building site in the Midlands. The boys like the Irish rebel songs, too, and many's the good night's craic starts off with next to no money. These lads sing along, stamping their feet in time and thanks be to God, passing the hat around afterward! There is no Irish music to be heard on juke boxes this time of day, and the workers really show their appreciation for a wee touch of home.

Most of these chaps work on short contracts in England to keep their families fed back home in Ireland. They call themselves long-distance men.

They are a hard breed of men, working out in all weathers and living out of the pubs and the fish and chip shops. Often they stay in the cheapest lodgings, or spikes, as they refer to these doss-houses. They have their own folklore about the good and bad construction companies to work for. These become the subject of the ragged-arsed toastmasters:

Come all you brave young navvies
And you long-distance men,
And don't you work for Bovis,
MacAlpine or Maclean.

"A toast: You work for Laing, but not for long!"

The glasses clink and a tidal wave of Guinness washes away the dust of a day's hard labor.

"A toast to WIMPEY: *'We Import Millions of Paddies Every Year!'*"

With a sweep of well-trained elbows, the flagons are drained and replenished.

"A toast:

Oh Mother dear, I'm over here,
And never coming back.
What keeps me here's,
The rake of beer,
The women and the craic!"

"A toast:

'Twas the Irish built the roads of Britain,
and before them, the bloody Romans!"

They are good men, these gentlemen of the pick, shovel, hod, and trowel. They are amongst the finest lads to be met anywhere; hard-working, honest, and diligent. Politicians could learn much from them!

My activities at school continue to incur the wrath of the headmaster. I have been warned that I'm on the expulsion list. It's dinnertime and I am called to his office. On my way, I prepare my speech for the defense:

"I cannot settle to this tame, indolent existence amid the stench of fuming factories and the wantonness of pissy backstairs that lead to the concrete concussion of urban urbanity. It is easy for me to see how rats caught in a maze go mad and kill each other in frenzied savagery. This will not be my fate. I who have flown with the war heroes, survived the fury of the accursed damp, run with the sleek brown hunted otter, and roamed wild with the children of the Gael amongst the shafts of Celtic willows springing straight and lethal from the osier beds."

In the cluttered calm of the Head's study I deliver my oration, standing erect like Robert Emmet in the dock.

"Yes, very good, Watkins. Go home, your grandmother has died."

Mary-Anne the dancer had passed away, aged seventy-three.

I ask Mr. Druce, the science teacher, if I can start a science club during recess and a couple of hours after classes each night. He is delighted at my interest and readily agrees to our needs, subject to the headmaster's approval. I often helped the staff set up experiments and equipment, so he has no problem giving me a key to the main laboratory on the top floor of the science block.

One day we casually ask permission to form an amateur radio society. This, like our previous request, is granted by the headmaster, who is delighted that he has whipped one of his dissidents back into line.

We rig a huge dipole antenna and set up an ex-army W.S. No. 19 transmitter-receiver and attendant accessories: microphones, record player, tape recorder, and so on. Thus is Radio 190 born!

Our pirate radio service runs for an hour at lunchtime and two hours in the evening on a frequency of 190 meters — easily tunable on any transistor radio.

My staff of four are very professional in their delivery, and the programs soon have a wide listenership. We can be heard up to a mile away in daytime and two miles at night. For nearly three months we stay on the air.

One lunchtime, two green vans appear in the staff car park with ominous-looking direction-finding loop antennas on the roofs. We had just started transmitting when in bursts the headmaster, a policeman, and four members of the General Post Office Radio Interference Division, "The Pirate Busters." We are nicked!

I take the rap for the whole shebang and tell the doubting officials that the other kids didn't know we were radiating.

"I'm leaving soon to become a radio officer in the merchant marine."

"Best bloody place for you!" says one of the GPO men.

In view of this admission, I am not charged with offenses under the Wireless Telegraph Act of 1949 (illegal transmitting apparatus), but I'm given a hell of a row and the equipment is confiscated.

The headmaster invites me to resign from the school and thus save me the embarrassment of being expelled. This I duly do and that is the end of my formal education. I am sixteen.

My only regret is in betraying the trust of Mr. Druce. I seek him out and begin to apologize.

"You're a silly bugger, Watkins."

"Yes, sir, sorry, sir."

"Have I taught you nothing, boy?"

"Sorry, sir."

"Sticking to the same wavelength. You should move frequency, and then they'll never catch you!"

"Eh?"

"It's a shame. I like some of that folk music you played. You don't hear too much of that on the ordinary radio stations!"

So he knew all along, the cunning old fox.

"Good-bye, Watkins," he says, shaking my hand.

He is the last staff person I speak to that day, and I'm glad that we part respecting each other.

I knew I was wasting my time at school. The staff, too, knew that I was not going to pass my exams and meekly go into industry.

Dave Knaggs, the new poetry teacher, urged me to go into the theater.

"Become an actor, dear boy! God knows you have it in you!" was his advice.

Mr. Davies, our Welsh music master and part-time sadist, who had once caught me playing the blues on a harmonica, informed me that I had no musical ability whatsoever, and "a bloody cowboy like you, Watkins, should join the bloody army. It would make a bloody man of you. Look see—there's lovely, isn't it?"

I go home and that evening and tell my parents that I am no longer at school. They are surprisingly more amenable than I thought. Maybe they saw it coming.

"So what are you going to do now?" asks Dad.

"Well, I think I'll take out my wee bit of money from the Post Office Savings Bank and go back home to Ireland!"

"Hhmm! Come on!" he says, and we go for a walk into the cornfield at the back of the flats.

"Listen, Will, when I was young I wanted to be an artist. My father discouraged this and wanted me to join the Great Western Railway where he was a rising star. He had great plans for me. I would become a Freemason like him and this would help shoot me to the top. But he never thought of what I wanted. I didn't want to go against him. So I gave up my dreams for a while, thinking that after a couple of years on the railways, I could go to art school on my own money."

"So why didn't you?"

"Because Franco, Mussolini, Hitler, and the rest of the fascist bastards had a different idea about my future. By the time I'd finished fighting those sods, my chance was gone and my youth with it!"

"Oh! I never thought about it like that before." We crunch on through the stubble of dried-up cornstalks.

"Do what you feel you should do and do it well. Live your own dreams and no one else's. Never give up and don't believe the buggers who tell you it's impossible, all right?"

"Sure, Dad, I'll do that!"

"Just don't come back here later on and say I put you wrong, OK?"

"Yes, Dad, I will do no-such-a-cowardly-act, as Mam would say!"

"Remember, Willie, a man of honor may oft times have to walk alone!"

We trudge on in silence until we reach the stile. After crossing over, Dad puts his strong hand on my shoulder and heaves a shuddering great sigh. Then squaring me around face to face, he looks me straight in the eye and adds, "Remember above all things, you are a Celt, laddie!"

→ Chapter 19 ←

JOHNNY (J.C.) CARR, EX-SCHOOL CHUM AND HARMONICA
player extraordinaire, sits next to me on the braided, horsehair-stuffed
seats of the Irish boat train. He is engrossed in tuning an autoharp, the
effort of which has his bottom lip sticking out like a washbasin. This
time it is my mam who waves farewell and watches the train draw away
into the long New Street Tunnel.

Peering out of the misted-up windows, I see Mam disappearing in
a vortex of white steam as we move away. A thousand swirling images
of our past travels and partings cascade through my mind. I had gone
places before without my folks, but this time I know it is different, and
so does my mam. She knows fine that she is saying good-bye to her little
lad forever and that the person who returns from this adventure will be
changed, grown up, someone new. It is all rather sad.

"You ain't gonna cry, are ya, ya big wench?" needles Johnny in his
Brummy accent.

"Of course not. I've just got a bit of soot in my eye from sticking
my head out of the window!"

"You are, you're gonna blub. Blimey, and to think I took you for a
bit of a bleeding hard knock!"

"I'll give you a hard knock if you don't shut yer gob!" My reaction
gives Johnny the rise he was looking for and he sits, contentedly chuckling to himself as the train bursts out of the tunnel into the grimy "sa-
tanic mills" of the industrial North Midlands.

I doze for a while with my eyes closed, thinking of when I was a
wee kid and fond of putting my head out of the carriage window into
the fragrant clouds of steam that billowed by.

"Don't do that, you'll get smuts!" said my mam, not explaining that smuts are airborne soot particles.

"OK, Mam!" I'd say and sit down puzzled.

The only smuts I'd heard of was General Jan Smuts, a hero of the South Africans, who fought the British in the Boer War, and I couldn't see how he fit into the picture.

I jolt awake with an involuntary laugh.

"Well, Wocko, it's good to see you've cheered up!"

"Aye, aye, J.C.," I mumble and begin checking my gear to make sure I have everything. It doesn't take long. I have a guitar, a sleeping bag, a woolen blanket, one change of clothes, and a bag of cheese and onion sandwiches.

"Do you want a sandwich, Johnny?"

"Fuggin' right I do!"

Johnny has even less gear than I do. Whereas I have left home with the blessing of my folks, J.C. has run away after a barney with his mother, and he thinks the police might be looking for him. His only possessions are a bag of harmonicas, an autoharp, a blanket-wrapped sleeping bag, and the clothes he stands up in. About his neck is a heavy crescent-shaped pendant fashioned by himself from a pound of pure copper; this he wears for good luck. On his head is a black derby, and the huge pocket watch hanging on a toilet chain from his waistband completes the ensemble. It's like traveling with the Mad Hatter.

Johnny and I had spent a short time on the road before. Last summer we had hitchhiked to Stourport and slept rough in the old sandstone caves with other weekend ravers. It was fun but cold in those caverns; even with the aid of a crackling log fire, the earth was damp and the air chilly. The real troglodytes, who had lived there until the 1930s, must have been a very tough breed of folk. Eventually, the way of life of these cave dwellers was made illegal by the various Health and Safety Acts of the wartime government and they were rehoused.

Sometime later J.C. immortalizes the events in song:

> *Billy and Johnny, fresh from school*
> *Slung with guitars and playing it cool*
> *Out on the road, down Stourport way*
> *To live in the caves for a holiday-hay-hay.*

The truth was, our first expedition into the wild world was a desperately ill-equipped affair: one blanket each, no tent, no matches, no cooking gear, loads of tins of beans and not a bloody can opener between us. After this initial bollock-freezing folly, we made sure that, if nothing else, our bedrolls would be adequate. "'Still, everyone makes mistakes,' as the hedgehog said, climbing off of the hairbrush." So what the hell? We're on the road!

This journey to Ireland was to be the making of us both; we planned on being away an entire year. No more would we be considered weekend ravers, traveling on optimism instead of experience. Whenever we do return to Birmingham, we'll be real heroes—long-distance men!

I'm looking forward to returning home to Ireland, and when I realize that it's nearly six years since I was last over home, my enthusiasm bubbles up.

"You won't believe Ireland, Johnny. It's beautiful. Everything is green, forty shades of it, they say. Not just the fields and the hills, even the railway engines, airplanes, buses—all emerald green."

"Yeah, yeah, and the shamrocks are green and the leprechauns are green and me arse is green—"

"Well, your face might be green by morning, matey. The sea yonder looks a wee bit on the rough side. Do you get seasick?"

"I dunno. I've not been on a ship before."

"That's right, you've never been out of England, have you? God knows what you're expecting to find in Ireland—lions, elephants maybe, camels, or whatnot!"

"Little green women, an' little green men, an' little greenhorns like you, so don't be taking the piss out of me, Wockins, ya cheeky wee bastard. I'm older than you, remember, so have a bit of respect!"

"Oh, aye, that eighteen days makes all the difference. Who do you think you are, bloody Methuselah?"

"Who the hell's Mafoosela?"

"You know, the bloke in the Old Testament who lived nine hundred and sixty-nine years—blimey, Johnny, haven't you read the Bible?"

"No!"

"Why?"

"Because it's full of bollocks, like blokes living nine hundred and sixty-nine years!"

Holyhead, the gray granite springboard of so many of my past adventures, comes into view. The boat train pulls into the seaport and the west wind whips hard at the wave tops, sending white breakers crashing over the harbor mole. Rising from the quayside like a floating city is a shiny new passenger ship, owned by British Railways, but called the M.V. *Hibernia*. The old steamship *Princess Maud,* which had survived countless hurricanes, two world wars, and the curses of my mother, had finally met her fate in the scrap yard.

The new vessel is clean and spacious. We promenade the deck like Edwardian gentlemen, nodding to fellow passengers and crew members alike. Below decks, we find the seclusion of an empty linen closet and roll our sleeping bags out on the wide wooden shelves. It's perfect.

There's a singsong in the lounge bar, and grabbing our instruments, we join in. The Irish are famous for impromptu get-togethers like this and we have a good session, marred only by Johnny being refused service by the English bloke at the bar.

"Can I get two pints of Guinness, please?"

"Are you of age, mate?" says the barman in a London Cockney accent.

"What d'you say?"

"How bleedin' old are you, sonny?"

"I'm sixteen."

"Then come back in two years, sunshine. Now bugger orf or you'll get my boot up yer arse!"

We dock in Ireland next morning. Although the sea remained rough, the crossing had been smooth as the ship was fitted with stabilizers. Johnny was not seasick and, indeed, proved to have a "cast-iron" stomach after surreptitiously drinking all the dregs he could find in the bar. A comfortable night's sleep was had in our makeshift cabin, and before long we were making our way down the gangplank onto Irish sod.

"Welcome to my country, Mr. Carr." I make a sweeping arm gesture.

"Merci beaucoupus fullbus maccabeeus, Mr. Wockins." Johnny bows in mock reply.

"What's that mean?"

"I've no idea."

The tang of sea air, fresh and salty, is great for the appetite, and along the dockside a greasy-spoon café offers an Irish breakfast we'd be fools to ignore. After supping on a belt-bursting meal of sausage, bacon, eggs, fried black pudding, tomatoes, soda bread, and hot black tea, we waddle like penguins over the cobblestone forecourt to the Dublin train.

The port rail terminal is not quite as I remember. Dun Laoghaire has changed a lot in six years. Long rows of horse-drawn jaunting cars once queued here waiting for fares; now it is rows of motor taxis that ply the trade.

Sadly, the hissing green CIE steam trains of yesteryear have been replaced with oil-dripping diesel locomotives in grimy orange livery. Nearing the engine, the sweet ocean ozone, wafting in from the bay, is quickly soured by the belch of acrid exhaust fumes from the revving loco. Johnny pulls an equally acidic face and belches himself.

"Hey, Wocko, you bullshiter! You told me they had green steam trains here, not these stinky things." I have no answer for him, so I just shrug my shoulders.

From the vantage point of the long curve of raised railway line, J.C. stares down on the shops and houses comprising the outskirts of Dublin. The quick ride into the city has convinced my friend that Ireland was England with more shit in the streets. The brisk walk from Westland Row station to the city center confirms his belief.

"These buses look exactly the same as the buses in Birmingham!"

He was right. The buses, once green with gold trim, were now a drab cream and black, but something else looked different, too, something about the view down O'Connell Street. What the hell was it?

"These building are just like the ones in Brum, same stone, same shape, same—"

"Of course they are. They were built by the same British architects when Ireland was a colony! But something has changed since I was last here," I mumble, still puzzled by the "new look" Dublin.

"What's changed about it?"

"I'm not sure. People seem better off than I remember, better dressed. There's more motorcars than there used to be and hardly a horse and cart to be seen. These shopfronts all had quaint old Dickensian windows. I wonder why they got replaced with plate glass?"

"Maybe it's just modernization, you know? Getting with it, as they say."

"I guess you're right, J.C. You can't expect a place to stay frozen in time, like the Olde Worlde pictures on a toffee tin, but it's a shame that things have to change."

"That's the trouble with nostalgia, Wocko, it ain't what it used to be."

"Yeah, maybe that's it. Wait a minute! Oh, my God, he's gone! Totally gone!"

"Who's gone?"

"Admiral Nelson! Horatio *bloody* Nelson. He's gone, completely gone!"

"I think you're bleedin' gone, Wockins, gone in the head! Nelson's been dead for donkey's years!"

"Johnny, you don't understand. He was standing right there, outside the GPO, on a bloody great two-hundred-foot column, like the one in Trafalgar Square, and it's gone!"

"What d'you think happened to him?"

"I dunno, wait and I'll ask someone. Hey, mister, what happened to old Nelson?"

"Aw Jasus, son, sure wasn't he blown up last March by the brave boyos!"

"What boyos?"

"The Eye Or Ay, so it was, in the middle of the night. Blew the ould Brit from his perch—an' good riddance to the one-eyed ould tosser. Ould Nelson is up there now, orbiting the fookin' earth with John Glenn an' Yuri *fookin'* Gagarin!"

"What did he say, Wock? I didn't get a word of that."

"He says the IRA blew up the statue in the middle of the night."

"That's right, son. The lads blew the beJasus out of the column, without even cracking a pane of glass in the GPO. When the fookin' Irish Army were called in to blow up what fookin' remained of the fookin' thing, they broke every fookin' window in Dublin! Boom!" says the stranger, throwing his arms in an arc about his head.

The spot where Nelson's plinth had once stood is now a flowerbed burgeoning with daffodils. We take our ease for a while, sitting on the concrete wall surrounding the nodding yellow blooms. On the parapet, some Dublin wag has scribbled "Nelson's Grave."

"The GPO, over there, is where the rising of 1916 started fifty years ago."

"Oh, that's nice," he says, surveying the scene.

"Nice? There was bugger-all nice about it. The British shelled the city flat and killed hundreds."

Johnny isn't listening; his mind is elsewhere and, in a feat normally the sole province of the owl, he nigh-on turns his head full circle when checking out a bevy of passing office girls.

"Wow! They've got some nice looking bints here and no mistake. D'ya think we'll get the ride?"

"No bloody chance. You know what they say in Holy Catholic Ireland, 'No Fling Without a Ring!'" J.C. pouts and cranes his gaze in the opposite direction; there is a sharp crack like the snapping of a stick of chalk.

"Oh, shit! I think I've got fighter pilot's neck!" He rubs the bones at the base of his skull as pain dampens his ardor and more mundane thoughts reappear.

"So where's this other station we have to go to. Is it far?"

"Aye, it is. Kingsbridge station is a good long walk from here, a couple of miles away up the back of Guinness's brewery."

"That's a drag. Why didn't they build the station in the city center?"

"Well, they thought of that, but decided it was better to put it where the railway tracks were."

"Oh, very funny, Wocko. You're so bloody sharp, be careful you don't cut yerself."

"Forward march!" I signal. Johnny follows and we swing briskly up the banks of the Liffey to the railway station. Although encumbered by our bedrolls and instruments, we exude a jaunty air and enjoy the inquisitive looks from passersby and the curious gaze of the many young lassies we meet on the way. Imbued with all the confidence of victorious soldiers on a looting spree, we know there is nothing in Ireland the likes of us!

The Limerick Express thunders across the great open expanse of the Curragh Plain. All around, fine thoroughbred horses are being exercised for the flat-racing season. Like the white chalk figures our ancestors carved into the hills, these creatures look so well adapted and content in the lush, green landscape. It is easy to see how these Irish horses excel in soft-going racing conditions when they have been running on moist malleable moss all their lives. Sure I like the soft-going myself.

"Glac bog an saoghal agus glachgig an saoghal bog tú!"

"Yeah, Watkins, and the bleeding same to you with knobs on! What sort of bloody bog Latin is that? Roman?"

"No, it's Irish! That was the favorite saying of a venerable old Irish tailor. It means, 'Treat the world softly and the world will treat you softly!'"

"So you bog-wogs have yer own lingo, do you? I thought you were just ignorant paddies that can't speak English proper—like what I do!"

"And a lovely job you make of it, too, Johnny! No, Irish is a very ancient language, far older than Greek or Latin, a remnant of the old Celtic tongue once spoken all over Europe and the British Isles, until the Romans pushed the native people into the most out-lying fringes of the continent, where they live to this day."

Johnny chants a kiddies' street rhyme much used by girls jumping rope or skipping, as we would say:

> *The Germans speak Krautish*
> *The Frenchies speak Frog*
> *The Romans speak I-tie*
> *The Noggies speak Nog*
> *But the English speak English*
> *The language of God!*

"Hmm, very nice, but 'dogs' would be a better rhyme and a lot more accurate."

"Bollocks!"

"That's an Irish word, Johnny!"

"Well, how about *bugger off?*"

"Now you're talking. That's good old Anglo-Saxon, or as you would say, the language of God. By the way, do you fancy a beer?" He looks up suspiciously.

"How are you going to manage that? We're both obviously under-age."

"You're not in England now, sonny!" I say, mimicking the Cockney accent of the barman on the ship. "This is Ireland!" I make my way to the buffet car, where I buy two bottles of Time beer. The barman hardly looks at me.

Beer in hand, J.C. is very impressed.

"How did you pull that one off?"

"You see, my friend, no one thinks it odd that a sixteen-year-old would be up at the bar getting drinks. The parents often send the kids up to get the rounds in."

"Cool! Is it the same in the towns—kids allowed in pubs and the like?"

"Yeah. All the big pubs employ young lads as potboys to fetch and carry pints for the grown-ups, and if someone is sick, a child might be sent to the local pub for a bottle of medicinal whiskey. No one's bothered if a teenager has a beer or two, as long as he don't get stupid and start showing off. You can have a good piss-up as long as you don't advertise it to the whole bloody world! You'll not get away with that in Birmingham, will you, eh?"

J.C. nods his head and sucks at his beer bottle, cross-eyed, like a calf getting its early morning feed. He makes me laugh, and humor is a good leaven and succor in times of travail. I reckon, deep down he's carrying a heavy load and hides his problems under a facade of japing and jesting that gives him a reputation for being a bit of a bumsteer. At school his taste for practical jokes was legendary, and he drove the teachers to distraction.

Johnny could emit a high-pitched scream, ventriloquist-like, and then become part of the crowd of puzzled passersby, looking around and speculating on the origin. When some poor innocent bugger runs past him at speed, "Stop thief!" Johnny shouts. The unfortunate victim of this prank was often grabbed or banjaxed by some civic-minded member of the public, who instead of receiving praise for their actions, are at pains to explain the nature of their random act of violence to the injured party. He transforms the mundane world around us into a maelstrom of mischief and mayhem, whilst seemingly aloof to the consequences. Johnny was born on April Fool's Day the same year as myself; a date that, considering his taste for the bizarre, has to be more than coincidence.

I first met him when he was made to sit next to me at school. He was loud and brash with a puckish sense of humor and liked to get up the teachers' noses. However, he wasn't much of a student and left school early to become an apprentice cable joiner for a firm of street-lighting electricians. He says that working in the roadside trenches gives you great opportunity to look up girls' skirts, and heating up pennies with a blow lamp, for some mean old sod to pick up, is a good source of fun on an otherwise boring day.

Johnny sits staring at the label on his beer bottle, his eyebrows alternately meeting and blenching; like two shy caterpillars waiting to be introduced.

"Why call a beer Time? Seems like an odd name. Time goes by, maybe? Ah, ha! That's the joke—Time for another!" Finger aloft in realization, he makes for the bar and returns somewhile later with: "Look, Wock, more Time on me hands!"

He lies full length across the carriage seats, gawping at the green fields flitting by. His well-rounded face has a girlish "peaches and cream" complexion, which, combined with his shoulder-length blond curls, makes him look rather effeminate. This most certainly is not his nature. He's a tough little bugger and can be a downright nasty little bollix when it suits him. It's as well that he makes me laugh or sometimes I'd have to strangle him.

I had helped him to play music and he was quick to learn the guitar and mouth organ. Now J.C. has an autoharp to add a little zest to our folk duo, and we look forward to singing for our supper in the green womb of Holy Ireland, where so much music and poetry have been conceived, nurtured, and often banned by the BloodyEnglish.

We arrive in the same old Limerick station and go to my nana's house, where there is tea, soda bread and jam, and a bed made up for us in the spare room.

After swapping family news, I sit scanning the entertainment column in the *Limerick Leader* newspaper, for word of a folk club or traditional music event where we might make our debut.

To my chagrin, I can't see anything that looks even remotely promising. It seems that country and western music has taken over and there is no shortage of these gigs. The big venues are being packed out by the many showbands, like "Big Tom and the Mainliners" and "Dickie Rock and the Miami." This is a blow. What has happened to the come-all-ye folk clubs? Is our trip to end in disappointment?

"So what's the big event in this one-horse town?" Johnny enjoys taking the piss out of my mounting frustration.

"Well, Latchford's Cinema in Newcastle West is opening with *Mary Poppins* on the twenty-first of August. Admission prices: threepence, two and six, and one and six. Do you want to go?"

"I'd rather eat my own shite, thank you very much!"

"You wait there, Johnny, and I'll get you a spoon!"

Dad is right. The Lamp of the Gael is burning at an all-time low. Poetry is becoming the province of academics, and traditional music is disappearing from areas of the countryside, like frost on a fire grate. Something has got to be done, but what?

"What has happened, Uncle Seán? What's happened to Celtic culture?"

"Jasus, Willie, you will be hard put to finding a piece of Celtic culture outside of a museum. Sure the Gaelic tunes, songs, and stories are being torn asunder by immigration and death and apathy and sure Hollywood movies have a lot to answer for. Radio Eireann hardly ever plays Irish music anymore. Now it's all Frank Sinatra and Elvis Presley and all them Bobby whatsits—Vee or Vinton or Darrin. Jasus, there's no end to them! Sure I have the feeling that Irish music is on the run and has little chance of surviving for long, unless a miracle happens!"

He's right, judging by the fact that it is almost impossible to get traditional Irish music on modern LP records. Most of the stuff we have is on old cracked wax seventy-eights. I worry it might all be going down the tubes, doomed to oblivion in my own lifetime.

"Auntie Maura, would you ever sing me 'Bridgín Bhan Mo Stór?'"

"Ah, go'way now, Willie, sure no one sings them old come-all-ye songs anymore, sure they went out with the Ark! How about 'When Irish Eyes Are Smiling' or maybe 'Tu-ra Lu-ra Lu-ra'?" They're grand little ditties altogether! You need to get with it, Willie!"

"Maura, if Tin Pan Alley is with it, I'd rather be without it!"

It seems that the old ways are dying out and a new era of modernism is sweeping the last vestige of the Gael into the wild Atlantic, with folks looking on who think that Bing Crosby is an Irish priest who sings nice songs and does a bit of acting on the side!

It isn't all bad news though. Seán tells me that Irish music and folklore are still alive and safe in small pockets scattered throughout the country and even more so overseas in Britain and America.

"You need to get out into the country and seek ye the festivals called 'Fleádh Cheoils.' Organizations like Comhaltas Ceoltóiri Éireann are working both sides of the Irish Sea trying to promote traditional music and dance. Seán O'Rioda, Paddy Tunney, and Séamus Ennis are doing grand work, and so are the Dubliners and Paddy Maloney's group Ceoltóri Chuilinn. I'll ask around the boys at the post office and we'll see if we can't find you a Fleádh Cheoil to get your teeth into!"

"Thanks, Uncle Seán. I promised my dad that I would do something to help save our culture and that will give me a start."

"Strike a blow for the Gael, Liam! Ceol an Gael Abú!"

Seán brings news of a Fleádh in Kilrush, County Clare, where I had once seen the tinkers and the drunken horse. With spirits high, we hitchhike down to Kilkee and sleep the night in one of the beach changing huts. In the wee small hours, the door bursts open, giving me the fear of Christ.

"Oh, sorry lads! It's the police here—I'm just checking!" The civic guard looms large on the other end of his flashlight, his torch picking out our musical instruments in the gloom.

"Are you down here for the Fleádh, boys?"

"We are, sir, yes. We've come down from Limerick!"

"Good lads. I'll maybe see you in the morning, so! Goodnight now."

After sunup we arise to leave. I find that some kind person has left a pint of milk and a bunch of bananas outside the hut for our breakfast.

"It must have been the policeman. What a nice chap, eh, Johnny?"

"A.C.A.B."

"What's that supposed to mean?"

"All Coppers Are Bastards, Wockins, you mark my words." Shaking my head, I leave him sitting on the sand dunes, the policeman's milk running down his peach-fuzzed chin.

Alone I walk up to the cliff tops and stand eating my banana, watching the ever crashing, luminous green Atlantic rollers basting the bay with rhythmic repetition.

The sky is alive, iridescent with bands of mingling color: red, gold, green, and blue. Great white gulls and kittiwakes wheel and squawk overhead, spiraling upward, then descending dartlike into the foam-topped waves. Although I am alone, I have no feeling of loneliness. I feel a part of all this. Like the prodigal I am, I have returned home to where my heart lies. Way out, far past the edge of the silvery bay, I see a ship hull down to the horizon.

"Must be going to America. More immigrants, I suppose. Just why do people pull up their roots and leave such a beautiful place?" I am still full of the inward glow of the returned wayward son, wandering and wondering, being young, naive, and most of all oblivious to the economic realities of recession-cursed Ireland.

"Wockins! Wocko! Where are ya?" J.C. is calling me from below, his foghorn voice cutting through the hiss of waves on the shape-shifting shingle.

I make my way back down and pack up my gear. It is a testament to the times that sleeping bags, guitars, or what have you can be left unattended almost anywhere without fear of theft or damage. Johnny is waiting.

"What yow bin doing, Wock?"

"I was communing with nature." I am still dreaming the small dreams of the protopoet.

"Yer, me too. I had my shite over there!" replies my nefarious neme-sis, pointing to a little pyramid of turds and newspaper, steaming amongst the golden sand dunes.

As I roved out one midsummer's morning,
For to view the fields and to take the air,
Down by the banks of the sweet primroses,
'Tis there I spied a sweet maiden fair.

Singing at the top of my voice, I march my way along the green-dyked undulating road, from the seaside town of Kilkee, to the inland market town of Kilrush.

Strolling along a few feet behind me, Johnny is striking great swelling chords of accompaniment on the autoharp. We are a pair of medieval minstrels on our way to the fair to find fame and fortune. Bardic vagabonds, celebrating a tradition as old as humankind itself. Songsters, rhymesters, clowns, and jongleurs. The Gentlemen of the Toby, as all true Gypsies call the road. We are the dedicated artisans of the muse, resolved to play our souls to the very heavens and, if at all pos-sible, please God, get ourselves fixed up with a couple of young lassies.

The soft wind pulls the summer trees over to hear our song. The sun tumbles blithely across the blue sky, the meadowlark soars from the furze in sublime vivacity, and we, just as carefree, ramble through County Clare.

Cars full of reprobates, rakes, and revelers occasionally pass us by, the folks all waving and beeping their horns in merriment.

Although we do not stick the old hitchhiker's thumb out, to our great surprise, a venerable old Morris Minor car stops next to us and its equally ancient driver asks, "Arroo going to the Fleádh, boys? If you am, get yerselves in. I'm away down to sell da sheep and ye'll be most welcome to come along fer da ride!"

We are quick to take up the farmer's kind offer, but when I open the door, I realize that the driver has the only seat left in the vehicle. Where the passenger seat and the rear seats once were, there is just a bed of straw and a disconsolate-looking blackface sheep that stares back at us as baleful as Bacchus during the holy hour.

Anyway, we make the most of it and our journey down is full of songs and jokes. On the outskirts of town, we run into the crowds, and it takes almost thirty minutes to navigate through the festive throng to the central square.

So like Christ's triumphant entry into Jerusalem on the back of a lowly donkey, we young hopefuls arrive at the epicenter of the "1966 All-Ireland Fleádh Cheoil," not as the rising stars of the folk music revival, as we had hoped, but covered in straw and sheep shit and smelling like the bottom of an owl's nest.

The Fleádh is a unique experience. Since I have little interest in sporting events and seldom do the Stations of the Cross, I'm not used to large crowds at all and it is at first a bit intimidating. Before long, however, the good nature of the participants and the other musicians quickly wins me over and I feel as at home as a pig in a midden. Johnny is in his element, doing his long-range ventriloquist act and puzzling the beJasus out of the folk in the market square. I am plucked by the arm by a big fellow with a shock of wiry red hair and a square ginger beard.

"Come on, youngfella, there's a grand session inside of the green barn here. Come and sit in, and we'll hear some of your stuff."

I recognize this man from an LP record of my mam's. It is Luke Kelly from the Dubliners! Johnny follows us inside, grinning with devilment.

In the dim light of the old corrugated iron barn, several tiers of wooden benches have been erected, and on some of the lower ones sits a clutch of musicians battering out the reel "Rakish Paddy."

The thing I find most peculiar with this scene is that the audience sits behind the players and can only see their backs. When I ask Luke why this is, he says, "This is a session, not a concert, so you don't need folks staring ya in the face!"

I am very glad of this fact, when after being invited to sing, my nervous state of excitement causes complete amnesia in the middle of "The Wreck of Engine 143." My red face is saved by my fellow musicians filling in an extra-long instrumental break until I can recover my wits and sing the ending to the old American railroad song.

Johnny and myself, gaining in confidence by the minute, play almost everything we know and soon are the *corps célèbre* of the assembly of fine musicians, made up mostly from the Pipers' Club in

Thomas Street, Dublin. These wonderful people take us under their collective wing, and we become sort of mascots for our much older and wiser companions.

Brendan Byrne, or Brendan Bodhrán, as he is known, being a virtuoso on the ancient one-sided Irish skin drum, is taken up with J.C. and, like him, has an autoharp. He spends a good while teaching Johnny new techniques and how to get the best out of his old yoke, as most folk refer to any unknown or seldom seen instrument.

I have a good deal of time chatting with Luke Kelly, who is very interested in some of the old songs that I can remember and is pleased when I help him fill in some missing words or verses from a song he is trying to master.

Luke is a truly great singer and a lovely man and, like myself, sports a "Ban the Bomb" badge on his jacket lapel. He is as politically aware as he is talented, and it is reckoned that his voice is loud enough to blow the froth off of a pint of Guinness at forty paces!

I'm glad to say that he is very patient with me when I put up my half-arsed arguments against his communist beliefs. Also, he is delighted when I sing Spanish Civil War songs like "Viva La Quince Brigada" or "Los Cuatro Generales" in which he and Brendan would join in with gusto, their clenched fists waving the air!

For the four days of the Fleádh, our mentors do us proud, imparting that which you cannot learn at school or from your family and treating us as young adults, not as older children.

We are successful in everything, except chatting up the girls. I am far too shy and Johnny is far too blunt. Between the pair of us, we either bore them to death or scare them off. A couple of blond girls with Swedish flags sewn on their rucksacks seem poised to speak with us. J.C. jumps in quick, snatching defeat from the jaws of victory.

"It gets on yer wick, don't it?" he says, indicating the enormous press of the crowd around us. I stand beside him nodding assent and grinning like a torn slipper. The darling daughters of Odin regard us in mystified silence, whilst trying to decipher our meaning. Then, assuming they are in the company of a pair of village idiots, they leave us in their wake.

"Fuggin' Viking virgins!" Johnny curses. It's as well he has a "cast-iron neck"; rejection never seems to bother him.

In every house, pub, and street the festival is a seething sea of wild goings-on that would have inspired a dozen paintings by Brueghel, or in some back lanes, the lewd triptychs of Hieronymus Bosch. There is a huge wooden stage made of farm carts in the town square, on which beautifully uniformed Irish dancers clack out their knotwork of intricate steps. On smaller stages all around, competitions are being held for poetry, dancing, singing, piping, flute playing, and fiddling. Harps send their silvern notes drifting heavenward suffused with the smell of roast ox, chicken, and pork. Reminiscent of the medieval pageants, velveteen-tabarded dancers, in vividly embroidered smocks, mingle in the throng, calling to mind the colors of a patchwork quilt. Like camels at the oasis, the imbibers know no limit, and the many hundreds of pubs are serving strings of people well outside their premises and down into the streets.

To one such tavern we push our way through the merrymaking, and it is pleasing to note that folk give way to the musicians, so as to let them into the heart of the sessions. There are so many people crammed inside this old pub that half of the assembled players are having to stand up on the sill of a great stained-glass window to get room to swing the elbow. The music is mighty, and the jigs and reels that we're playing reach a climax of speed, involvement, and dexterity.

Suddenly without any warning, there comes an earsplitting crack and a dozen or so musicians and the multicolored window disappear out onto the cobbledstoned street below. I am one of them, but luckily for me, I land on top of the pile and am thus saved from injury. The ones who fell first seem to fare no lasting harm and even instruments are spared any bad damage. I guess many are too drunk to notice otherwise, as overindulgence leads to great immunity! We climb back through the gaping casement and into the newly air-conditioned pub, where we continue playing until a visiting civic guard calls us to order.

"Quiet! Quieten down now, all of youse!" he shouts, waving his arms in a sit-down movement. "This is no good, no good atall atall!" he continues. "Youse will all need to make some reparations to the good folk of this establishment!"

And with that, he takes off his policeman's hat and passes it around to take up a collection for the damages. By the time it is handed over to the grinning landlord, it is overflowing with pound notes and fivers. He and his staff give us a round of applause in thanks and we bend back to the task of raising the roof—musically, that is!.

It was very strange to see a cop indulging in such a noble gesture and although neither of us could contribute to the fund, I'm glad to have witnessed it. At the insistence of one of the farmers present, we later adjourn to a private house that is having a chélidh. We eagerly dig into the huge buffet of food that is provided for us.

"God, Johnny, this is good scran."

"Yeah, no kidding. I'm as hungry as a pig with worms!"

Our group of six or so plays for the dancers, who thunder across the bare floorboards of the front room. Sitting on the floor, the vibrations of the assembled jarring the bones of my arse, I'm wondering how the deck can take such punishment when a teacup hits me on the head! Looking up I see the Welsh dresser, from which the cup had tumbled, swinging some six inches out from the top of the wall with each syncopated stomp of the dancers. I decide to move to a safer spot as the dresser continues to jive around, shedding its china contents and no one paying any heed to it. Amazingly, the two-hundred-year-old floor stands firm and is probably used to such extreme testing.

But all good things must come to an end, even Fleádhs. On the following Tuesday it is time to say good-bye to our new friends and hit the road once more.

I have learned a lot in these four days. Not just about playing music, but how to conduct myself with a wee bit of decorum. As Luke says, "Always remember that a musician is the guest of his audience and not the other way around!" I am grateful for this wisdom and thank him as we say "Slán leat" to each other. He is a great man with his loud voice, wild red hair, and graceful demeanor.

About five or six miles out of town, there is a Bronze Age "fairy fort." This takes the form of a circular enclosure with a central stone-slabbed chamber that you can access by a shallow tunnel. The locals are very superstitious about these and seldom go near them. This is a useful taboo, as it prevents vandalism and helps to preserve the monuments for future generations. It also means that we can camp out there with little chance of interference from the police or the intrusion of blaggards.

A southwest wind, soft on the cheek, blows warm and moist from the Gulf of Mexico. It has all the makings of a fine night. Content with our lot, we lie in our sleeping bags on the dewy grass, wishing, like most sixteen-year-olds, that we had the company of a couple of lassies. However, I have the moon for companionship; a silver, pockmarked surfer riding the curls of the scudding clouds above. Johnny is soon snoring, but I've a bet on with myself and won't go to sleep until I can remember all of a poem about the moon.

> *Whenever the moon and stars are set*
> *Whenever the wind is high . . . dum te dum*—oh, bugger!

Try another one:

> *The moon was a ghostly galleon*
> *Tossed upon cloudy seas . . . de-dah-de-dah-de-dah*—no better!

There must be one I know all the way through:

> *The man in the moon came down too soon*
> *And burnt his tongue on his porridge*—there, done it!

Good night!

I doze off in the throes of trying to remember any other moonish verse. An hour later, I'm rudely awakened by rain splattering in my face. The moon and stars *have* set, and the wind *is* high. In the cloudy seas above, the ghostly galleon has foundered after the man in the moon abandons ship.

In the sudden squall, my sleeping bag is fast sinking in the mud and Johnny, cursing like a whore on holiday, is trying to wriggle out of his waterlogged bedroll. The storm gathers pace, and we crawl into the open mouth of the underground burial chamber.

Our shadows gyrate on the walls of the mortarless stone vault, as the breeze from outside snatches at the flickering flame of a candle stub. By our feet, a rivulet of peaty rainwater vanishes, gurgling, between the cracks of the flagstone floor. Sitting hunched up in the confined space, we speculate on the existence of yet another crypt below us. This conjecture is short-lived when a successful grab of wind snuffs out the candle. Attempts to relight it fail, and embalmed in our bedrolls, we sit like motionless mummies in the thick blackness, two entombed mortals sporadically illuminated by the blue sheen of lightning flashes from without.

Thunder pounds the grassy roof of the dank Bronze Age sepulcher. Between thunderclaps, the dribbling water splatters onto the stones of the mysterious chamber beneath. Sitting on the numb bones of my arse, knees under chin, I eventually slip into a fitful sleep.

A white-robed Druid invades the dank sanctuary of my tormented dreams. Grasping my wrist, he pulls me down into the dripping catacombs below. A fire flares at the end of a long tunnel, upon which sits the great boiling bronze cauldron of Dagda. The priest causes me to gaze therein. Under its bubbling surface, I see a hideously demonic visage twisted and contorted in a ghastly grimace. Against my will, my own face is drawn inexorably nearer to the wraithlike specter, grinning maniacally up at me. The horrid head opens its raw mouth and, instead of speaking, belches a stench of the foulest imaginings, searing into my stinging nostrils.

"Ahggh!" I shake myself awake into an equally malodorous environment. The fetid air of the musty tumulus has taken on the clinging miasma of a putrefying corpse.

"Silent but deadly, eh, Wockins?" says Johnny, sitting smugly in the clammy midst of his early morning fart.

⤜ Chapter 20 ⤛

A BRISK ATLANTIC BREEZE SWIRLS DUST DEVILS ALONG THE
cracked concrete streets of Milltown Malbay, chasing the last of the
summer heat haze from the late afternoon. The town seems deserted as
we two vagabonds drift through empty lanes with nothing to do and all
day to do it. Autumn is coming and the fresh westerly trade wind threat-
ens to dislodge a goat, feasting on the fruits of windblown cabbage
seeds growing green and luscious in the diseased roof thatch of a white-
washed cottage shop. Having failed to intimidate the animal, the wind
snatches up a faded newspaper, rending the pages asunder in rage. In a
fit of spite, the gust deposits most of the fragments over the half door
of the tumbledown emporium below. A girl's voice from within strains
over the tinny dirge of pop music from a transistor radio.

"Would ye ever close the top door out, Connie? The bloody wind
has all the shite in the universe blowing in and me trying to clean up."

"We've an hour to go yet, Patty-Jo. If I close the door, how will anyone know we're open at all?" comes a second voice.

"Put the sign up in the window, Concepta, fer Jasus' sake and don't
be coddin' me!" The yellow-stained sunshade jerks aside and a slender
hand places a card in front of the cobweb-embroidered corner of a con-
spicuously empty window.

'Yes, We Are Open!' the Day Glo orange message proclaims to a heap
of dead wasps and bluebottles gathered behind the grimy glass.

Johnny makes his way over the road to investigate the derelict shop
and its young female proprietors. As he ventures to peer into the dark
interior, the top half door, squealing in torment on its rusty hinges,
bangs out in his face, revealing the name of the establishment neatly
picked out in fine Art Nouveau lettering: A Touch of Class Boutique.

J.C. gets a fit of the giggles at the shop's optimistic claim and his derision is met by a bleating rebuff from the roof above. The goat leaves off chomping cabbages and from his vantage point regards Johnny with defiant contempt. Lord of all he beholds, the capricious creature reaps his revenge. With a triumphant bleat, the puck lifts its tail, releasing a shower of sticky black grapeshot, skittering down the rotting thatch roof and all over the pair of us. Pursued by the bouncing nodules, Johnny and I scurry for the safety of an old pub up the road that is advertising a music session.

Sitting in the back bar of a west Clare public house picking goat shit out of my collar was not how I'd imagined the life of a wandering balladeer, but as luck would have it, we had stumbled into one of the finest traditional music sessions in Ireland. Amongst the customers in the tavern, the mood is quiet and expectant. Conversation is muted, and Johnny, somewhat awed by the ambience, sits like he's in church .

"That old geezer over there is going to play the fiddle," he whispers over his pint of stout.

With a conceding creak, a coffin-shaped violin case opens. There is a soft rustle of velvet, then the sonorous squeak of a ball of rosin rubbed gently upon the ghost-white horsehairs of a centuries-old bow. In the center of the room, the old man stands tuning the antique walnut instrument resting beneath the stubbled jowls of his chin. Silent, except for the wind in the chimney, the audiences wait impassively for the release of the fiddle's secret soul. The fiddler pays no heed; he takes his time plucking the strings and adjusting the pegs until, content with the tuning, he stiffens his frame and presents bow to string. With his eyes seemly fixed upon a far-distant point in time, a torrent of triplets spill out heralding the arrival of "The Lark in the Morning." Feet tapping in six/eight time, we return to our pints. The maestro takes us on a gay-spirited ramble down "The Road to Lisdoonvarna," and by way of a merry hornpipe, introduces us to "Madame Bonaparte." Finally comes the heart-wrenching lament for lost youth, "An Buachaill Caol Dubh."

I had never before experienced such a mystical force emanating from one human being. It was obvious to me that the fiddle played itself, but the man played the very souls of his listeners. For the first time, I realized the power of music and why it struck fear into those whose hearts were cold to it. If the pen is mightier than the sword, then the fiddle bow is a veritable cutlass in the hands of a noble warrior such as this. This fact didn't escape the BloodyEnglish. Under the Penal Laws of the seventeenth century, possession of a musical instrument was punishable by death! Mind you, come to think of it, under the Penal Laws anything an Irish person did was punishable by death.

A prolonged applause abates, and acknowledging the audience for the first time, the old musician hands the violin to a fresh-faced girl of about eleven. She plays a fine slip-jig, without scratch nor screech, then amid hoots and cheers, hands back the fiddle with a curtsey. A young lad, who might have been her brother, pulls a tin whistle out of his sleeve and begins to play "The King of the Fairies." Every musician in the house joins in and a whale of a session primes the autumn night. I am reborn!

Milltown Malbay, Lahinch, Lisdoonvarna, and Ennistymon become the radials of our circuit as we pass from session to session through the pubs and taverns of wild West Clare. We find a little-known village called Doolin at the back of the Cliffs of Moher. Here we play in a tiny bar in the rear of O'Connor's grocery store.

Although we are seldom paid any money for our entertainment, we are bought lots of pints and provided with plenty of food by our various benefactors. It is a grand apprenticeship to serve, playing the music I love and living rough. However, as winter draws on, we decide to go back to Limerick and the warmth of Nana's house.

There is a poetry and ballad session in the Turret Room of King John's castle and we offer our services. The resident musicians include accordionist Joe Collopy with his pal Jimmy Martin on the bodhrán, and a lovely young girl called Martina, who plays guitar and sings the Irish ballad "Buachaill on Eirne." She is an invocation of pure beauty and I'm immediately smitten with her.

I play one of my own compositions, "The Beatnik's Lament," which despite its lack of subtlety, is well received, rough edges and all. Afterward a reporter from the *Limerick Leader* asks for an interview, which duly appears in the local paper under the headline "Castle Recitals Appealed to Birmingham Pals."

It is a start. From this we get a couple of gigs at Limerick's White

House Tavern, a long-famous place of poetry, music, and sundry bo-
hemian carryings-on. Robert Graves, the poet and author of *The White
Goddess,* is a frequent visitor and we also are befriended by the local artist
and poet Peter Jackson. We are at last getting recognized; this just might
be a twin-edged sword.

We had made friends in town, but unbeknownst to us, we had also
fostered some enemies. After a night in O'Brien's Bar, we are making
our way down the back lanes behind Denmark Street, when two big
men call across to us from the doorway of a derelict shop.

"Hey, lads! Come over here and see this," says one of them, and like
fools we oblige.

"See what?"

"This!" says the other one, punching me in the head and dragging
me into the shop doorway. Recovering quickly from the shock, but finding myself in a headlock, I get a side-angled view of Johnny grappling
with the taller of the two, in the orange silhouette of the streetlight.

"Gerroff, ya bastard!" I roar, but my cries are lost in the rank stench
of my assailant's tweedy armpit. Wriggling away from the acrid reek of
sweat and urine tearing at my senses, I try to grab his balls, but he ma-
neuvers sideways, turning us like a two-man Rugby scrum. Luckily, I
get in range of the other guy and let fly a well-aimed kick into his bollocks. Still spinning, I lose sight of him briefly, but on the next turn, I
see Johnny has the upper hand and the blaggard is scrambling away on
all fours. As I'm dragged around again, there is a whooshing crack
above my head and the grip on my neck relaxes as my attacker, blood
gushing from his ear, stumbles cursing into the darkness. Johnny stands
gasping in the shadows of the doorway, the great half-moon copper
pendant swinging like a blood-spattered medieval mace from his trembling fist.

We never discover the identities of our attackers, let alone their
motive. An overcast day becomes the first of many and finds us loiter-
ing in the local railway station. Now, boredom is an awful thing, and
the devil soon finds work for idle hands. Temptation comes in the form
of an old penny vending machine standing in the corner of the main
hall. The ancient contrivance is a green-painted, cast-iron apparatus,
with a large brass dial lettered A – Z and numbered 0 – 9. By swinging

the pointer to select letters, a person can emboss words on small strips of aluminum. I waste a penny printing a tag with my name on it, and Johnny wastes another making one that reads, "THE POPE IS A JUNKIE." That night at the dinner table I show off my neat little name tag, which I intend to put on my guitar case someday. Johnny has lost the tag he made, which is no big deal until Nana finds it in the bathroom and goes doolally. We think it prudent to cut out until she calms down. After a spell of staying with friends, J.C. and I find an old deserted farm cottage and move in.

On a rainy evening, Garda officer Patrick Carmodhy clanks down the road on an antediluvian bicycle and, seeing us, shudders to a testicle-jarring halt across our path.

"I want a word with ye lads," he says, pulling the bicycle clips off the cuffs of his blue policeman's trousers.

"It has been braawt to my notice that you have been blaggarding in the street and shouting rude things about His Holiness the Pope." We stare at each other making noncommittal wiggly faces.

"Don't be shtandin' there like butter wouldn't melt in yer mouths, an' don't be denying it eithur. Shure I have it on the besht arthority: ye were seen by the priest! Two longy-haired amadawns, he said, and there's no one else in this town with hair down to their shoulders like a gerral. It's disgustin' so it is?"

"It was good enough for Jesus. He had long hair—and a beard!" tries Johnny.

"Don't ye be taking the Lord's name in vain, by Christ, or I'll be marching ye off to the slammer right now!" He turns a maddened eye on me.

"And ye, I seen ye sitting laffin' like a fooly one, across on the steps of Tait's clock. Is it the drugs ye'd be after taking?"

"No, no, I've never taken drugs in my life. It's just . . . that old clock makes the funniest clangs and boings when it strikes. It's a source of amusement." The old civic guard shakes his head in resignation.

"Jasus, if shoutin' yer bollocks off in the street and laffin' at old clocks is the best diversion ye can find, then God help the yooth of today!" He replaces his bike clips and pedals off.

"I have my eye on ye—be warned!" he roars over his shoulder, nearly spilling himself from the saddle in the process.

"Silly old sod. Who rattled his cage?"

"I sure as hell don't know, Johnny."

We trudge through the splattering rain to the derelict cottage, which we had commandeered as our own. Last week it was cozy and dry, but the change in the weather has revealed it as a bit of a bum gaff. With the roof a mass of holes, the decayed stone building has become a miserable old kip for sleeping in. I try to light a fire, but the thin cold rain, pissing down the chimney, puts it out. I sit by the dead hearth wrapped in my blanket.

"This place is a hellhole, Johnny. We should go back to my nana's."

"No, not likely! Look on the bright side—we can come and go when we like and if we do pull a couple of tarts, we can bring them back here and ride them. We can't do that at yer granny's!"

"If . . . that's a big bloody *if.* You wouldn't get a decent lassie to come back to a dump like this if your arse was dripping with diamonds!"

"I'm not looking for a deeecent lassie, I want a tart who ain't a fuggin' virgin!"

Silence falls and I take to watching the rain-soaked clouds scud the gray heavens through the gaping hole in the roof. Just to cheer me up, God sends a lightning storm that keeps me awake all night. I've been through this movie before and it's shite!

A dreary drizzle mists the windows of the main railway station as we begin the chore of drying ourselves out. We hang our socks and underwear on the heaters in the waiting room, and the smell rising up soon ensures that we have the place to ourselves.

The sun comes out and we trail our way down to Authur's Quay, a looming complex of rat-infested warehouses that had once been converted into small cupboard-sized dwellings by some unscrupulous bastard of a landlord. Sitting on the stone quayside, we drop rocks into the fetid, still water of the dock and watch the oil released from the sediments bursting on the surface of the dark brackish water like a psychedelic light show. Nearby in the flaccid back reaches of a tidal eddy, a dead dog floats, bollocks to the sky, in a slowly rotating dance of decay.

When the tide is out, the smell of putrefaction oozes from beneath each stepping-stone as we mudlark in the mucky shingle hoping to find treasures. Sometimes we find old bullets and cartridge cases from the civil war, but more often, we end up just getting covered in shite.

When not engaged in wasting time on the waterfront, we sit in the Muileann d' Ór Café, or the city library, wasting more time.

After being told by Robert Graves that the beatnik movement lacked ethics, I'm not sure what he means, so I steal a book on the subject from the public library, but after reading it, I realize I'm duty bound to put it back. We have our own code of conduct anyhow and don't need Immanuel Kant to tell us right from wrong. In the impecunious state we have found ourselves in, it would be all too easy to sell drugs, rob people's houses, or mug unsuspecting folk in dark alleys—like what had happened to us—but that is not our way. We were poor, others were rich, but were they any more moral?

The poor man toasts the rich man thus:

> *Here's to us, as good as you are, and as bad as I am*
> *But as good as you are, and as bad as I am*
> *I'm as good as you are, as bad as I am!*

If we were guilty of any sins at all, I suppose lust, unrequited as it was, would be top of the list, followed by sloth and on rare occasions gluttony. Our lives have become akin to that of the snake: always on the lookout for food and when gorged, sleeping night and day until hunger spurs the quest forward again. Pride, avarice, envy, and covetousness, all seemed the damnation of the wealthy and so hardly our affair. What was our concern was the state of the moldy old cottage now crumbling around our ears. Attempts to fix the holes in the roof have been repeatedly sabotaged in our absence, probably by the landowner to discourage unwanted tenants. No matter, Johnny comes back all excited after discovering a new doss-house.

"I've found a great place, Wock, just up opposite the castle in the old graveyard. It's a little stone shed with wooden benches and it's bone-dry inside."

"Maybe it's a workman's hut for the sexton or the grave diggers?"

"I dunno, it was too dark to see. Come on before the rain starts again and the doss bags get soaked."

We bundle our kit up and run through the dark lanes to the grave-yard wall. With much humping and pushing, we scale the stone para-pet and drop into the Protestant cemetery.

"Over here! This is it!"

He swings open the iron gate of a rectangular limestone sepulcher. It's as black as all hell inside.

"I'm not sleeping in there, that's a crypt!"

"Is it? Like in, 'The cat crept into the crypt, crapped, and crept out again'?"

"Yes, and it's full of—"

"It ain't full of fugg all, it's empty—feel?" Johnny waves his hands around in the air. I try to strike a match, but they're too damp to light.

"Just roll your sleeping bag out on one of these benches and we'll be fine." In the inky blackness, we doss down for the night. The first fingers of a deathly dawn poke impious probes into the vapid vault. My one eye peering from my blanketed cocoon reveals that fear to which, last night, I could give no voice. The wooden benches of J.C.'s dream home were the rotting lids of ancient coffins.

"Johnny, fer Jasus' sake!"

"What is it!"

He sits bolt upright in fright as, with a noise like a pistol shot, the ancient wood beneath his arse gives way. Johnny is interred in a cloud of dust as he drops in to visit the previous incumbent. Lying cheek by jowl with an eighteenth-century woman is the nearest he's got so far to fulfilling his ambition of sleeping with a tart who wasn't a fuggin' virgin!

The Muileann d' Ór Café boasts even more unsavory characters than us, most of whom are tinkers and petty criminals. One particular little her-bert, who was as shifty as a shithouse rat, informs J.C. of an empty house up in Farron Seon that is still fully furnished and had been mys-teriously abandoned long ago. It remains undisturbed by the thieving classes only because it is supposedly cursed and haunted. No doubt, the informant wishes to test the veracity of the haunting rumor before bur-gling the place over.

Johnny neglects to tell me this bit of the plot as we creep into the back kitchen of the long-empty house. Like the famous ghost ship, *Marie Celleste,* everything from daily life is left as it had been thirty years before: dishes on the table, pots and pans on the stove, coats hanging on their pegs, and beds still neatly made upstairs and in the attic. All is covered in a thick layer of dust and cobwebs. The detritus and decaying fur of three decades of neglect, unexplainable, uncanny, and sure to make the hair rise on your neck!

We select a room at the end of the long upstairs hall. For reasons of security, I put a piece of straw into the lugs of the backdoor lock, which, if found broken, will show us that someone has entered. I also place some of the glass-framed pictures face up, along the corridor, so's no one can launch a surprise attack without a foot breaking the glass and giving the alarm.

The house does indeed feel creepy, but it is weather tight and the next morning, in daylight, it seems not so scary. In getting ready to leave, we feel confident enough to leave our gear behind and even some small change sitting on the bedside table.

It is easy for us to wriggle through the tight gap we have created by pulling the heavy, marble-topped table over and jamming it in behind the bedroom door. Anyone bigger than ourselves will never be able to slip through this narrow passage.

For the first week all is well and we've grown used to our new abode. I have a part-time job doing a bit of modeling at the art college, which consists of sitting on a dais, playing guitar, whilst the students paint the scene. Some of these portraits even look like me, which is flattering. One lassie paints enormous purple pussycats, and I wonder at how much paint she uses. It must be great to be a student.

J.C. hangs out with his mates at a small café in the town center and does odd jobs for them. On a misty, cold night, I go into the house alone and venture upstairs. We both know where the glass frames are lying and can easily step between them. We reason that a would-be intruder will not be so nimble and so give the game away.

I have left Johnny talking to his mates under the streetlamp outside. As I wriggle into my sleeping bag, I hear what I take to be Johnny's footsteps coming along the hall. The door handle turns and, not in any way perturbed, I start a conversation with him. To my puzzlement the door opens, but there is no one there. I get up and peer into the hall—not a soul. I look out of the window and, as before, there is Johnny still chatting with his pals below. When he finally comes up, I tell him the news of the odd occurrence and that I think it is supernatural! J.C. says that I'm full of shite and being a wimpy prat.

Later that night, the footsteps return twice, and this time Johnny hears them as well. Leaping up, he challenges the interlopers.

"Who's there? Who's there, ya bastards!" Just as before, the hallway is devoid of human form! We have a restless night with our fleet-footed phantoms.

The next morning, I try to put it all down to being overtired. As I walk down the stairs a silver tabby cat shoots past me and runs into the upstairs passageway. I turn and follow it back up. It sits at the end of the hallway regarding me with jaundice eye and as I approach it, quick as a cobra, it darts into a hall cupboard. I ease the door a little more ajar and gaze in. The closet is totally empty except for the skeleton of a small cat!

When I tell Johnny this, he thinks I'm pulling his leg.

"You'm off yer rocker, Wockins. Bloody spooks, my arse! Who's ever heard of a ghost cat, fer God's sake?"

"Well, I'm only telling you what I saw! You heard the footsteps last night, didn't you?"

"I heard something, but it might have been the wind!"

"The wind from your arse maybe. Anyway, I'm not dossing there tonight. I'd rather sleep in the park!"

"Look! Let's give it till the end of the week and if it's still getting weird, we'll move out, OK?" Johnny is beginning to have his doubts, too.

When we get back at night the glass is still intact, as is the piece of straw across the backdoor lock, but our room is totally ransacked. The heavy marble-and-oak table has been pushed with such force that the iron bedstead is buckled in the middle. Whoever is responsible for this act possesses superhuman strength. Nothing is missing—not the musical instruments, nor the wee bit of money sitting on the bedside table. The only thing that can't be accounted for is my red neckerchief that traditional traveling people like to wear, "for to keep away the evil spirits!"

Snatching up my scant belongings, I run so fast out of that damned room that I break every plate of glass in the hall! With my heart pounding like a steam hammer, I can only hope and pray that whoever is running behind me, breathing acrid hot air down my neck, is Johnny Carr and not the spawn of Beelzebub!

That night we do indeed sleep out in the concrete changing rooms at the football park. It is unbearably cold, but with the aid of some candles nicked from the local church, I manage to hard-boil two eggs in a water-filled milk carton. It's hardly a warming supper and doesn't stop the dank cold seeping right through me.

We wake to a light snow falling and dejectedly trudge down to the Coliseum Cinema where we often sneak into the gents' toilets for a wash. The warm water feels good on my frozen face and fingers. After some minutes, there's a knock on the lavatory window from the outside. When we pop it open, unseen hands push in buns, cakes, and other fancy confectionery from the bakery next door. This is akin to the miracle of the loaves and fishes to me, and, although some pieces fall in the soapy water, like half-starved dogs, we eat everything greedily.

It is plain that our daily routine is becoming well known to the general populace, and before long we are banned from the cinema washrooms. We begin to look more like tramps than travelers, grimy ghosts haunting any warm place until ejected by store owners or pub landlords who get pissed off when we don't buy anything.

St. Mary's Cathedral is one of our few places of sanctuary, because no one bothers us here. It is damp and in a bad state of repair, but it's wind- and watertight, and we spend hours sitting on the pews talking or dozing in fitful catnaps. There is an odd plaque on the west wall of the church that reads: "Here lies the body of Dan Hayes who died in 1767. An honest man and a lover of his country, who was the author of 'The Tragedy of Hamlet,' originally written by him and inserted into the works of William Shakespeare."

I am dreaming of walking with old Willie Wagglestaff through the summer-filled country lanes that surround Stratford-upon-Avon.

"Did you write *Hamlet,* Willie?"

"Hamlet? Hamlet! Quotha! I fain I knowest not aught of this Hamlet. Perchance it be an omelette containing ham, foresooth?"

I am laughing at Shakespeare's jibe as the sun slips behind a dull, gray cloud and an icicle chill seizes me.

"Wocko! Wocko, wake up! You're rambling in your sleep. We'd better go and warm up. Let's get out of here. It's fuggin' freezing." We stumble through the winter streets to a new location. I dream and I stagger through my dreams. Cold, cold and damp seeping into my body, the pavement slides underfoot and I fall. Numbness, no pain from the fall, nothing to drive out the chilly humors. Cold, damp, death, dancing in my footsteps. I can feel its icy breath on the back of my neck. I hold on to J.C.'s arm and stumble on, eyes closed.

I wake up in the boiler room of a school. This is the warmest I've felt in weeks, but we are discovered by the janitor and the next nightmare is spent in an abandoned Austin A40 hatchback car, out in the wintry wilds. Somehow, in the middle of the night, the police appear.

I wake first and wind down the window. Three civic guards surround the derelict vehicle.

"Is that a girl you have in there?" says a hopeful cop, shining his flashlight into Johnny's effeminate face.

"No, it fuggin' well isn't, ya dozy prat!" says Johnny and then wonders why the cop opens the door and thumps him!

I'm feeling too weak to do more than answer few a questions in a hoarse whisper. They leave us alone that night, but when we return the following evening all of the windows of the car have been smashed.

"You see, I told ya. ACAB—All Coppers Are Bastards!" Johnny smiles with the grim satisfaction of belated vindication. I cannot walk back to town, and so we try to sleep where we are sitting, in the midst of the frozen crystals of shattered glass.

The winter days wear on, and I drift in and out of reality. We have taken refuge in the basement of a vacant shop near the city center, but although it is warmed by the boiler rooms in the buildings adjacent to it, I am cold and ill.

It's all I can do of a morning to get up and make my way down to the library, where I can sit and pretend to read. That night we sit in the small dockside café, and the waitresses try to sneak us the odd cup of tea and a bite to eat when the boss isn't looking. Day turns to night turns to day. I see the faces of two art students, John Connolly and his girl-friend, Adrianne, who know me from the college. They are speaking to me, but I can't make out what they're saying. They realize that I'm sick and take me to their flat and call a doctor. I'm suffering from pneumonia and am seriously ill. Christmas comes and goes, and in my illness I'm oblivious to it. These good people nurse me back to health and pay my expenses out of their own pockets.

"How are you feeling, Bill?"

"I feel better, Adrianne, very much better. Was I out of it for long?"

"Oooooh, yes! And you kept saying that the damp had eaten your cowboy suit!"

"Dear God! So the dreaded damp had nearly done for me, after all was said and done!" I mutter.

"What was that?"

"Oh, nothing! Just thanks, thanks for everything!"

Whilst I've been poorly, J.C. has been working with some dodgy-looking traveling folk dealing in scrap metal. I imagine the job isn't all quite aboveboard, as it is only referred to in hushed tones and deals are furtive affairs in back streets and on pub corners.

Amongst the other Flash Harrys that Johnny has befriended are a bunch of young spivs who hang around the street corners in their shiny Italian suits, spitting on the pavement and smoking king-sized cigarettes. They remind me of Derrick Davies's Bulldog Gang, who hung around the post office corner when I was young.

J.C. is chin-wagging with this gang of young turks one evening, as I'm walking down past Cannocks's clock. I stop to chat with him for a while when I spy the young lassie I'd once seen at the castle, walking down the road with two other lassies. She is dressed in a dark green Aran sweater and a gray skirt, her long ash-blond hair flicking over her shoulders. As she sweeps past me into the ice cream shop, my head turns with her like the periscope of a U-boat scanning for a ship.

"You fancy her, don't ya? That's young Martina, ya know?" says a lanky chain-smoking eejit who goes by the name of Wayney.

"Er . . . no! . . . I mean, er . . . yes . . . sort of!"

"Do youse want me to put in the good word for ye? I used to go out with her big sister, so I know her well enough!"

"Would you do that for me, Wayney? I'd be ever so grateful to you!"

With a giggle, the three girls come out of the shop licking their ice creams and turn to go back up the hill.

"Hey, Martina! I've something to tell you!" The matchmaker is doing his work. This is great! I can hardly believe it!

"What is it now, Wayney?" she asks coyly, looking a vision of loveliness.

"BILLY WATKINS WANTS TO BREAK YOUR FEATHER FOR YOU!" he roars across the street, nearly choking on his own laughter.

She glances at me for a split second and I hoped she could see my hurt and bewilderment. I am devastated by this foul-mouthed traitor, but too taken aback to do anything but stare like a fool. Wordlessly, with a toss of her lovely head, she is gone and, with her, my hopes of romance. The night is sickly sweet with the derisive laughter of know-nothing knaves.

Head bowed, I shuffle off to the café. Each black crack in the pavement becomes a yawning crevasse, wide and deep enough to swallow my shame and sorrow. It's my own fault, putting my trust in the likes of corner boys. You'd think, with all the time I'd spent studying Taliesin, I'd have learned by now!

> They despoil Mary's chaste maidens
> Their lives and times they waste in vain
> They scorn the frail and the guileless
> They drink by night, sleep by day
> Idle, lazily, making their way
> They despise the Church
> Lurch towards the taverns;
> In harmony with thieves and lechers.

Johnny strolls in and sits opposite me in the steamy café, all smiles.

"Cheer up, Wocko! Things could be a lot worse!"

"What the hell could be worse than this? What could be worse?"

"He was only having a little bit of fun, Wock!"

"Don't try to placate me, Johnny. These folk are morons, especially that Wayney fella! I don't think it was funny, embarrassing the poor girl like that! There was no need for that at all."

"It was you that got embarrassed, Wocko! You looked as red as a baboon's arse and just as sore!"

J.C. sniggers away to himself as he stuffs yet more pieces of bread and butter into his already overfull gob!

"Grow up, for crying out loud!" I mumble to my teacup.

Suddenly Johnny starts and stares goggle-eyed at me. His cheeks begin to puff out like a hamster and his eyes begin to bulge. He is bursting like an overripe boil!

I lean back from this swelling apparition, wondering whatever can be amiss? As I open my mouth to inquire, J.C. explodes into my face, the loudest, wettest cross between a sneeze and a cough imaginable. I am suffused with half-masticated bread and butter particles, snot, and phlegm. On the verge of throwing up, I jump up from the table. Johnny is howling with laughter and pointing to the mirror behind me, on the surface of which, outlined in his expectorated slime, is the fine silhouette of my head and shoulders.

Thank God, winter is now a distant memory and the weather is getting warm and wet. The moist Caribbean southwesterly winds blow up along the Gulf Stream, draping films of fluffy white clouds across the Shannon estuary and over the mountains, where they hang swirling and twitching like lace curtains at a gossip's window.

"It's soft over Clare—there'll be rain today!" says a familiar voice behind me. I spin around. It is my uncle Seán, out taking his bicycle for a walk.

"When did you get back in town? Why didn't you pop over to see us?"

"I'm just back now!" I lie, anxious not to hurt his feelings by letting on that I have been there all the time.

"Well, come over for Sunday dinner so. I'm sure Nana will want to hear all of your news. How's yer mam and dad?"

"Er . . . grand enough when I last saw them, a wee while ago!"

He held out his hand to shake mine, and as he does so, I feel him slip something into my palm. It is a five-pound note, riches above the dreams of avarice!

"Get yerself some sweets, Willie—or is it beers now?" he says with a twinkle.

"Go raibh mile math agut, Seán." (A thousand thank-yous, Seán.)

"Fáilte romhat, Liam." (You're welcome, Willie.)

Johnny is off on one of his forays into the country with his traveler pals. I am making my way over Baal's bridge in the cacophony of a barrage of bell peals. It seems like every church in Limerick is trying to outdo the other; Methodist, Proddy, and Pape all going like the clappers of hell . . . bell, book and candle . . . and buckets of blood. What is it they're saying?

> *Catholic, Catholic, going to mass,*
> *Riding on the devil's ass!*
>
> *Prody, Prody, ring the bell,*
> *All the vicars, down to hell!*
>
> *A rope, a rope to hang the Pope,*
> *and a lump of cheese to choke him!*
>
> *Jacky the minister, four foot high,*
> *A baldy head and a winky eye!*

Cannonade and broadside bounce off each corbeled stone edifice with little damage to anything except the ego and the eardrum. You'd be hard put to, thinking that these rivals are all praising the same God! But I suppose it makes for a more interesting life. Sure aren't we all flowers in the same garden—with the occasional weed thrown in?

On the way to Nana's house, I walk behind two venerable old women, both wearing waist-length, black knitted shawls draped over their heads and large hobnailed boots. These are the last real "shawlies" in Limerick. The one is as large as the other is small, and in their antiquated garb they look like the peasant women from the Ukraine and wouldn't look out of place doing washing on the banks of the Dnieper. It would have been a wonderful thing to sit down to a slice of soda bread and a heat of the tea with these women and listen to their chat. I bet they have stories galore. When they are gone, we won't see their likes in Ireland again, and we'll be impoverished by their passing and that's a fact.

I cross the Shannon at the Thomondgate bridge and put my fingers in the indented scratch marks made by the fingernails of the Bishop's Lady when Drunken Thady tried to throw her into the river. As a child, I always wondered about this folktale and its incongruities. How did a woman, struggling for her life, manage to scratch deep into a solid rock parapet with her nails? What was the bishop doing with a lady anyway? Why did Drunken Thady want to drown her? And how come, judging by the twelve gouges in the granite bridge, did she have six fingers on each hand? Ah, Limerick, thou city of mysteries!

Sunday dinner at Nana's is just as I remember and as luck would have it, it is bacon and cabbage, the Irish national dish and a great favorite! After dinner, Nana, Aunt Frances, Uncle Seán, and myself sit around the peat fire chatting, and I play some classical pieces on the guitar.

When questioned, I'm more than a bit evasive about what I have been doing recently and make certain sure that I don't mention sleeping rough.

Nana has no such reservations, however.

"Guard Carmodhy says he saw you downtown dressed like a tramp and laughing at a clock. So what, in the name of the Good Savior, is that all about?"

"Sure I don't know, Nana. Maybe he's been having a wee drink of the poteen."

To avoid further questioning I take the boiled potato skins outside for the seagulls. There they are, lined up on the Shannon wall, waiting to be fed, just like when I was a tiny child. This visitation only takes place at Nana's house, and somehow the kittiwakes and blackheaded gulls always know when our dinnertime is. This inherent skill must have been handed down through the generations, and I would guess it is these gulls' great-great-grandparents that I'd fed all those years ago, when I was wee!

I'm invited to stay the night and I take up the offer of a hot bath.

Lying in the warm suds, I decide it is time to give up the traveling life for a while and see if I can find regular work. The next day, leaving my gear at Nana's, I go down to Jacky Glynn's music shop to see if I can get a job as a musical instrument salesman. He is very sympathetic, but says there is just not enough work to justify taking someone on. He says to call back in the summer.

Meantime, rumors are spreading in the town that Johnny and I had pissed in the holy water tank outside the Augustinian church. I knew I hadn't, but had J.C.? So one night, sitting in the dockside café, I ask him outright.

"Did you take a leak in the holy water tank?"

"No, I couldn't get the top off . . . it's padlocked."

"Why did you try? You're not even a Protestant!"

" 'Cause I don't like any of the religious bastards, Caflick or Proddystans!"

"Why not? You never had to suffer all the kneeling on cold floors, praying for the conversion of Russia, or that Jack Kennedy would be elected president, like we did!"

"No, I never went to church. I didn't have to do the relige bit!"

"Why not?"

" 'Cause they're wankers and if you go to church you're a wanker as well, you're all a bunch of wankers!"

"You're f——ing nuts!"

"I'll show you fuggin' nuts, Wockins!" he says, picking up the teapot and holding it above his head with a deafening shout of, "The pope's a wanker!"

He does a little jig in the middle of the café floor. Then emitting a high-pitched cackle, rather like the Australian kookaburra, he leaps through the café door and vanishes into the misty night.

"Where's my bloody teapot?" demands the café owner.

I can only shrug my shoulders.

"Come on, where does that hairy eejit live?"

"In truth, I have no idea. I didn't ask him. I don't know where he is dossing at all. He moved from where I stay some time ago."

"Well, if he doesn't bring me pot back soon, I'm calling the civic guards!"

"It's bugger-all to do with me, and so I'm leaving!"

The owner puts a big hand on my head and presses me back down into the seat.

"Oh, no, you're not! You're staying right there!"

"Would you like another cup of tea, Bill?" asks one of the pretty waitresses.

"NO, HE BLOODY WELL WOULDN'T!" my captor shrieks.

I watch the grease-covered café clock, as the seconds turn to minutes and the minutes to an hour.

"Right! That's it! I'm calling the police! Your mate has had enough time to return my goods and he hasn't!" The man is indignant as he picks up the telephone.

To his consternation, no sooner has he replaced the receiver than the door flies open and in rush three policemen! The bewildered owner stands blinking, looking perplexedly from the telephone to the latest arrivals. Then seizing the moment, points at me, crying out, "Him! There! That longhaired sputnik fella! He's one of them! He's the accomplice to the thief, so he is!"

The spluttering owner rubs his hands and does a little jig of delight.

"Would you come with us, sir?" says the sergeant, and I get up resigned, to my fate.

As I'm marched past the grinning patron, I hiss, "The word is *beatnik*, you ignoramus!"

"By Jasus, I'll not have that sort of language in my establishment!" he is roaring. "Come ye back here and I'll give ye a good hiding!" he says, going purple in the face.

"I fight with men, not their underpants!" I needle, as I'm whisked out the door.

He hops up and down, fists raised, shadowboxing the air!

"You cheeky young bollix . . . I'll . . . I'll . . . !"

"Shit his pants if he doesn't calm down!" says the sergeant, and even I laugh.

I am taken to William Street Garda Barracks and into the interview room. A detective comes in and offers me a cigarette.

"I don't smoke, thanks."

"Do you know why you're here, son?"

"No, not really . . . I don't . . . no."

"Well, we have a report that someone has committed a very serious crime, something we haven't had in this town since the Black and Tans were here, a crime I have never had to deal with in all my years on the force, a crime, not just against man, but against GOD! Jasus, lad, they used to hang people for it!"

"Hang people for what?"

"Sacrilege! Do you know what sacrilege means?"

I nod yes with my head. I know fine what it means. It means that holy water tank.

"We have a report that one of ye beatnik fellas ran into the Augustinian church, just after benediction tonight, and put a red teapot on top of the tabernacle and that a cry of 'F——the Pope!' was heard by the sexton. So was it yourself?"

"How could it be me? I was in the café all the time."

"Can you prove that? Do ye have witnesses?"

"Of course I have. Wasn't I being held a prisoner by the manager?"

"Oh, yes, sure I never thought of that! Well, if it wasn't ye, it must be the other fella." He opens the office door and shouts down the hall, "Is there any sign of the other eejit, Michael?"

"There was, sir, yes. Officer Carmodhy saw him in the street a bit ago and chased him. If he hadn't stopped to put his bicycle clips on, he would have caught him, too."

"OK, keep me posted, so." He turns back. "So this is nothing to do with you!"

"No, sir, nothing."

"Well, I believe you, thousands wouldn't," he says, indicating the door.

"Can I go now?" I ask the detective.

"Well, that's up to the duty sergeant. I have no more use for you!"

I'm told to stay put and from where I sit, strange shadowy shapes pass the frosted glass of the charge room windows. I imagine it's Johnny being led to the interview room in handcuffs.

"OK, youngfella, what's your address?" asks the burly desk sergeant, filling in a form.

"What am I being charged with?"

"Just give me your fuckin' particulars, laddie, and less out of ye, and don't you worry your little head, I'll soon find something to hang ye on."

I give him my folks' address in England so as not to embarrass Nana with a visit from the police.

"So where are you staying in Ireland, son?"

"I'm just traveling about, all over."

"How much money do you have on you?"

"I think I have about one and six left, that's all."

"Well, you need at least seven and six so's not to be a vagrant! It is my belief that you are living without visible means of support and that is an offense against the Vagrancy Act."

"Oh, dear, I didn't know! What will happen to me? This is all very worrying."

"Let me see now. We can send you up to court, or get rid of you quietly and no questions asked!" he says, cleaning his earhole with his pencil.

"What! What d'ya mean, 'Get rid of me quietly'? Good God, man, it's only vagrancy!"

"No, don't worry. We give you a rail pass and a second-class ticket back to Britain, from out of the public purse, and then you're someone else's problem! You will stay here in the cells tonight. And tomorrow, I have a man going up to the Bridewell in Dublin and he will escort you to the boat. Get it?"

"Yes, OK, so I'm being chucked out of the country through no bloody fault of my own!"

"Yer breaking my heart! Now empty your pockets into the tray and give me your belt. You'll get them back in the morning. Now sign this and good night!"

"What do you want my belt for?"

"So you don't hang yourself, of course!"

"Jasus! Do ye think I'd hang myself for vagrancy?"

"You haven't seen the state of the cell yet. Now come along quietly or it will be the worse for you!"

He slaps the palm of his hand with a heavy black truncheon as he leads me to a black, iron-studded door that has a peep hole in the center. The policeman swings it open with a sinister screech like a cat caught in a mill wheel. To my horror, the cell already has an occupant. As the door clangs shut, the acrid stench of piss and neglect overwhelms me. A shadowy figure resembling a hastily assembled bag of rags rustles in the corner of the only bunk in the room.

"Get away! Get ye gone! Yer not having my blanket—yer not!"

"I don't want yer poxy old blanket! Now shut up, fer God's sake, before the guard comes back and takes the night stick to ye!"

The poor old tramp mutters a string of demented oaths as he pulls his maggoty army horse blanket around himself. Even in the half-light, I can see it is crawling with body lice. Sitting on my haunches on the other side of the chilly cell, I pass a tortuously wearisome night. My dreams are the only escape from the living nightmare of waking up. These, too, would suddenly lurch from the pastoral bliss of a day fishing by a gentle stream to the mockingly, maniacal spectacle of a giggling Johnny Carr dressed in priest's vestments, celebrating Holy Communion with chocolate wafers handed out from a red enamel teapot.

Of the events the next morning, I recall little as I seem transfixed in a dreamlike state. Having survived that hellish night, I am given a cup of tea that tasted like creosote and has most likely been stewing on the gas all night. This at least gives some heat to the couple of bits of cold toast the guardians of the law have provided for breakfast. On the trip up to Dublin, I sleep most the way to Nenagh. The policeman is a cheery Dubliner and is transferring back up to the big city. He jokes that although I am a bloody Englishman, I'm the best prisoner he's ever had.

"No need for the bracelets to be put on a sleeping man!"

"Thanks!"

"So what are you being deported for? Tell me, I can't be bothered to read your paperwork."

"Well, apart from being broke, which I didn't know was a crime, I haven't done anything wrong at all! It's all just lies and rumors."

"They still haven't caught your pal. Is he some sort of a Protestant Orangeman or the like?"

"No, not at all, he wouldn't know an Orangeman if one leapt up and bit his arse! He just jokes around. He likes to shock people, that's all. He's no threat to anyone."

"Now I'm supposed to take you all the way to the boat. If I just see you just up to Kingsbridge and onto the boat train, you won't be running off anywhere now, will you? It's just I don't want to be traipsing all the way down to Dun Laoghaire and back, baby-sitting a fine big fella like yerself!"

"No, no, I'm just as anxious to get home as you are. You can trust me not to scarper. God knows I've no intention of going back to Limerick for a good while."

The cop accepts my assurance of good behavior and kindly buys me a cup of coffee and a hot bacon roll. It is the ambrosia of the gods.

He is more than pleased to be out of the Confraternity City, as Limerick is known for its straitlaced Catholic airs. He's going back to the bright lights of dear debauched Dublin. Stationed up at the Bridewell nick, he explains, is nice and handy for getting a pint or two in John Mulligan's pub in Poolbeg Street or a quick gargle in the Palace bar, on Fleet Street.

After arrival at Westland Row we take the bus to Kingsbridge railway station. Here he gives me my second-class boat ticket and we shake hands. He is a decent sort of a chap with a merry twinkle in his eye. He straightens up and touches his cap.

"Slán leat. That's Irish for good-bye!"

Well, if all coppers are bastards, at least this guy was a decent bastard.

"Bu'ochas a' chara, agus slán abhaile anois!" (Thanks, my friend, and safe home now!) I shout from the door of the departing Dun Laoghaire train. I am pleased to see him crack up laughing at being had on! He's a good egg.

Alone in my compartment, high on the railway viaduct above the slate roofs of backstreet Dublin, I gaze down as the game of daily life plays out on the cobbled streets below.

Raincoated men with greyhounds and whippets scurry in and out of pubs and betting shops. Others, in suits or overalls, hurry off to work or off to avoid work, either joining or avoiding the commuter queues, standing at bus stops, waiting in vain for the black and cream, *just like Birmingham,* buses to come along.

Garrulous groups of women, in floral pinafores and paisley pattern headscarves, chitchat on street corners, pausing only to plug fallen baby bottles into infant mouths, light cigarettes, or scold scruffy-arsed kids hanging on rope swings from lampposts.

Descending into a railway cutting, the train slows, giving the passengers a chance to read the spiderous graffiti scrawled across the blackened brick walls. It caters for all tastes: "Up the IRA"; "Mickey is a wanker"; "Whitworth F.C. We are the Champions"; and my favorite, an insult complete with the element of choice, "Helen is a pig or cow."

After idling in the cutting for some minutes, the train jerks forward again. I am fighting the fatigue now closing in upon me. For all I know, this might be my last view of Ireland for a long time. Maybe I won't be allowed to return at all! Spurred by this fear, I greedily grasp every last image of my Irish motherland.

Through half-closed eyes, I spy a Rugby game scrumming down on a college pitch. The young buckos, in their green striped jerseys, have the advantage over the lads in red and white and push them over. Oblivious to all but their own world, two lovers dawdling along the banks of the Grand Canal steal a long, lingering kiss. Behind the canal wall, a tinker lad, standing upright on the back of a speeding horse-drawn cart, darts down the lane toward Pembroke Road. By Beggar's Bush Barracks, a black-faced coalman dumps bags of "Tadcastle's Best Anthracite" into a coal cellar, watched by a tail-flicking cat proudly enthroned upon the dented roof of a rusty, wheelless Volkswagen.

Behind the long rows of terraced houses, one woman hangs out damp washing on her backyard clothesline, whilst a few doors down another gathers dry washing in.

An old man, in shirtsleeves and cloth cap, shakes the creases out of his daily newspaper before entering the privacy of an outside lavatory. In the adjacent alleyway, a small brown dog strains in tail-quivering ecstasy on the threshold of his own evening evacuation. Life, when viewed from a passing train, has a wonderful symmetry about it.

Yellowed by the honey-faced sun peeping demurely from behind the shadowy crests of the far-off Wicklow Mountains, all of Dublin seems to be busy doing something; as busy as bees around a hive. I close my eyes, but the honeycomb of my brain remains abuzz with a swarm of bittersweet images; montaged mementos, frozen in the moment, always there to be recalled, something that no one can take from me, my personal experience, my own ramshackle vignettes of my island, my Ireland.

✦ Chapter 21 ✦

SAILING, AS MANY'S THE TIME BEFORE, FROM THE OLD QUAY-
side that I know so well, again, I leave Ireland. But on this occasion, instead of leaving a piece of my heart behind, I'm leaving my child-hood innocence. I have experienced a good slice of adult life with its mixture of great beauty and callous ugliness; losing old friends and finding new ones. I've discovered that both the kind and the crass na-ture of people is as universal as it is unpredictable. I feel likened unto a snake that has outgrown its skin; a serpent leaving Ireland, not at the behest of St. Patrick, but because of the need to expand my horizons way past the confines of miscreant youth.

Leaning on the ferry's stern rail, the green, white, and orange tricolor above my head snaps in a fresh, westerly breeze. The great golden orb of the sun sinks below the ribbon of pastel-colored houses that form the skyline of the township of Dun Laoghaire.

I gaze down.

Keen, phosphor bronze screws slice through the emerald green water, turning effervescent eddies of boiling white foam into a hissing dissipating wake.

The last lone finger of the setting sun stretches out from between the darkening hills and anoints the ship with a rich amber light. I too feel anointed, as if heaven has seen fit to forgive my misdeeds in her ver-dant green colony upon this small earth.

Great gulls and kittiwakes follow our progression, the souls of dead sailors shining in their round black eyes. Above, a cloudless sky is turn-ing a deep indigo and small strings of streetlights twinkle out from the headland, like dancing decades of a fluorescent rosary.

Wild, tempestuous Irish Sea, you have broken the backs of ships, the spirits of men, and the hearts of wives and sweethearts, but tonight, without my mother to torment, you lie fetid and flaccid, as content as a fishmonger's cat. You beguile the foolish with a placid calm that belies your true nature. Who can trust you, you fickle witch of wicked water?

In the secret realms of your deep, the sea-god Mananan Mac Lir rides his wave-cutting currach *Ocean-sweeper* out from the Isle of Man. Aloft he waves the Answerer, the magical sword that no armor can resist. Through storm and tempest, he guides sailors to and from Ireland. Not only does he protect that sacred isle, but also the Islands of the Dead that lie beneath the rolling waves.

To you, Tír na nÓg, the souls of the dead seafarers descend. To you, Land of Eternal Youth, is given the name Davy Jones's Locker or Fiddler's Green. Yours is the enchanted land that lies beneath the white-crested breakers. Yours is the roar of defiance when chilly arctic drift currents and the warm Gulf Stream clash in the midst of your ebullient maelstrom. Yours is the magic that seduces the hearts of men. Yours is the—

"Excuse me, lad. I don't want to disturb you, but I need to take the flag down," a Scouse deckhand wakes me from my reverie.

"We take down the colors at sunset."

"Oh, sorry, mate! I was away with the fairies there for a moment. I didn't see you." I smile as he gathers in the ensign.

"Are you going on holiday or coming back from one, like?"

"Yeah, I was on holiday, the holiday of a lifetime!"

"Now what? Are you working or trying a job over in England?"

"No, I suppose I'll have to find something to make a living."

"Ever thought of going to sea? Being a sailor, like?"

"Yeah, when I was a kid it's all I wanted to do. I used to dream about it."

"Then why not do it? What would youse like to be? A skipper, I'll bet?"

"Naw, maybe a wireless operator."

"What, a sparks? Blimey, you know a cushy job when you see one. Nothing to do but sit around listening to the radio. Fair play to ya, son!" He wanders off.

I take one last look into the west and, with a sigh, make my way to the ship's aft-deck saloon. Unlike the trip to Ireland, there is no party atmosphere celebrating the exiles' return home and no session in the bar. These passengers sit in muted groups, reading or quietly playing cards. Some stare out of the lounge windows and others into space, no doubt contemplating the return to the daily grind of work in the pubs, factories, and construction sites of England:

> 'Twas the Irish built the roads of Britain
> And before them, the bloody Romans!

I go below and locate the comfortable linen cupboard, but find it fitted with a Yale lock and a sign reading, "Crew Only."

Above deck I have better luck and find a warm place to curl up in the lee of the vessel's smokestack, just behind the wireless cabin. Lulled by each soporific swell, I soon drift off to sleep.

My subconscious dreams rise and fall on the peaks and troughs of the undulating waves. Across the dark rolling sea, the voices of the fabled sirens of old beckon to the mariner within me, not in the ancient language of Greek myth, but in the modern staccato notes of the International Morse Code. Dah di Dah dit . . . Dah dah di dah . . . the temptress nymphs call: CQ . . . CQ . . . Seek you! Seek you! they solicit.

On the morning of March 14, 1967, I walk warily down the gangplank of the M.V. *Hibernia* and, for the first time in nearly a year, set foot back in Holyhead, Wales.

There is no police reception committee, no passport control, just a ticket inspector who punches a hole in my chit and wishes me a good morning.

Seagulls wheel overhead, squawking their enticements as a new flame kindles the ashes of my childhood yearnings. I look at the ships riding at their moorings, each craft a mystery. Where has it been? Where is it bound? I need to know. The sirens of the previous night have done a good job, and one day I will surrender to their entreaties. But for now, I must turn my back to the sea and its calling and strike out across the long causeway connecting Holy Isle to the beautiful Isle of Anglesey.

Ynys Môn, as it is in Welsh, is the age-old sacred island where the Druids had their holy groves and chief seats of learning until its destruction at the hands of the Roman general Suetonius Paulinus, in A.D. 61.

> *Romans, long departed,*
> *Your name liveth on in Welsh*
> Rhufeinig, *you are in that tongue.*
> Roughnecks *and* Ruffians
> *The English will call you, in their turn.*

Wales! Wales! Here I am in the land of my fathers and like my father before me, deported from Ireland through no fault of my own. A Celt, son of a Celt, deported by Celts, from one Celtic country to another. It's a ridiculous scenario. I mind well the words of my father, the great exponent of internationalism and erstwhile professor of fermented beverages: "Never be seduced into playing the English imperialist game. It's a game of divide and rule, and the dice are loaded in favor of the conqueror. Scots, Irish, Manx, Cornish, and Welsh, we are hewn from the same stock. We may be different tribes, but we are the same people—Celts! It has always been in the interest of the English empire builders to split us up and use one tribe to subjugate the other. It's something they learned from the bloody Romans!"

Sure enough, Welsh is just the Saxon word for foreigner; Scot means an Irishman; Cornish comes from the Celtic tribe, the Cornovii; and Manx from Mananan Mac Lir, the Irish god of the sea. The Angles, the folk that most English people claim descent from, were never a people; the name is derived from Gaelic: *An Gaul,* which just means the foreigners. Likewise *regal* comes from *Ri Gall,* or stranger king.

Strange parlance, English. In the medieval period it was so akin to that of the Frisian areas of modern-day Germany and the Netherlands that there is an old folk rhyme recording this similarity:

> *Bread, butter and green cheese*
> *Is good English and good Frise.*

Language be buggered! A cheese sandwich sounds great. I'm starving and neither have I a penny to my name, nor a pot to piss in.

A steady stream of vehicles trickles through the Holyhead ferry terminal. I pause for a while at the dock gates, hitchhiking the little knots of traffic leaving the customs post. I'm wasting my time. No one returning from their holidays can be bothered picking up a scruffy-looking bugger like me, and I can't say I blame them. Ah, well! As Dad was wont to say, "nil carborundum illegitimi"—or should that be ille-gitemus? No matter, no bastard is going to grind me down, either way!

Head up! Stiffen the sinews! Summon up the blood! It will be a long hard slog to the mainland, but if the Roman legions could march twenty-four miles a day, then surely a Celt like me can make the twenty-one miles to the Telford Bridge before evening. The long march begins into the interior of the Isle of Anglesey.

As the crow flies, it must be seventy miles to the English border, but since I have little chance of wings in this life and even less in the next, shank's pony is my only means of transport. Borders, what a pain in the nawney! I'll be glad when no one gives a bollocks about divisions anymore. Aren't we all born naked on the same planet?.

I'm put in mind of my American poetry teacher. He liked to quote the words of the Russian poet Yevgeny Yevtushenko. What was that he said about international borders? "Frontiers are imaginary lines in the minds of men," or something along those lines and fair play to him, he's right enough. Sure aren't all of us just Jock Tamson's bairns or the sons of Adam or whatever you like to call it. It seems very odd that individ-uals can be racist, let alone the governments of the world classifying people by what side of a dotted line you were born on.

"If a cat has kittens in a bakery, does it make them currant buns?" No, Mother, it does not and all hail to the day when the word *xenopho-bia* can only be found in a crossword puzzle. Aye, aye, we're all flowers in the same garden, so we are, but I wish one of these fine specimens, whizzing by in their fancy cars, would stop and give this wilting violet a ride!

The spring sun beats down relentlessly and there is little shade on the flat central plain of the island to comfort the traveler. The sacred oak groves of the Druids, once burned down by the BloodyRomans, never grew back. God's curse on the ruffians!

Ah, but despite it all, the sense of freedom you have on the road is intoxicating:

I have traveled over the earth
Before I became a learned person
I have traveled, I have made a circuit
I have slept in a hundred castles
I have dwelt in a hundred cities.

Taliesin's words set me off thinking about my seventeen-year quest through life. Did my father plant the seeds, full knowing the effect the poetry of this ancient adept would have on me? Did he envisage how closely my own life would parallel that of Taliesin, the wandering bard? The poet began life as little Gwion; he became Taliesin. Who am I?

I try my hand at a shape-shifting poem:

I was William, I was Willie
To my father, I was Will
In Wales I was Gwylym
In Ireland, Liam
To J.C. I was Wocko
I was Billy, I am at last Bill.

Shakespeare asked, "What's in a name?" I wonder if he managed to collect as many nicknames as I've had over the years?

"To be or not to be? That is the question."

Who am I? Who was he? Some of the world's scholars reckon he never wrote a play in his life and others maintain that he was never born at all and was an invention of medieval Stratford's Tourist Board!

Great Britain's Poet Laureate lies
In fear of church and crown
It must be hard to satirize
The state when kneeling down
And so his art becomes the crap
Of sycophant and craven
Unless you count the bearded chap
From Stratford upon Avon
But Shakespeare's wit was in his plays
His verse was quite limp-wristed

Its drama's muse deserves his praise
—If ever he existed!

Well, poor Willie Wagglestaff might not have been born, but he definitely died! I've seen his grave, and judging by the size of the massive stone on top of him, he'll have a fierce job getting out of bed when Gabriel blows his horn to wake the dead on the last day. So when he doesn't turn up, ye'll have all those intellectual clever bollixes saying, "See, I told you so. Those plays were written by Francis Bacon over there!" And old Bacon would just smile and wave and wouldn't be fool enough to tell the buggers any different, after them giving him the cold shoulder first time around. Dan Hayes, from Limerick, would be scandalized and jumping up and down screaming that Bacon was an impostor, too, and that he'd written *Hamlet* himself! Then Shakespeare, being a very merry wit, would arrive late at the gig and wisely decide to say nothing to nobody and instead make a grand play out of the whole carry-on—which, since Shakespeare didn't appear to exist, would end up being attributed once again to Bacon!

Bacon? Oooh, Jasus, I could just go a big bacon butty, dripping with grease. What was it Dad used to say in times of hardship?

"If we had some bacon, we could have bacon and eggs—if we had some eggs."

It's amazing the stuff that tumbles through your mind when you are hungry. Maybe that's why religious folk like to fast as a way to clean out the attic of the soul. It's little wonder they have visions. Daydreams are handy vehicles drowning out the cries of an empty stomach and two sore feet.

I am so involved in my dilly-dallying that I fail to notice an open-topped Land Rover that has stopped for me.

"Do you want a lift or don't you?" the farmer quizzes me.

"Yes, sorry, I was dreaming away to myself."

He has a crate of live chickens in the front seat, so I sit in the back in the company of a trussed-up, blackfaced ram and three black-and-white border collies. The ram glares at me, but the dogs seem to like my company and give me their own version of my mother's face-cleaning technique.

We cross the Menai Bridge into North Wales. The farmer is delivering the livestock locally and can only take me a further six miles, but I'm more than grateful. As I wave good-bye to the departing jeep, the three sheepdogs sit in line abreast, barking their farewells in triple harmony. Ah, yes, the Welsh love choirs!

Dad was right. "A man of honor must oft times walk alone," but he didn't mention getting corns on the toes. I walk on until my boots feel like they are full of hot sand.

At a wayside stream, I stop to drink and bathe my feet. The cool mountain water is sweet and refreshing, and I fancy that the bubbles arising from my toes are caused by me boiling the water with my feet. Completely knackered, I rest up for a while in a lush spring meadow near Penmaenmawr, which is the Welsh for "The Head of the Big Rock."

I catnap and in turn, dream of Palug's Cat, a spotted kitten given to the people of Arvon by the evil goddess Hen Wen. The feline grows into a savage monster, killing all in its path and becoming one of the three plagues of Anglesey. This mighty leopard is eventually killed by the warrior Cei, who was destined to become the Sir Kay of the Arthurian legends:

> *Cei went to Ynys Môn*
> *To kill lions*
> *Polished was his shield*
> *Against Palug's Cat*
> *Nine score warriors*
> *Would fall as food for her.*

Awakening, I feel renewed enough to walk onward toward the distant fortress town of Conway. My eyes follow the curve of the coastline to the Weir of Gwyddno, where Elphin found Taliesin cast ashore in his baby coracle on All Soul's Eve, all those centuries ago. The railway line that had been my umbilical to Ireland runs along the same route. How many times had I traversed that track? Dozens, maybe scores!

Still I amble on. The wind at my back, the merciless sun above, and the hard metal of the A55 North Wales trunk road driving into my feet. I am dehydrating quickly and, like a parched pilgrim, beginning to feel the mystical effects of drought and hunger.

My thirst is quenched at the drinking fountain in the village of Gwalchmai. As clarity returns to my addled brain, I ponder upon the origin of the place-name. It must be called after King Arthur's nephew, who the medievalists renamed Sir Gawain. The lines of an ancient stanza fleet in my mind:

> Gwalchmai they call me, enemy of the Saxons
> For Anglesey's king I have lunged out in battle
> And to please a girl, bright as snow on the trees
> When Chester was fought for, I have shed blood.

I trudge on toward Chester, feeling like my boots are shedding blood and wishing I had a girl to please, "bright as snow on the trees."

I had slaked my thirst with a drink at a fast-flowing stream outside of Llangefni, again at a tap in the gents' toilet in Colwyn Bay, and now in desperation, with a bottle of yellow-green pop that I find lying in a ditch near Llysfaen. I smell and taste it with the greatest of trepidation, being more than wary of yellow liquid in bottles, but it is good!

The punctual orb of the sun is beginning to slip silently below the horizon, drawing its covers of purple night behind it. This is a welcome relief. There is still a stiff breeze to assuage my sunburned forehead and cool a brain that is boiling like the cauldron of Ceridwen.

I have fasted for almost twelve hours, and I am now seriously feeling the pinch. "An army marches on its stomach," said Napoleon. I feel like an army has marched over mine! "An empty stomach has a loud voice," another old saying goes. Well, if that's true, mine is singing the old Welsh marching song "Men of Harlech."

Descending into the seaside town of Rhyl, I root amongst the discarded trash of the early holiday makers and glean some half-eaten fish and chips. Although they are cold, I am more than glad of what I have found. As luck would have it, I pick up a silver sixpence from the gutter and use it to buy a packet of Cadbury's chocolate wafers. This is good high-energy food and I ration them out to myself. The long jaunt continues back up onto the main road and into the crooked arm of North Wales. No one notices my passing except a few inquisitive brown bullocks, with whom I share a respite and some handfuls of juicy green grass.

Night falls thick and treacle black as I tramp my way from Rhyl to Prestatyn. There is hardly any traffic, and what there is speeds by. The length of highway I am now navigating is undergoing repairs. New curbstones are being laid, and every other one is lying out in the road. I take some small diversion by walking up and down on each of these, just to break the monotony of walking and cursing my pathetic plight. Up-down-up-down, I swing—like Long John Silver on his wooden leg.

The stars sizzle bright overhead in a moonless sky, and several times I see the streak of meteors blazing across the inky heavens, leaving luminous, powdery trails arching behind them. Mars glitters like a discarded cigarette end in the crystal cosmos above.

I know the names of the stars in their places.

I think of the night that Dad showed me the constellations and Mam sang "O'Ryan the Hunter." I was so young then and now I feel so old and weary. Seventeen—the lucky number of the Druids. I went to Ireland a child. Now I am cast ashore on the coast of Wales, a changeling; neither child nor adult, neither fish nor flesh, reborn, but still growing, hardening my form, shaping my spirit.

On the road behind me, I perceive a single light making its erratic course up the way toward me. It is either a one-lamped motor car or a motorbike.

Motorcycles and their riders often give lifts and, judging from its speed, the bike would take about another six ups and downs of the curbstones to put me within hitching distance of it.

Having walked the calculated interval, I turn with my thumb out, expecting the motorcycle to be about ten yards away.

"Whoa!" It's right on top of me! I get such a fright that I lose my footing and spiral into the ditch.

"You crazy bastard! You nearly knocked me over!" I scrabble for a stone to fire after my assailant, when something odd occurs to me. I rise up to get a better view.

The motorbike's taillight is a pale pink. The rider, in old-style goggles and helmet, wears a long army-type trenchcoat with a gas mask bag over his shoulder. The bike has a fishtail silencer, ancient flat-sided rear mudguards, and rigid suspension. I stand in the road, and the pebble drops from my grasp as I realize that the machine and its rider make no sound whatsoever. Shock overwhelms me; the entire vision vanishes in full view on the open road, fifty feet away. It was a ghost—a ghost on a motorcycle!

For a long while afterward, I walk alone down the center line of the road, now dark and lined with trees on both sides. "God is good, God is good, and the Devil isn't such a bad fella when ye get to know him!" Every noise of the night, every creak and hoot seem sinister portents of doom. I try to apply cold logic over sweat-forming fear. Whereas the events at the haunted house in Ireland may have had some rational explanation, this time, seeing is believing and the evidence of my own senses had to be reckoned with. Surely it can't be possible that I might be dreaming with all that amount of adrenaline coursing through every vein in my body!

I am still in a state of shock when another strange thing happens. Without me even noticing, a posh white sports car stops and the driver offers me a lift. I climb in with trepidation, expecting to see Old Nick or one of his demons behind the wheel, but the car is driven by a well-dressed young business type. Zombie-like, I sit quietly stunned whilst the poor young fella tries to elicit some sort of conversation out of me. Then suddenly, I'm off, bursting forth like a torrent from a fractured dam! I can't stop babbling about what's just happened. The unfortunate driver has every reason to think that he has either picked up a demonically possessed drug addict or an escapee from the local lunatic asylum. When he drops me on the Chester bypass, the poor man is as white as a sheet and tears off with the passenger door still open!

In the ensuing silence, I have time to recap and make some sense of my experience. "Right, Billy boy! There's nothing to be frightened of. Form a theory, try to think like a Druid. OK, here's what occurred. What happened was, the two worlds of the parallel universe brushed briefly together; one materialized in the other and by chance, I had been there in the middle, like the pin in a pair of tongs! Yes, that must be it." Comforting myself in this way I cease to be frightened as I walk on.

To my great relief, as soon as I lie down on a thick wooden bench in a country bus shelter, I go fast asleep with no thought of ghost, ghoul, or goblin. Even without the aid of blanket or pillow, I sleep the sleep of the just, or if you like, *the dead!*

I awake at first light to the tinkle of rain and the awareness that people are shuffling about somewhere near me. When I look around I realize that the early morning commuters have stood out in the shower rather than wake me up. I nod my head in appreciation of their kind gesture and vacate the bus shelter. I've nothing to eat except food for thought.

Resuming my walk toward the M6 motorway, my mind goes back to Ireland and J.C. I didn't like the thought of leaving him on his own, but who knows what fates lie in store. Johnny will have to pursue his own dreams in his own way. Everything happens for a reason, says my mother, and this is probably just the kick in the pants I am needing to set me on a new vision quest. I hope Johnny does all right. He too had played his part in reviving the fortunes of the Gael, and together we had made sweet music and opened many a deaf ear to it. In our small way, we rallied the songs and tunes of our heritage and brought them back to the people who had almost forgotten them. Was it worth it? Time will tell.

"Retrospection is the handmaiden of history," which I think means about the same as, "Even the fool is wise after the event."

Who knows if the Celtic culture will survive into a new millennium? It's the smallest stone that starts the avalanche. Maybe we did nothing to help and were just playing at it. Time will tell, time will tell.

> *Fish swim, bees gather honey*
> *Vermin crawl; everything bustles*
> *To earn its keep . . .*
> *except minstrels and thieves.*

Aye, Taliesin! As you say, *"except minstrels and thieves"*!

A spot of rain is the hitchhiker's friend. Drivers are much more likely to give you a lift during a downpour, and I cover several miles in small local rides.

Later that day, somewhere near Warrington, I get a lift from a bored Yorkshire long-distance lorry driver in need of a chat to keep him awake. He's heading south to Walsall and he can take me near enough to where I need to be. At his insistence, I tell him some of the bizarre events and whimsical stories of the past few years: the school Christmas pageant, the exploding pike, the haunted house, and the ghost of the North Wales bypass. He laughs like a drain as his eighteen-wheeler rumbles on.

At the Keele service station on the M6 motorway, the truck driver buys me the first hot meal I've had since leaving Ireland: steak-and-kidney pie, mashed potatoes, brussels sprouts, and gravy. It is the ambrosia of the gods, and despite the hunger, I eat it slowly for fear of throwing up!

He finishes his pie and mash, but leaves his sprouts.

"Don't you want them, the sprouts?"

"Er, no, I don't much care for them. They came with the meal."

"Is it the taste or the shape?" I scrape them onto my plate.

"What do you mean, the shape?"

I tell the trucker about Uncle Seán and his spherephobia. He laughs.

"Come to think of it, I've read about folk like that in the paper. It only effects certain types of people. He must be very odd?"

"No, not at all, there's nothing odd about him! He's a postal worker!"

For some reason this sets him off laughing and he goes up to the counter, coming back with two big steaming mugs of hot tea.

"By heck, lad! You've got some tales to tell and no mistake! How old did you say you were?"

"I'm seventeen."

"I'll tell thee this, lad! You be nowt but an old head on young shoulders. Them be some adventuring thee's has, and you hardly out of the egg."

Back on the highway the eighteen-wheeler eats up the miles on the downhill run to the Midlands of England. When he drops me off at the Brownhills interchange, the kindly trucker flips me a half crown. I try to refuse, but he won't take no for an answer.

"Thanks a million, pal, and drive safely!"

"You're welcome, mate, and thanks for the stories. Good luck!"

The truck pulls away, leaving me standing on the outskirts of Birmingham's new industrial sprawl. I marvel that the city has grown so huge since I'd first visited just a few years after World War II. Skipping across the road, I catch a black and cream bus—just like the ones in Dublin, Johnny!—to the city center. I sit upstairs at the front.

Brick upon brick, the crusty old metropolis rises from the Mercian plain. Two hundred years ago it was a hamlet of thirty people, belonging to the Norman-French family of Berminghame, who also owned lands around Limerick.

The Industrial Revolution saw the tiny village mushroom into the second largest city in Britain, a mighty powerhouse of industry and invention that became a magnet for rich entrepreneurs and itinerant laborers alike. Curiously, it is the only town in England to have a bullring.

Between angular lines of corbled stone banks, long reaches of sluggish green water crisscross the landscape, marking the course of the once-bustling inland waterways called navigation cuts. Tradition has it that the water filling these puddled-clay channels came from the living sweat of the Irish navvies who dug them.

For reasons lost on locals and Italians alike, the city fathers like to boast that Birmingham has "more miles of canal than Venice." That may well be true, but imagine two lovers enjoying a gondola cruise along the stagnant backwaters of the second city, serenaded by a Brummy gondolier's rendition of "O solo mio!"

Maybe I should write a tourist brochure?

"The romantic fantasy is further enhanced by perusing the canal's accumulation of abandoned cars throughout the ages. Lean back and enjoy, as we punt gently through the floating lilypads of household garbage to terminate our idyllic voyage in Birmingham's delicately named Gas Street Basin."

Gas Street, Oxygen Street, Broad Street, New Street, Corporation Street—when the city bigwigs named this lot, what were they thinking?

The bus stops near the bullring, now a shopping center. "Brummy-jum," as the natives call it, has the same run-down, grimy warmth as usual, and the air is filled with the incessant chatter of millions of little starlings clinging to every parapet and ledge of the soot-blackened Victorian buildings. The trees in the park are so densely infested with the wee birds that they look like sticks of black cotton candy.

"Sharpen Your Elbows and Show Your Teeth" should be the slogan of the spring sales. Purchase-hungry shoppers mass the doorways of C&A and Marks & Spencers. Swift as sharks, they close in on the scent and furious feeding frenzies erupt as they haggle over marked-down bargains. It's a tough call to make my way down through the greedy hordes of latter-day hunter-gatherers toward the entrance of New Street Station.

Reaching the station clock, I have returned to the very spot where my journey with J.C. had begun almost a year ago. I have come full circle, and in keeping with the old traditional ways of the traveler, I spit on the ground for good luck.

"Dirty hippie bastard, get off out of it!" shouts the old geezer sell-ing hot potatoes and roasted chestnuts from a cart-wheeled, black iron oven.

"No, you don't understand. I was just—" I smile back at him, but he's in no mood to parley.

"You were just gobbing on the floor, ya dirty bastard. Go on, get out of it, and get a bloody bath while yer at it, you bloody hippie!"

"I'm telling you, mister, I'm not a hippie."

"Piss off, before I call the police, hippie bastard!" A small crowd of toffee-nosed suburban commuters gathers around him, tutting and clucking in agreement.

There's no arguing with this bloke, and I retreat from his peculiar world as mystified as a visiting Martian.

What did he mean, hippie? What, in the name of God and his holy angels, is a hippie? I'm not a bloody hippie, I'm a long-distance man!

I quote a verse by the nineteenth-century Irish poet Arthur O'Shaughnessy, partially in memory of Johnny and our bizarre journey, but more to raise the spirits than anything else:

We are the music makers
We are the dreamers of dreams
World losers and world-forsakers
On whom the pale moon beams
Yet we are the movers and shakers
Of the world forever, it seems.

⇥ Chapter 22 ⇤

"HAAANDY CARRIER! HAAANDY CARRIER!" AN OLD SOLDIER sells brown paper shopping bags at the corner of Corporation Street, his rows of medals from two world wars glinting in the spring sunshine. I pass on.

"Daaaily Worker, Vanguard of the Revolution! *Daaaily Worker!"* The clarion call issues from beneath the cloth-cap of an old commie agitator hawking his red-star tabloid to an oblivious tide of people, who as ever, always seem to be going in the opposite direction to myself.

"Le papier! Le papier!" cries the oldest of all street vendors. I remember him since I was a little kid, standing in the same spot, peddling his pile of *Birmingham Evening Mail* newspapers. Sick Dick the Beatnik once spoke to him in French, only to discover that *Le papier* was the sole extent of the old boy's repertoire.

Fumes from the vehicles idling in traffic jams tear at my throat, whilst the human current streams against me, rude and unapologetic. I feel like a salmon trying to get up the rapids, swimming in an aggressive river of clamoring clods. Diving out of the melee into the relative quiet of a doorway, I get my breath. A tufty-haired waif, selling flowers from a street stall, shouts over to me.

"Hey, mister! Hey, you, hippie! Flower power, man!" He throws over a daffodil and I stick it in my buttonhole.

A pretty young girl in a cotton cheesecloth sari stops. She flashes a seductive smile at me and says, "Peace and love, man. Are you a real hippie?"

"Ah, yeees! Yes, of course I am. Yes, indeed!" She kisses me on both cheeks and gives me the two-fingered peace sign. Before I can overcome my surprise, she is gone, swallowed up by the mad rush, to God knows where.

Well, that was a turnup for the books! Whatever this hippie thing is, I better keep my options open.

With renewed vigor, I press up Corporation Street, leading a thirst that would choke a camel, to the oasis bearing the legend:

Yeats's Wine Lodge
(Licensed for the Purveyance of Alcoholic Beverages)

My soul, once soaring aloft, thirsty for Mr. Yeats's poems, now prepares to land with parched palate squarely in the brothers Yeatses pub. In from the bright street I fly, touching down in the cool entrance hall of the saloon.

The Wine Lodge is a distillation of the city itself, thronged as it is with a multiethnic ensemble of late afternoon tipplers, poets, scallywags, besuited businessmen, thieves, and fur-coated old hookers. All human life is here.

This is a truly great house. The design is every bit as varied and eclectic as the clientele: a jumbled mishmash of classical, baroque, and rococo motifs thrusting out their tobacco-stained glory at the drinking fraternity below. Few customers are English, and most are Irish, but the languages of Sikhs, Hong Kong Chinese, and jaunty Caribbean Rastamen can all be discerned in the hubbub.

The ornate vaulted ceiling resembles a medieval cathedral nave, as does the great stained-glass windows portraying nymphs, satyrs, centaurs, and other zoomorphic imaginings of the ancient Greeks. These fabled beasts blaze from their intricately carved casements above the walnut bar. It is how Nero's mausoleum would have been, if indeed he had one.

One hundred feet of bartop, the longest in Britain, supports gargantuan oak casks upon a gantry, their brass stop-taps supplying the world's finest wines, ports, and sherries. Each sweet elixir emits an aroma, which, suffused with beeswax polish, fresh ground coffee, and cigar smoke, produces an olfactory cocktail heady enough to put you spinning!

Service is obtained by entering a long wooden-railed chicane. Here you wait to be served by one of the white-aproned counter staff. They give you a ticket with your order, which you pay for at the checkout at the end of the rail, rather like in a supermarket. It is all rather quaint and reminiscent of the old luxury ocean liners: *Lusitania, Mauritania,* or, if you've had too much to drink, the *Titanic.*

Standing atop of the white Connemara marble steps, it takes a few minutes for the eyes to adjust to the interior ambience.

To my left is the great bar and to my right the smaller speciality bar, whose blond-curled keeper is smiling and craicing away with her admiring customers.

Sideways is the only method to slip through the press of folk, and with some jostling, I gain a foothold on the edge of the walnut bar.

"Hey, watch out, mate! You nearly spilled my drink."

"Sorry, pal, it caught my sleeve, I just want a word with the bar lady there."

"It's OK, no harm done, son. Hey, miss! There's a hippie-looking bloke here wanting a word with you!"

The server strolls down the long counter as if she owns the place.

"Good day, sir, and whaat can I do for yew?" She says, nonchalantly, polishing a cocktail glass and half-looking in my direction. Somehow this barmaid has recently acquired a rather refined English accent. She turns to put the glass up on the shelf.

"How's about you and me going for sausages an' stuffing at the Oxford Restaurant!"

She spins around like a cartoon cat, her eyes round and large!

"Jasus, Willie! I'll kill you, you bleeder, giving me a bloody fright like that, you bugger. Ye put the heart crossways in me, so you did!" Gone is the affected BloodyEnglish accent and thanks be to Christ and his Holy Family, she lapses back into her native Irish brogue.

"Holy mother of God! Will you look at him—he's all grown up! You were never that tall when you left home. And look at all that hair. You look like a Beatle!" She clasps her hands momentarily over her mouth. "Jasus, I don't know what your dad's going to say? No matter, bollocks to him! Are you well so? Will you have a drink, a pint or something? Do you want a pork pie? Are you hungry? Oh, Jasus! I can't get over it! Would you Adam and Eve it? The cat came back."

Hopping about like a flea on a griddle, she takes out a small white handkerchief, and for a moment I'm feared that I'm about to get the dreaded spit-and-rub treatment, but mercifully, she dabs at her eyes instead. The crowd at the bar are all smiles and nudge up to let me in.

"Easy now, Mam, I'm fine! Grand all together, tickety-boo, just."

"By all the saints, Willie, you look so different. Just take a gander at yourself. You're like no one's child!" She moves sideways, revealing the glint of the scalloped-edged mirror enshrined in the dark wood cove of the bar. I stare at a stranger!

"You are no one's child," mocks my reflection in the glass. "Not any more. This weather-beaten bloke with the wee red whiskers is you—and you have become a man!"

Every bit as mystified as Alice, I'm mesmerized by the apparition reflected in the looking glass. For an all too brief moment, on the threshold of metamorphosis, my existence hangs in the space between the mirror and myself.

"I was many shapes before I was born . . ."

The distance between my mother and me widens, but not in an uncomfortable way; it's more the sense of sweet loss felt when sailing from the familiar pierhead of a beloved country. The seventeen-year voyage into manhood has all but ended, leaving in its wake a mere decaying reflection in the smoky glass mirror. I have come full circle again, back to the mother that bore me, back to the harbor of her heart.

My wee Celtic childhood is over, gone like snow on the water in a cascade of infinitely repeated images reflecting the world betwixt the child and the long-distance man. And that was that! Having shed the soft skin of infancy, I emerge from the chrysalis transformed; reworked in the image my father had envisioned, that time long ago, when we walked and talked in the woods.

The umbilical cord to the past is finally severed. Destiny ties the end in a trefoil knot: a trinity of three faiths. I hope my father will approve of my efforts. I trust I have become "a man to ride the river with." I pray that I am on my way to becoming "the once and future Celt."

Above our heads, the great oak gantry clock strikes two and, as is the custom, Mam closes the bar down for the afternoon holy hour. We step into the street.

Arm in arm, we trip through the backstreets, avoiding the crowds. Before us lies the legendary Oxford Restaurant. It's just like old times, except I'm the tall one now. I'm the long-distance man.

Mam squeezes my arm. She is proud of me, I can tell.

"Is an leanbh athair an fhear!" she says. "The child is the father of the man!" I squeeze her arm in reply.

"Mam?"

"What is it?"

"Sing 'Bobby Shaftoe' for me."

Some of My Family's Traditional Songs as Alluded to in the Text

Bad Luck to This Marching
Air: "Paddy O' Carroll"

Bad luck to this marching
Pipe claying and starching
How neat we must be to be killed by the French
I'm sick of parading
Through mud and snow wading
And standing all night to be shot in a trench.

Now I love Garryowen
When I hear it at home
'Tis a marvelous tune, with an elegant lilt
But the strength of the beat
Doesn't sound half as sweet
When you're facing the French and about to be kilt.

Though we're up bright and early
Our pay comes so rarely
The devil a farthing we've ever to spare
Some say a disaster
Befell the paymaster
But I fervently think that the money's not there.

Like a sailor that's nigh land
I long for ould Ireland
Where even the kisses we steal as we please

With no Sarge to abuse us
We fight to amuse us
And we've nothing to do but to stand at our ease.

Now I'd dance like a fairy
To see ould Dunleary
My discharging papers cannot come too soon
To the tune of a fife
They'll dispose of your life
So think on, my lads, 'er you join the dragoons.

Brighidín Bhán Mo Stór (Bright Bridget My Treasure)

I am a wandering minstrel man and love's my only theme
I've strayed beside the pleasant Bann and the Shannon's winding
  stream
I've piped and played to wife and maid, by Barrow, Siur and Nore
But never met a maiden yet, like Brighidín bhán mo stór.

She wears her ringlets rich and rare, as nature's fingers wove
Loch Cara's swans are not so fair or gentle as my love
As she walks out in her Sunday sheen, all by my cabin door
I'd forsake a high-born Saxon queen for Brighidín bhán mo stór.

It's not alone her smile so sweet, or soft her voice in song
That causes me to oft times repeat her name the whole night long
But that does rest all in her breast, a heart of purest core
Whose pulse is known to me alone, my Brighidín bhán mo stór.

Oh, I'll take ship to Amerikay, good fortune for to find
And every day lament the heart I had to leave behind
But soon in riches I'll return, unto my native shore
With pomp and pride, I'll make a bride of Brighidín bhán mo stór.

An Maidrín Rua

Ar ghabháil ó thuaidh dom trí Shliabh Luachra
'Gus mise 'cur tuairisc mo ghéanna
Ar bhfilleadh aduaidh sea fuaireas a dtuairisc
Go raibh Donncha Rua á n-aoireacht.

Curta.

Maidrín rua, rua, rua, rua,
An maidrín rua atá dána
An maidrín rua 'na luí sa luachair
Agus bárra a dhá chluais in áirde.

Nil cnoc ná coill ná cnuasach poill
Ná lub ná leadhb in Eireann
Ná go rabhas is mo mhuintir de ló 'gus d'oíche
I ndialadh an mhasa rua ar saothar.

Curta.

O' greadacdh croi craite chugat 'mhaidrin ghranna
A sciob uaim m'ál breá géanna
Mo chearca beaga bána mo choilligh is mo bhárdal
Is mo lachain bheaga b'fhearr a bh' in Eirinn.

Curta.

Dinny Burns the Piper

In the year '98 when our trouble was great,
It was treason to be a Milesian and the blackwhiskers said we would
  never forget,
And our history tells us there were Hessians
In these troublesome times; everything was a crime and murder it
  never was riper
In the town of Glensheed, not an acre from Meath, lived one Dinny
  Burns the piper.

Neither wedding nor wake would be worth a shake if Dinny was first
  not invited

For at squeezing the bags, or emptying the kegs, he astonished as well
  as delighted.
But in these time poor Dinny, he could not earn a penny
Martial law had him stung like a viper, and it kept him within,
Till the bones of his skin, were grinning through the rags of the piper.

Now day it did dawn as Dinny marched home back from the fair at
  Lafangen
And what should he see, from the branch of a tree, but the corpse of a
  Hessian there hanging.
Says Dinny, "These rogues, they've got boots—I've no brogues" and
  the boots he laid hold with a gryper
And he pulled with such might and the boots were so tight; legs
  boots and all came away with the piper.

Well, Dinny did run, for fear of being hung, till he came to Tim
  Haley's cabin
Ah, says Tim from within, sure I can't let you in, and you'll be shot if
  your caught out there rapping.
So he went to the shed, where the cow was in bed; with a wisp he
  began for to wipe her
And they laid down together, in seven foot of heather, and the cow
  took to hugging the piper.

As day it did dawn Dinny did yawn, and he pealed off the boots of
  the Hessian
And the legs, by the law, sure he left in the straw, and he gave them
  leg-bail for his mission.
Now breakfast being done, Tim sent out his young son, to get Dinny
  up like a lamplighter
When the legs there he saw, he rose up like a jackdaw, "Jasus,
  Daddy—the cow's ate the piper!"

"Well, bad luck to the baste, she has musical taste to eat such a jolly
  old chanter
Arrah Phadrig a vic, get a lump of a stick, drive her off on the road
  and we'll cant her."

The neighbors were called, Mrs. Kennedy bawled, they began for to
    humbug and jyper
And in sorrow they met, and their whistles they wet, and like divils
    lamented the piper.

Now the cow it was drove 'bout a mile or two off till they came to the
    fair at Killaley
Where there she was sold, for four guineas in gold, to the clerk of the
    parish, Jim Daly.
They went to the tent, where the pennies were spent, the clerk being a
    jolly old swiper
And who should be there, playing "The Rakes of Kildare," but yer
    bould Dinny Burns the piper.

Tim gave a jolt, like a half-drunken colt, and he stared at the piper like
    a gamuck.
Says he, "By the powers, I thought for the last eight hours, you were
    playing in the ould cow's stomach!"
And Dinny observed that the Hessians, when served, began for to
    humbug and jyper
And in grandeur they met and their whistles they wet—and like divils
    they danced round the piper.

Seán Ui Dhuir a Ghleanna (John O'Dwyer of the Glen)

After Augrhim's great disaster
When our foe in sooth was master
It was you who first plunged in and swam
The Shannon's boiling flood
And through Slieve Bloom's dark passes
You led your gallowglasses
Although the hungry Saxon wolves
Were howling for your blood.
And as you crossed Tipperary
You rived the clan O'Leary
And drove a creacht before us

As our horsemen southwards came
Through flood and field we bore them
To the very heart we gored them
Ah Seán O'Dwyer a ghleanna
You were worsted in the game

Long, long we kept that hillside
Our path hard by the rillside
The sturdy knotted oaken boughs
Our curtain overhead
The summer sun we laughed at
The winter hail we chaffed at
Depending on our strong steel swords
To win our daily bread
But the Dutchman's troops came round us
And with fire and steel he bound us
And he blazed the woods and valleys
Till the very sky was flame
But our sharpened swords cut through them
To the very heart we hewed them
Ah Seán O'Dwyer a ghleanna
You were worsted in the game

Here's a health to yours and my king
A sovereign of our liking
And to Sarsfield underneath whose flag
We cast once more a chance
For the morning dawn will wing us
Across the sea and bring us
To take a stand and wield our brand
Amongst the sons of France
And although we part in sorrow
Still, Seán O'Dwyer, a chara
May our prayer be God save Ireland
And pour blessings on her name
May her sons be true when needed

May they never fail as we did
Ah Seán O'Dwyer a ghleanna
You were worsted in the game.

The Jackets Green

When I was a maiden fair and young on the pleasant banks of Lee
No bird that in the greenwood sang was half as blithe and free
No love have I for to call my own, nor he call me his queen
Till down the glen rode Sarsfield's men, and they wore their jackets
    green

Young Donal sat on his high gray mare like a king on a royal seat
And my heart went out on its regal wave for to worship at his feet
Oh love you have come in those colors dressed and woo with a sol-
    dier's mien
I will lay my head on your throbbing breast for the sake of your jacket
    green

No costly attire did my true love wear but the good sword that he
    bore
But I loved him for himself alone and the colors that he wore
Ah love had you come in England's red for to make me England's
    queen
I would roam the high green hills instead for the sake of the Irish
    green

When William stormed with shot and shell at the walls of Garryowen
In the breach of death my Donal fell and he sleeps near the Treaty
    Stone.
That breach the foemen never crossed while he swung his
    broadsword keen
But I do not weep for my darling lost for he fell 'neath the flag of
    green

And when Sarsfield sailed away I wept as I hear the wild Ochone
And I felt as dead as those who slept 'neath the walls of Garryowen

Whilst Ireland held my Donal blest no wild seas rolled between
I still would fold him to my breast all robed in his jacket green.

I saw the Shannon's purple tide flow by the Irishtown
as I stood in the breach by Donal's side when England's flag went
    down
But now it glowers as it reaches the sky like a blood-red curse be-
    tween
And I cry, "It is not women's tears will raise the Irish Green."

Watkins Ale (This version c.1590)
A Ditty delightfull of mother Watkins ale
A warning well wayed, though counted a tale.

I

There was a maid this other day
And she would needs go forth and play
And as she walked she sithed and says
I am afraid to die a mayd,
With that behard a lad
What talke this maiden has
Whereof he is full glad
    And do not spare
To say, faire mayd, I pray
Whether goe you to play
For I will, without faile,
Mayden, give you Watkins ale:
Watkins ale, good sir, quoth she
What is that I pray you tell me?

II

'Tis sweeter farre then sugar fine
And pleasanter than muskadine
And if you please, faire mayd, to stay
A little while, with me to play

I will give you the same
Watkins ale cald by name
Or els, are I to blame
    In truth, faire mayd
Good sir, quoth she againe
    Yf you will take the paine
    I will it not refraine
    Nor be dismayd
He toke this mayden then aside
And led her where she is not spyde
And told her many a prety tale
And gives her well of Watkins ale

III

When he has done to her his will
They talkt, but what it shall not skill
At last, quoth she, saving your tale
Give me some more of Watkins ale
Or else I will not stay
For I must needs away
My mother bade me play
    The time is past
Therefore, good sir, quoth she
If you have done with me
Nay soft, faire maid, quoth he
    Againe at last
Let us talke a little while
Good sir, she then do say
With that the mayd begin to smile
What do you care?
And sayse, good sir, full well know
Your ale, I see runs very low

IV

This young man then, being so blamd
Did blush as one being ashamde

He takes her by the middle small
And gives her more of Watkins ale
    And sayse, faire maid, I pray
  When you goe forth to play
    Remember what I say
      Walke not alone
    Good sir, quoth she againe
    I thanke you for your paine
    For feare of further staine
      I will be gone
Farewell, mayden, then qouth he
Thus they parted at last
Till thrice three months are gone past

This mayden then fell very sicke
Her maydenhead begin to kicke
Her colour waxed wan and pale
From taking much of Watkins ale.